JC 330 CAN.

IDEAS OF POWER IN THE LATE MIDDLE AGES, 1296–1417

Through a focused and systematic examination of late medieval scholastic writers – theologians, philosophers and jurists – Joseph Canning explores how ideas about power and legitimate authority were developed over the 'long fourteenth century'. The author provides a new model for understanding late medieval political thought, taking full account of the intensive engagement with political reality characteristic of writers in this period. He argues that they used Aristotelian and Augustinian ideas to develop radically new approaches to power and authority, especially in response to political and religious crises.

The book examines the disputes between King Philip IV of France and Pope Boniface VIII, and draws upon the writings of Dante Alighieri, Marsilius of Padua, William of Ockham, Bartolus, Baldus and John Wyclif to demonstrate the variety of forms of discourse used in the period. It focuses on the most fundamental problem in the history of political thought – where does legitimate authority lie?

JOSEPH CANNING is Affiliated Lecturer in the Faculty of History at the University of Cambridge. He taught for many years at Bangor University, where he was Reader in History until 2007, and from 1996 to 2001 he was Director of the British Centre for Historical Research in Germany at the Max-Planck-Institut für Geschichte in Göttingen. He edited *Power, Violence and Mass Death in Pre-Modern and Modern Times* (2004) with Hartmut Lehmann and Jay Winter, and his other publications include *The Political Thought of Baldus de Ubaldis* (1987) and *A History of Medieval Political Thought, c. 300 – c. 1450* (1996).

IDEAS OF POWER IN THE
LATE MIDDLE AGES, 1296–1417

JOSEPH CANNING

CAMBRIDGE
UNIVERSITY PRESS

CAMBRIDGE UNIVERSITY PRESS
Cambridge, New York, Melbourne, Madrid, Cape Town,
Singapore, São Paulo, Delhi, Tokyo, Mexico City

Cambridge University Press
The Edinburgh Building, Cambridge CB2 8RU, UK

Published in the United States of America by Cambridge University Press, New York

www.cambridge.org
Information on this title: www.cambridge.org/9781107011410

First published 2011

Printed in the United Kingdom at the University Press, Cambridge

A catalogue record for this publication is available from the British Library

Library of Congress Cataloguing in Publication Data
Canning, Joseph, 1944–
Ideas of power in the late Middle Ages, 1296–1417 / Joseph Canning.
p.   cm.
ISBN 978-1-107-01141-0 (Hardback)
1. Power (Social sciences)–History–To 1500.   2. Authority–History–To 1500.
3. Power (Social sciences)–Early works to 1800.   4. Authority–Early
works to 1800.   I. Title.
JC330.C337 2011
303.301–dc23
2011019697

ISBN 978-1-107-01141-0 Hardback

For Lucy, Martin, Peter and Polly

Contents

Preface

This book is the result of my growing fascination with questions of power and authority. This marks something of a change in my attitude to political thought. When I undertook my first research project I was driven on by the idea of consent. Maybe, over time, I have become more sensitive to the realities of political life.

In writing this book I have benefited so much from discussion with other scholars and students, both graduate and undergraduate. Pride of place must go to all my students over the years at Bangor University: those who took my Special Subject, 'Ideas of Church and State, 1294–1356', and my course on 'Medieval Political Thought', through their highly intelligent and informed discussions, helped me enormously in the development of my ideas. I am grateful to Bangor University for its support in granting me study leave at an early stage of composition.

I should also like to thank Philip Pettit for his gracious invitation to give a paper to the Political Philosophy Colloquium at Princeton University. I was much encouraged by the intense and constructive discussion with colleagues there.

I have found it very stimulating to try my ideas out on scholars from a variety of disciplines: history, politics, law, philosophy and literature. Having to go beyond my intellectual comfort zone helped me make real progress in my understanding – those from other disciplines always posed new and unexpected questions which led me to review my ideas and interpretations. I was especially helped by discussions when I gave papers at a range of universities: Leeds, Sheffield, Southampton, Trinity College Dublin, University College Dublin and University College London. In recent years

I have also benefited enormously from regular participation in the highly congenial and intellectually demanding 'Europe, 1150–1550' seminar at the Institute of Historical Research at the University of London – the benchmark, for me, for medieval history research seminars.

My return to Cambridge in 2007 gave me the time and resources to finish this work. I know of no better place for a scholar to work than Cambridge University Library: the holdings are wonderful, the atmosphere ideal and the staff exemplary in their helpfulness. I have also gained so much from my participation in the History of Christianity research seminar in the Divinity Faculty. But, above all, the Political Thought and Intellectual History research seminar in the History Faculty has provided me with great stimulus. It has been such an intellectually enlivening experience participating each week in the comprehensive range of seminars on both political philosophy and the history of political thought. In particular, I have derived so much from the company of younger scholars, including research fellows and postgraduate students – the future of our subject.

I would like to thank my original editor at Cambridge University Press, Bill Davies, for encouraging me to press on with this book, and my final editor, Liz Friend-Smith, for her invaluable help during the last stages of writing.

Above all, I wish to thank my wife Roberta for putting up with the various forms of 'authoritis' which I have exhibited from time to time. If she had not sustained me, I would have got nowhere with this book. But I would also like to thank my wonderful grown-up children for their confidence in me and their support. To them I dedicate this work.

Abbreviations

Auth.	*Authentica ad Codicem*
Brev.	William of Ockham, *Breviloquium de principatu tyrannico*
c.	*capitulum*
C.	*Codex Iustinianus*
CHMPT	J.H. Burns (ed.). *The Cambridge History of Medieval Political Thought, c.350–c.1450*
Clem.	*Clementinae constitutiones*
col.	column
Coll.	*Collationes Authentici*
Cons.	*Consilium*
Const.	*Constitutio*
D.	*Digesta Iustiniani*
DCD	John Wyclif, *De civili dominio*
Decr. Grat.	*Decretum Gratiani*
DIPP	William of Ockham, *De imperatorum et pontificum potestate*
Dist.	*Distinctio*
DM	Marsilius of Padua, *Defensor minor*
DOR	John Wyclif, *De officio regis*
DP	Marsilius of Padua, *Defensor pacis*
EHR	*English Historical Review*
Ep.	*Epistola*
Extrav. comm.	*Extravagantes communes*
Feud.	*Libri feudorum*
gl.	*glossa*
Inst.	*Institutiones Iustiniani*

xi

l.	*lex*
MGH	*Monumenta Germaniae Historica*
Mon.	Dante Alighieri, *Monarchia*
Nov.	*Novellae Iustiniani*
OND	William of Ockham, *Opus nonaginta dierum*
OP	William of Ockham, *Opera politica*
OQPP	William of Ockham, *Octo quaestiones de potes-tate papae*
PL	J.P. Migne, *Patrologia latina*
Pol.	Aristotle, *Politics*
qu.	*quaestio*
Reg.	*Registrum*
Sext.	*Liber sextus Decretalium Bonifacii P. VIII*
Specul.	Gulielmus Durandus, *Speculum iuris*
ST	Thomas Aquinas, *Summa theologiae*
v.	*verbum*
WS	Wyclif Society (London)
X.	*Decretales Gregorii P. IX seu Liber extra*

Introduction

The argument of this book is that radically new ways of discussing questions of power were developed in the period from the end of the thirteenth century to the early fifteenth century – the long fourteenth century of the European Late Middle Ages. This study is particularly concerned with the most fundamental problem of political thought – where does legitimate authority lie? In short, who is in charge? These years saw a remarkably intensive increase in the production of what may be called political thought texts, both in terms of quantity and quality. The works of these authors were characterized by an engagement with political reality and especially with a series of spectacular political and religious crises: they were not theorists writing in relative isolation from the world. The sophistication and depth of their discourses rested on the development of academic disciplines in thirteenth-century universities, but during the course of the fourteenth century, these writers took the elaboration of political ideas to a far higher level than had existed before in medieval political thought. The stimulus for their thinking came from reflection on the demands of reality in a manner and to a degree that was new for the Middle Ages; the rigour and originality of their ideas derived from the education they had received and the creative use they made of it. Historians' treatments of ideas of power in these years have so far tended to be piecemeal. A study like this, focused on ideas of power and authority in this period, has not been attempted before.

In the last thirty or so years, a great deal of research has been done on aspects of the political thought of the long fourteenth century. But largely because of the sheer variety of the sources, approaches have tended to be fragmented, following different lines of enquiry. A new overall interpretation has been lacking. Certain grand themes stand out in the work of modern scholars. Great advances have, for instance, been made in examining the origins of republicanism.[1] Our knowledge of constitutionalism in both the secular, political arena and the church has been much advanced.[2] A flood of light has been shed on the implications of the different languages or forms of discourse used to elaborate political ideas.[3] Our understanding of questions of poverty and property has been deepened.[4] Our appreciation of the nuances of natural law theory has also been greatly increased.[5] I have learned so much from the work of other scholars, but their approaches and leading concerns have been different from my own. By concentrating on the fundamental questions of power and authority, I have sought to produce a distinctive and integrative

---

[1] For example, the seminal work of Quentin Skinner has helped to stimulate a whole school of research in this regard: see, for instance, his *The Foundations of Modern Political Thought*, 2 vols. (Cambridge University Press, 1978), vol. 1: *The Renaissance*.

[2] Brian Tierney has made a matchless contribution in this respect. See, for instance, his *Religion, Law, and the Growth of Constitutional Thought, 1150–1650* (Cambridge University Press, 1982). Francis Oakley has also produced magisterial studies: see, for instance, his *The Conciliarist Tradition. Constitutionalism in the Catholic Church, 1300–1870* (Oxford University Press, 2003). Arthur P. Monahan's wide-ranging works have also greatly advanced our appreciation of the themes of republicanism and constitutionalism: see his *Consent, Coercion and Limit. The Medieval Origins of Parliamentary Democracy* (Leiden: E.J. Brill, 1987) and *From Personal Duties towards Personal Rights. Late Medieval and Early Modern Political Thought, 1300–1600* (Montreal and Kingston: McGill-Queen's University Press, 1994).

[3] Antony Black deserves to be singled out as having had great influence in the formulation of this approach: see his *Political Thought in Europe, 1250–1450* (Cambridge University Press, 1992).

[4] The work of Janet Coleman has been particularly influential in this respect: see, for instance, her 'Property and poverty', in *CHMPT*, pp. 607–48.

[5] Brian Tierney's huge contribution in this area has been summed up in his *The Idea of Natural Rights. Studies on Natural Rights, Natural Law, and Church Law 1150–1625*, Emory University Studies in Law and Religion, 5 (Grand Rapids, MI: William B. Eerdmans Publishing Company, repr. 2001). For an excellent study, see Annabel Brett, *Liberty, Right and Nature. Individual Rights in Later Scholastic Thought* (Cambridge University Press, 1997).

interpretation which applies to all the various forms of political organization in the fourteenth century.

In order to make sense of the content of this book and to justify the starting- and end-points, it is necessary to explain the historical context leading up to the period – both in terms of intellectual life and political developments. The authors considered were late medieval scholastic writers – theologians, philosophers and jurists. Typically, they elaborated their ideas in terms of intellectual authorities, largely through the application of Aristotelian logic. Indeed, in the period between the 1120s and the 1270s the whole corpus of Aristotle's philosophy had been rediscovered in the west. As regards Aristotle's political thought, fragmentary translations of the *Ethics* into Latin were produced in the twelfth and early thirteenth centuries, but Robert Grosseteste translated the work in its entirety by about 1246/7. The *Politics* was translated into Latin in a literal manner by William of Moerbeke, in an incomplete version in *c.*1260 and in a complete form in 1265. This acquisition of Aristotelian philosophy contributed to a growing intellectual ferment, notably at the universities of Paris and Oxford. The problem was whether it was possible to reconcile traditional medieval Christian theology and philosophy (based on the Bible and the fathers of the church), which may loosely be termed Augustinian (because of its debt to St Augustine), with the pagan philosophy of Aristotle. The results produced a very broad spectrum of interpretations indeed. But there is some value in distinguishing between Augustinian and Aristotelian approaches in broadbrush terms, although so many writers combined both. As far as political ideas were concerned, the medieval Augustinian tradition saw rulership and government as existing within the overall context of a Christian community, whereas Aristotelian ideas provided a systematic model for the treatment of the natural order, including the state, government and political life. It should however be said that Augustine's mature political thought was different from the medieval interpretation. He removed justice from his definition of the state, which he kept separate from the church. But there were ambiguities in Augustine's writings: he was interpreted in the Middle Ages as meaning that true justice was only achievable in a Christian society understood as an existing body of baptized Christians. Individual late medieval writers could use both Augustinian and Aristotelian forms of discourse eclectically. In jurisprudence the authoritative texts were the Roman law (the *Corpus iuris civilis*) and the canon law (*Corpus iuris canonici*). The writers covered in this book drew on these complicated traditions of thought. The question of course is whether it was possible for them to argue in an innovative or original way in interpreting authoritative texts. It certainly was, although the novelty could be masked in the process. Such innovation resulted from the way in which authorities were used to produce arguments to accommodate changing, contemporary reality and to provide answers to questions unforeseen by those who wrote the original authoritative sources.

What was new about fourteenth-century political thought when compared with that of the thirteenth century? The difference may be summed up in terms of the realistic turn taken by fourteenth-century writers. Their prime motivation was to provide solutions to problems presented by the realities of political life, and especially questions of power. This is to talk in general terms and, of course, thirteenth-century writers did to some degree reflect contemporary reality in their contributions to political thought. Indeed, Aquinas, for instance, in his political thought did primarily employ a metaphysical and theoretical approach to political questions with a tendency to argue from first principles, although his writings did show some limited reflection on the political life of his own day. But the intellectual orientation towards confronting the real world of politics and power became the dominant characteristic of fourteenth-century political thinkers. This was a trend which had its roots in the earlier period but which became intensified. In Roman law studies, the juristic school of the Glossators was in the first place concerned to explicate the meaning of the text of the *Corpus iuris civilis*, but with the growing sophistication of their method from the late twelfth century increasingly produced interpretations reflecting the requirements of the society of their own times. Similarly, the first task in dealing with Aristotle's *Ethics* and *Politics* was to try to understand the meaning of the texts translated into

Latin and then to apply Aristotelian concepts in the development of philosophy and theology. In the fourteenth century the school of the Commentators sought above all to accommodate the text of the Roman law to interpret their contemporary reality. In this they were building on the work of the Glossators and late thirteenth-century jurists. Canon law did not present the same problems because its growth in the thirteenth century was the result of the huge production of papal decretals dealing with legal problems as they arose. Obviously, the realistic turn was not a characteristic of all fourteenth-century political thought. There was much evidence of writers using purely deductive arguments from first principles in a theoretical way. But the dominant trend was for writers to employ both inductive and deductive reasoning in applying authoritative texts to the interpretation of political reality.

In particular, the fourteenth century witnessed great originality and creativity in the development of ultimately Augustinian political ideas, with truly diverse results which were new for the Middle Ages. At one extreme, some writers maintained that legitimate rulership depended on sanctifying grace. But it became possible to hold the polar opposite view: that God was the ultimate source of legitimate power and authority, whether pagan or Christian. This meant that a form of Augustinian argument was used to justify the autonomy of secular rulership and of political communities. These arguments are considered in this book. Whereas Aristotelian ideas continued in the fourteenth century to provide a justification for the autonomy of the political order on a naturalistic basis, an innovative interpretation of Augustinian ideas (closer to the master's own views) could now also serve the same purpose, but on a theological basis. This means that a new model for interpreting late medieval political thought is required to take account of the way in which, in the fourteenth century, both Aristotelian and Augustinian languages were used to justify secular power and authority.

The political world of late medieval Europe was complicated indeed. By the end of the thirteenth century, a variety of political entities, many with attributes of territorial states, existed. The forms of government varied. Monarchy remained the dominant kind, as, for instance, in the cases of the established realms of France, England and the Spanish kingdoms. But a range of sovereign and autonomous city-regimes also existed, as in the case of the Italian city-republics, such as Florence, Venice and Milan, and the great German cities, including many in the Hanseatic League. There were also principalities and feudal lordships with varying levels of independence. Forms of representative institutions could also be found in some monarchies, as in the case of England, for instance, and Aragon. The universal title of Roman Emperor had been borne by a succession of German rulers since Otto I in 962 but, in reality, central Europe, and Germany in particular, had become increasingly fragmented politically in the thirteenth century, and certainly since the death of Frederick II in 1250. The idea and title of Roman Emperor persisted but the reality fell far short. Italy was also divided between the city-republics and lordships in the north, the papal lands in the centre and the kingdom of Sicily in the south of the peninsula and in the island of Sicily itself. Furthermore, the church, and the papacy in particular, played a central role both through its claims to power and through its elaboration of the language to describe it.

This book begins and ends with two crises which were crucial in stimulating the development of political ideas – both involved the church. The first featured the disputes between King Philip IV of France and Pope Boniface VIII. This beginning has been chosen because it marked the commencement of the prolonged late medieval series of conflicts over the papacy's claims to power and authority. The opposed positions and actions of Philip and Boniface can only be understood in the context of the history of the relations between the papacy and secular rulers from the mid-eleventh century onwards. The reform papacy, especially from the pontificate of Gregory VII (1073–85), had sought to achieve liberty of the church (*libertas ecclesiae*), that is, the freedom of the church from lay control and its subjection to papal control. This resulted in a conflict with a series of German rulers, a conflict known as the Investiture Contest, which lasted from 1075 until 1122. What was at issue was sovereignty in the Christian community. The long-term result was the rapid development of the papal monarchy, which made universalist claims to superiority over secular rulers and which was consolidated by the growth in canon law in the twelfth and thirteenth centuries. The papacy was involved in major conflicts with the empire, in the twelfth century with Frederick I and in the thirteenth century with Frederick II. The disputes between Boniface VIII and Philip IV marked a watershed on two levels. In the first place they marked a change because it was now the French king rather than the emperor who was involved: the highly developed governmental entity of the papacy came into collision with the concentrated power of the French monarchy, rather than with the relatively diffuse power of the empire. Secondly, the terms in which the conflicts were conducted were different. The political, juristic and theological languages used were far more sophisticated than those employed previously and reflected the level of elaboration of political life in the thirteenth century. The second crisis was the Great Schism (1378–1417), which was without doubt the worst time of troubles for the church and the papacy in the Middle Ages. This was the most profound test for the papacy and raised issues about the very nature of papal monarchy.

Why did this period provide such stimulus for the development of political ideas about power and legitimate authority? It was through a combination of factors. The issues thrown up by deep-seated conflicts and profound political change were so challenging that they resulted in a radical questioning of inherited fundamental presuppositions. The intellectual armoury for coping with these problems was already available and was put to use in producing innovative solutions.

This book is divided into six chapters, which fit into a chronological progression through the period. The chapters are, as it were, windows onto the problem of legitimate authority in the late Middle Ages and reveal differing and innovative approaches to it. Chapter 1 deals with the political thought produced during the disputes between Philip IV and Boniface VIII, and looks at the large range of greater and lesser tracts written. Chapter 2 studies the approach of Dante Alighieri, specifically from the point of view of his highly original contribution to political philosophy. It is especially con-cerned with his arguments about the right and the wrong use of knowledge. Chapter 3 is devoted to the thought of Marsilius of Padua, the most thoroughgoing critic of the papacy, and considers his discussions of where legitimate authority did and did not lie. Chapter 4 addresses issues of power and authority raised by the poverty debate. The question of poverty was the major problem facing the church in the first part of the fourteenth century and highlighted fundamental issues of power and powerlessness. The ramifications for legitimate authority were huge and, indeed, sys-temic. This chapter focuses on the prime theological and philosoph-ical exponent of the poverty ideal – William of Ockham. Chapter 5 covers juristic discourse and is focused on the two greatest fourteenth-century jurists – Bartolus of Sassoferrato and Baldus de Ubaldis. It addresses the question of how useful notions of sover-eignty and state are for interpreting juristic ideas of legitimate authority, and explores the unique test case of papal temporal power in the papal states. Chapter 6 looks at two sets of ideas which had their origins before the Great Schism but had their main development during it. They were different in kind but both posed a considerable threat to papal claims. The first was the notion of grace-founded *dominium*. Particular attention is given to John Wyclif's elaboration of this thesis. The second was the set of theories elaborated by exponents of the conciliar movement in the church. Both raised fundamental issues concerning legitimate authority. These six chapters serve to reveal the sheer variety and sophistication of late medieval political thought. The different writers shared a common culture in that they could draw on a rich treasury of biblical, theological, philosophical, literary and juristic sources. Their approaches varied in the ways in which they used these authorities. Thus, for instance, theologians, highly critical of canonists, would themselves make great use of canon law. Aristotle's political and ethical concepts were used both by writers seeking to undermine papal claims and by those supporting them. Aristotle could be used to produce thoroughly this-worldly political ideas but, equally well, his works could be drawn upon in support of arguments in favour of the most extreme pro-papal claims. As we shall see, Augustine's ideas about power and authority were susceptible to a range of interpretations. The Bible, of course, could be used in support of divergent political positions. But the point was that all these writers could engage with one another – they were sharing a mental world. There were no fixed boundaries between disciplines. The exponents of theology, philosophy, church history and jurisprudence (of both Roman and canon law) all drew on one another's authorities. What is revealing to a modern historian is to discover what questions these late medieval authors thought important and how they sought to answer them.

Clearly, the thought world of the late Middle Ages was radically different from our own and in the course of this book I have endeavoured to be especially sensitive to the language of medieval scholastic discourse. The differences in language will become clear in the course of the book. But there is one area where misunderstandings can arise and which it may be helpful to highlight at the start. In the medieval sources there is constant reference to jurisdiction (*iurisdictio*). In modern usage the term is largely restricted to a legal sense, as, for instance, to the legal competence of a judge, court or state. *Iurisdictio* had a far wider meaning in the late Middle Ages. It could be synonymous with power and authority, albeit understood with legal overtones. Thus, papal power and authority were expressed in terms of jurisdiction. The notion of law in its widest sense as legitimating governmental authority lay behind this usage. In its original application in antiquity, jurisdiction had derived from the capacity to declare the law (*ius dicere*); by the late Middle Ages it had developed into the capacity to govern and rule in a legitimate way. Supreme jurisdiction was synonymous with sovereignty. Certainly, the role of the concept of jurisdiction shows the fundamental importance of juristic notions in late medieval ideas of government and rulership. Jurists produced the most sophisticated discussions of the concept of jurisdiction and its ramifications, but everyone used it.

This book confronts the problem of what was new and important about late medieval political thought. In so doing, it also raises the question of the nature of politics and political ideas. It is important not to unthinkingly project back modern presuppositions about the content of politics onto the late Middle Ages. Thus, for instance, there was strong evidence for notions of state and a this-worldly approach in the works of many late medieval writers, but this should not be seen as any form of anachronistic 'advance' in political thought and should not be privileged as the most salient development in political ideas in this period. This book argues that the most important contribution of these writers was to the elaboration of notions of power and authority in a new way, and, specifically, to the sophisticated analysis of the question of legitimate authority. If their ideas are approached in this manner, then a more accurate assessment of their contribution is possible: ultimately theological approaches can then be seen as possessing a validity side-by-side with overtly this-worldly discourse, framed in ultimately Aristotelian and juristic terms. The question of the location and nature of legitimate authority is the right one to ask in order to do full justice to the rich range of late medieval political thought.

CHAPTER I

Ideas of power and authority during the disputes between Philip IV and Boniface VIII

The disputes between King Philip IV of France and Pope Boniface VIII in the years 1296 to 1303 over who held legitimate power, that is, authority, provoked a debate which gave a new direction to political thought. This was a classic case of the development of political ideas in response to a crisis. It was a great paradox of medieval history that the church, originally instituted outside the governmental and legal structures of the Roman Empire, had itself over time become the prime developer of the language of power. Here was the crisis of this process, begun in the fifth century, revitalized in the papal reform of the eleventh and consolidated in the twelfth and thirteenth, whereby the church had developed as a legal and governmental institution under a papal monarchy with increasing jurisdictional pretensions. Papal claims to power were encapsulated in the concept of the pope's plenitude of power (*plenitudo potestatis*). The origin of this formulation lay with Pope Leo I (440–61), who used the phrase in a restricted manner to indicate how the delegated and therefore partial authority of a papal vicar, that is, legate, differed from the pope's, which was full in relation to it. The formulation was not used by Gregory VII, but emerged in the twelfth century as a way of expressing papal sovereignty, a usage which diverged from Leo I's original meaning, and was to be found frequently, and definitively, in Innocent III's decretals.[1] The conflicting claims of the church and of secular rulers had now brought about a conflict with the French king, stimulating

---

[1] See Kenneth Pennington, *Pope and Bishops. The Papal Monarchy in the Twelfth and Thirteenth Centuries* (Philadelphia: University of Pennsylvania Press, 1984), pp. 43–74.

both defence and refutation of the papal position, together with profound discussion of the nature, exercise and location of authority in society. Indeed, this intellectual ferment produced a mass of pamphlets, tracts and treatises which amounted to a new genre devoted to ideas of power. There was a creative application of traditions of discourse to contribute to discussion of the issues involved in the crisis, with a variety of diverse results. Clear perceptions of questions of power and authority were elaborated.[2]

The essence of this bitter conflict was clearly expressed in an anecdote current in England at the time – that Philip's chancellor and ambassador to the pope, Pierre Flotte, had said to Boniface, 'Your power is verbal, ours however is real',[3] an observation that raised a fundamental question about the nature and relative effectiveness of royal and papal authority. Both sides accepted that the church did have power; the questions at issue were how much and of what kind, and where the points of demarcation lay. In a way the French monarchy and the papacy deserved each other. They and their followers were arguing within the same mental world, in support of their respective institutions, perceived as legal entities with rights and duties.

That conflict should break out was the result of the collision of fundamentally diverging views about the relationship between temporal and spiritual power, views which were the culmination of developments in the thirteenth century. As regards the papacy, what may be termed a progressively hierocratic interpretation of the role of the pope had become dominant in papal practice and in canon law. This trend marked a divergence from what had previously been the case in the High Middle Ages. In interpreting the period from the reform papacy of the eleventh century onwards, modern historians

---

[2] For the political thought produced in this dispute, see Gianluca Briguglia, *La questione del potere. Teologi e teoria politica nella disputa tra Bonifacio VIII e Filippo il Bello*, Filosofia e Scienza nell' Età Moderna (Milan: FrancoAngeli, 2010).

[3] See the continuation of William Rishanger, *Chronica*, ed. Henry Thomas Riley, Rolls Series, 28, 2 (Millwood, NY: Kraus reprints, 1983), pp. 197–8; and Thomas of Walsingham, *Ypodigma Neustriae*, ed. Henry Thomas Riley, Rolls Series, 28, 7 (Wiesbaden: Lessing-Druckerei, 1965), pp. 217–18.

have been divided in applying forms of hierocratic or dualist models. These terms need some explanation. They are clearly modern categories applied to the Middle Ages; they are inexact but have provided a useful shorthand. According to the hierocratic model of papal monarchy, the pope as the direct successor of St Peter has the divinely appointed headship on earth of the body of the Christian community which has been committed to his care by Christ. Within this body, the clergy is superior to the laity and spiritual jurisdiction to temporal. Because the pope is responsible before God for the Christian community, he has the right to judge, depose and concede power to secular rulers. Indeed, the pope came to be seen as the mediator of the ruler's power from God. There was no autonomy for the secular ruler and no way in which the pope could be judged by any other human being. The dualist model stressed the fundamental distinction between clergy and laity in a different way. It understood temporal and spiritual power as being both derived ultimately from God but as existing in parallel. The pope's role was seen as essentially spiritual, with the result that he had no right to interfere in the exercise of a secular ruler's power. All accepted that the dignity of the spiritual power was greater, but that did not mean that the temporal power was subject to it. Boniface VIII in his actions and in his words represented a hierocratic interpretation of the papal office. Indeed, his pontificate and the first three decades of the fourteenth century witnessed the high point of the elaboration of hierocratic doctrine. The dualist model, limiting the pope to a purely spiritual role outside the papal states and providing the king with an independent function in his rulership, would clearly be more suited to the aspirations of secular rulers. In the case of the French monarchy, the thirteenth century had seen a dramatic consolidation of the state with an increased perception of the notion of the ruler's territorial sovereignty. The need for royal jurisdictional control over all the king's subjects, both clerical and lay, had come to be seen as paramount. Any pretensions to independent ecclesiastical jurisdiction within the kingdom had come to be seen as unacceptable if the king's sovereignty were seen to be thereby infringed. There could however be no totally clear differentiation between the hierocratic and

dualist models because there was some overlap. Any hierocratic interpretation would accept the fundamental distinction between the functions of the clergy and the laity: the role of the secular ruler was seen as
valid but subordinate to the spiritual ruler. There was an acceptance that
the office of the secular ruler was to exercise temporal power and that
the pope only did so indirectly outside the papal states. Likewise, any
dualist view accepted the headship of the pope in the Christian community. But this element of overlap meant that the boundaries of jurisdictions could appear fuzzy and it was this that accounted for so much of
the conflict between the two powers – it was largely a problem of
demarcation of spheres of operation. Insofar as both hierocratic and
dualist views operated within the context of a Christian society, they
may be understood as deriving from and expressing a medieval
Augustinian notion of government and rulership, although Augustine
himself predated any such development of ideas of papal monarchy.

Both sides in the disputes between Philip IV and Boniface VIII
thought the other was at fault. The conflict broke out because the
papacy sought to protect church rights under canon law which it
considered the French crown to have infringed. The French monarchy in turn believed that the papal response sought to diminish
the rights of the king and, indeed, to undermine his sovereignty.
There were in fact two disputes. The first concerned the issue of
royal taxation of the clergy. Both the English monarch Edward
I and Philip had been taxing their clergy to finance war against each
other. This infringed a decree of the Fourth Lateran Council of
1215, whereby lay taxation of the clergy was only permitted with
papal approval. Royal taxation of the clergy had of course become
commonplace, but Boniface chose to make an issue of it now, partly
because he considered that Christian monarchs should fight Islam
rather than each other in the aftermath of the final expulsion of the
crusaders from the Holy Land in 1291. In April 1296 Boniface
issued the bull *Clericis laicos* which, without mentioning either king
by name, forbade secular rulers to tax the clergy and the clergy to
pay such taxes without the permission of the apostolic see. The bull
expressly stated that lay rulers had no jurisdiction over clerics or
their property. However, Boniface was humiliatingly forced to back

down under the pressure of a royal ordinance, issued in August, which imposed an embargo on the export of precious metal from France, an important source of papal finances. In July 1297 Boniface in the bull *Etsi de statu* exempted Philip from the provisions of *Clericis laicos* and permitted the king to tax his clergy in the case of emergency, which amounted in practice to acknowledging that he had carte blanche in this matter.

This was more than a squabble over taxation. Larger issues were involved. From Boniface's point of view, the principle of the liberty of the church (*libertas ecclesiae*) was at stake: that the clergy were free from lay control and subject to that of the pope. Behind this view lay the assumption that the clergy were a superior caste to the laity, amongst whom were included secular rulers according to canon law. From Philip's perspective, his sovereignty within his kingdom was damaged if he could not tax his clerical subjects, a pre-eminent economic group, without the approval of another ruler. In his view, the pope was going beyond spiritual matters and was interfering in the material interests of France.

The second dispute also raised questions of the liberty of the church and royal sovereignty, but it did so in a more profound way. It centred round the issue of the privilege of clergy to be tried solely by ecclesiastical courts, again a fundamental principle of canon law. In 1301 Philip had the Bishop of Pamiers, Bernard Saisset, arrested and then tried in his presence for blasphemy, heresy and treason. Saisset was then held in nominally ecclesiastical custody at the king's pleasure. This infringed the canon law provision that a bishop could only be tried by the pope. Boniface could have avoided conflict on this issue but chose confrontation instead. In so doing, he went against his earlier practice before he became pope, when as a legate to the French court in 1290 he had negotiated with Philip an agreement whereby the king issued an ordinance confirming the privileges of the French clergy and the right of the Parlement of Paris to judge French prelates and hear appeals from their temporal courts. Ecclesiastical jurisdiction was protected but the principle underlined that the king was the supreme judge in temporal matters in his kingdom, where there were no areas of clerical immunity. The

French monarchy had long been seen as the greatest supporter of the papacy, especially against the empire: the breakdown in relations a few years later was not foreseen.

The dispute went from bad to worse for the papacy. Boniface was obstinately committed to the course of action he had chosen, especially as a bishop was involved. Philip was convinced that his sovereignty was at stake. If he could not try a bishop for treason, how could he be truly sovereign? Boniface demanded that Saisset be released and revoked the privileges granted in *Etsi de statu*. He went further, however, by summoning all the French bishops to a council in Rome to discuss the preservation of ecclesiastical liberty, the reform of the kingdom of France, the correction of the king's previous excesses and the good government of the kingdom itself. He was therefore treating the king's government as a matter of ecclesiastical concern. In December 1301 he issued the bull *Ausculta fili* (Listen Son), which in its tone would appear highly patronizing to the French court and in which he stated that Philip as the pope's dearest son had a superior, and that he was subject to the head of the ecclesiastical hierarchy. This bull could easily be read as maintaining that the king was subject to the pope in both temporal and spiritual matters, since Boniface did not specify what kind of superiority he claimed. The reaction of the French court was fierce indeed: public opinion in Paris was whipped up against Boniface when Philip's advisers produced and made public two forgeries – one known as *Deum time* (Fear God), a crude version of *Ausculta fili*, claiming that the king was subject to the pope in temporal and spiritual matters, and the other a blunt response to this entitled *Sciat tua maxima fatuitas* (May Your Very Great Fatuity Know). The culmination was the first meeting of a form of Estates General at Paris in April 1302, which was called to condemn Boniface. Furthermore, successful pressure was put on the northern French prelates not to attend the pope's council – only bishops from the south took part.

In the midst of this maelstrom, in November 1302 Boniface issued the bull *Unam sanctam* which, without any reference to the dispute, enunciated in lapidary fashion the papal view of the ultimate subordination of temporal to spiritual power.[4] It was a curious document quite unlike any other medieval papal bull: it was more like a very short tract, but one issued with papal authority. Boniface was seeking to set forth the principles underlying the papal position. Since he was proclaiming what he saw as traditional and everlasting truth, it was very important that the bull should contain nothing new. It largely consisted of a collage of passages from theological sources together with some juristic content. Boniface presented a long-established argument from unity. He described the church as a mystical body (*corpus mysticum*)[5] in a juristic, corporational sense, under one head, Christ, whose representative was the pope, with all power on earth, spiritual and temporal, lying within it. Boniface applied a strictly hierarchical view with overt reference to Pseudo-Dionysius.[6] He referred to the traditional two-swords argument, using a hierocratic interpretation of Bernard of Clairvaux's famous formulation of it, to show that secular power was derived from and exercised at the command of the priesthood. He then paraphrased a well-known passage by Hugh of St Victor in a hierocratic manner to demonstrate that spiritual power, because it instituted the earthly, could judge it 'if it has not been good'.[7] The bull ended with the statement 'We declare, state, define and pronounce that it is entirely necessary for salvation that every human creature be subject to the Roman pontiff', which itself was based on Aquinas's words in his *Contra errores Graecorum* (Against the Errors of the Greeks).[8]

---

[4] For the text of the bull, see *Extrav. comm.*, 1.8.1 (ed. A. Friedberg). It was dated 18 November but may have been issued a few months later. References are to this edition.

[5] For the history of this phrase, see Henri de Lubac, *Corpus mysticum: l'Eucharistie et l'Eglise au Moyen Age, Etude historique* (Paris: Aubier, 1949).

[6] Pseudo-Dionysius was an anonymous early sixth-century Christian writer in Greek who purported to be St Paul's disciple Dionysius the Areopagite (a claim which Boniface would have believed). He had the distinction of having invented the term 'hierarchy'. His influence on medieval western thought was profound through Latin translations of his works.

[7] 'Spiritualis potestas terrenam potestatem instituere habet, et iudicare, si bona non fuerit' (col. 1246).

[8] 'Porro subesse Romano Pontifici omni humanae creaturae declaramus, dicimus, diffinimus et pronunciamus omnino esse de necessitate salutis' (col. 1246). See

Despite these ringing words, the culmination of the conflict was a débâcle for the papacy. Boniface died in 1303 a few weeks after the outrage at the papal city of Anagni to the south-east of Rome, where he reacted bravely to being threatened with death by the French forces under the command of Philip's minister Nogaret and by those of the dissident Cardinal Sciarra Colonna. His death did not put an end to French pressure. Pope Clement V in 1306 in his decretal *Meruit* backed down totally. In it he stated that he did not wish anything prejudicial to the French king or his kingdom to arise from *Unam sanctam*, that the king and his kingdom should be no more subject to the pope than they had been before the bull was issued, and that the kingdom and people should be in the same state as they were before. Clearly, this second dispute had raised the issue of power both at the theoretical level and at the nakedly practical level through the exertion of acute pressure by the French crown. *Unam sanctam* itself had no effect on events. Indeed, it was only incorporated into canon law in the sixteenth century, when it was included in the *Extravagantes communes*. Writers did refer to it in the remainder of the Middle Ages but it is modern historians who have given it real prominence, seeing it as a definitive statement of the claims of the medieval papacy and thus according it a retrospective importance which it lacked when it was issued. Boniface was indeed unfortunate in the timing of his reign: if he had occupied the throne of St Peter in less exciting times, his papacy would have been remembered for his great positive achievement – the issuing of the *Liber sextus* of the *Corpus iuris canonici*.

THE LESSER TRACTS

Two kinds of tract were produced in the context of the disputes between Philip IV and Boniface VIII: they may be distinguished

Aquinas, *Contra errores Graecorum*, 2.38, in *Opera omnia*, ed. Roberto Busa, 7 vols. (Stuttgart-Bad Cannstatt: Friedrich Frommann Verlag, Günther Holzboog KG, 1980), vol. III, p. 508: 'Ostenditur etiam quod subesse romano pontifici sit de necessitate salutis.'

from each other both by length and by subject matter. The lesser tracts were directly related to the detailed issues of the conflict, while the major tracts addressed fundamental questions arising from the disputes but made little or no reference to current events. Both groups argued from authoritative texts – the Bible, the works of previous Christian theologians, Aristotle, canon and Roman law – and history. In so doing they were arguing in a typically medieval way and one characteristic of scholastic thought patterns. They were not ostensibly trying to innovate, although they might have done so incidentally or under the guise of arguments supported by authority. Both the lesser and major tracts gave extensive treatments to aspects of the question of power.[9]

Amongst the lesser tracts, the one known, from its opening words (or *incipit*), as *Antequam essent clerici* (Before There Were Clerics)[10] was an anonymous pro-royal response to *Clericis laicos*. It was most probably written between August 1296 and September 1297, because it alluded to Philip IV's prohibition of the export of bullion and would have been out of date once *Etsi de statu* was known in France.[11] It was very short but contained important arguments for the royal side. The references which it made to authorities were entirely to the New Testament.

The particular merit of *Antequam essent clerici* was that it attacked the pro-papal position on a fundamental point: the concept of the liberty of the church (*libertas ecclesiae*) itself. The author rejected the papal interpretation whereby this notion applied to the church as an ecclesiastical body. The idea of the church had, of course, a wider meaning as well – the community of all Christians. The writer

---

[9] For a survey of these tracts, see Jürgen Miethke, *De potestate papae. Die päpstliche Amtskompetenz im Widerstreit der politischen Theorie von Thomas Aquinas bis Wilhelm von Ockham*, Spätmittelalter und Reformation, 16 (Tübingen: Mohr Siebeck, 2000), pp. 68–126.

[10] For Latin text with an English translation, see R.W. Dyson (ed.), *Three Royalist Tracts. Antequam essent clerici; Disputatio inter clericum et militem; Quaestio in utramque partem* (Bristol: Thoemmes Press, 1999). All references are to Dyson's edition; all translations from Latin into English are my own.

[11] *Ibid.*, p. 2.

maintained that the church was composed of clergy and laity, and that God had willed that both should enjoy this freedom – as he said: 'Did Christ die and rise again only for the clergy? No way!'[12] He rejected, as an abuse, any attempt by the clergy to claim liberty of the church exclusively for themselves.[13] His main concern was to attack those clerical pretensions which, to his mind, infringed the rights of the French crown. He therefore then narrowed the general concept of 'liberty' to the more specific one of 'liberties' in the sense of legal privileges. He argued that the liberties of the clergy had been granted by popes but with the goodwill or permission of secular rulers, and that such liberties could not take away the capacity of kings to govern and defend their kingdoms. The kingdom was described in organic terms as a body composed of a head (the king) and members. Both clergy and laity together composed this body. The clergy therefore should pay taxes for the defence of the realm, because they could not fight themselves; any refusal to do so was considered to be aiding the enemy and therefore treason. Indeed, the kingdom's right to self-defence was enshrined in natural law.[14]

The theme of the subjection of the clergy to the temporal power of kings and princes received a more extensive treatment in another anonymous pro-royal tract, the *Disputatio inter clericum et militem* (Dispute Between a Cleric and a Knight).[15] We cannot be certain about its date of composition. Since it was concerned with the issue of royal taxation of the church, it seems at first sight to have been written during the first dispute between Philip and Boniface, but it also contained a passage which is reminiscent of Boniface's language in *Ausculta fili* and that of the pro-royal forged papal bull based on the latter and disseminated in a public relations exercise to whip up public resentment against the pope: 'A little while ago

---

[12] 'Numquid solum pro clericis Christus mortuus est et resurrexit? Absit!' (*ibid.*, p. 4).

[13] *Ibid.*, p. 4.   [14] *Ibid.*, pp. 4–6.

[15] For Latin text with an English translation, see Dyson, *Three Royalist Tracts* and N.N. Erickson (ed.), 'A dispute between a priest and a knight', *Proceedings of the American Philosophical Society*, III, 5 (1967), 288–309. All references are to Dyson's text; all translations from Latin into English are my own.

I had a big laugh, when I heard that it had recently been decreed by the Lord Pope Boniface that he himself is and should be lord over all principalities and kingdoms.'[16] As its title suggests, the tract had the dramatic form of a dispute between two interlocutors, a cleric and a knight, the latter of whom was given the better of the argument. It was written in a lively way and was influential in the history of political thought because it was to be incorporated into the *Somnium viridarii* (Dream of the Orchard) produced in about 1376 or 1377, a form of compendium of French political thought then swiftly translated into French as *Le songe du vergier*. The author of the *Disputatio* drew on a wide knowledge of relevant biblical passages.

The fundamental idea of the *Disputatio* was that temporal and spiritual power were separate and distinct. The most striking argument to support this notion appeared towards the beginning of the tract, where it was maintained that, in considering Christ, a distinction must be made between two times: one of humility (corresponding to his life on earth up to and including his passion) and the other of power (after his resurrection). St Peter had indeed been constituted Christ's vicar, but for the latter's state of humility, not of glory or power and majesty. There was however some ambiguity in the author's use of the term 'power' (*potestas*). Although he contrasted the times of Christ's humility and power, he said that Christ 'committed to his vicar that power which he exercised as mortal man, not that which he accepted when he had been glorified'.[17] The power committed to the pope was not that of temporal rulership but of a purely spiritual kingship and lordship, such as Christ had exercised in his humility.[18] Therefore, the author

---

[16] 'Vnde nuper mihi risus venit magnus, cum audissem noviter statutum esse a Domino Papa Bonifacio quod ipse est et esse debet dominus super omnes principatus et regna' (Dyson, *Three Royalist Tracts*, p. 14). Cf. *Ausculta fili* and *Tua maxima fatuitas* (English translation, in Brian Tierney, *Crisis of Church and State, 1050–1300* (Englewood Cliffs, NJ: Prentice Hall, 1964), pp. 185–7).

[17] 'Illam ergo potestatem suo vicario commisit, quam homo mortalis exercuit, non illam quam glorificatus accepit' (Dyson, *Three Royalist Tracts*, p. 16).

[18] *Ibid.*, pp. 18–20.

did accept the notion of power in both spiritual and temporal senses. The main biblical passages referred to in support of his argument were those one would expect: 'My kingdom is not of this world' (John 18:36); 'I came not to be ministered unto but to minister' (Matthew 20:28); and Jesus's statement when he refused to judge over an inheritance: 'Man, who made me a judge or a divider over you?' (Luke 12:13–14). Property was treated as being under temporal power. Peter was given the keys to the kingdom of heaven, not an earthly one (referring to Matthew 16:19). The *Disputatio*'s approach was extremely clever in that it accepted the pope's claim to be the vicar of Christ but interpreted that title in such a way that it rejected the papal hierocratic interpretation. The pope's power was understood in the sense of spiritual service and certainly not of temporal rulership over people and property.

Indeed, the specific purpose of the tract was to demonstrate that ecclesiastical possessions were subject to royal control: the knight sought to silence the protestations of the cleric in defence of the property rights of the church. The *Disputatio* argued that the church did not possess its property absolutely, but that such property had been conceded to the church in trust by secular rulers in order to fulfil a purpose of protection of the clergy, who therefore had an obligation to contribute to the defence of the realm. It was up to the king or prince to determine whether the clergy were using their property well, that is, for the benefit of the commonwealth (*res-publicae utilitas*), as examples from Old Testament kingship confirmed.[19] Indeed, the tract used the argument of necessity to justify the ruler's capacity to revoke clerical privileges for the common good, an example of how necessity was employed to increase the power of the ruler over his subjects in order to achieve a purpose which was itself a defining limitation of rulership.[20] The culmination of the tract's argument was expressed thus by the knight:

And so, lord clerk, hold your tongue and recognize that the king, through the laws, customs, privileges and liberties which he has given you, is preeminent

[19] See *ibid.*, pp. 29 and 35.   [20] *Ibid.*, p. 40.

in royal power and, having consulted equity and reason, or his magnates, can add, diminish, change and regulate, whatever he likes, as he sees fit.[21]

This is not to say that everything went the knight's way in the dispute. He had difficulty in responding to the cleric's use of the 'by reason of sin' (*ratione peccati*) argument. This was one of the strongest weapons in the papal arsenal. It had been classically formulated by Innocent III and maintained that the pope, as head of the church, had the right to intervene wherever he judged sin to be involved. As the clerk said, this gave the church the right to judge in temporal cases.[22] The knight's stumble here showed the difficulties which any anti-papal writer encountered if he admitted that the power of secular rulers existed within the context of the Christian community of which the pope was the head.

The writer of the *Disputatio* was a Christian and a Frenchman, and towards the end of the tract he felt impelled to consolidate the claims of his monarch by making it clear that the King of France in his kingdom enjoyed the same power as the Roman Emperor in the Empire. He traced this back to the division of the Empire under the Carolingians. This was an expression of the *rex in regno suo* argument which had become such a well-worn part of the ideology of kingship in France in the thirteenth century.[23]

Another anonymous tract, conventionally known to modern historians as the *Quaestio in utramque partem* (Both Sides of the Question),[24] was a longer, well-structured scholastic treatment of the relationship between temporal and spiritual power. Although it came down on the royal side, its approach was measured and

---

[21] 'Et ideo, domine clerice, linguam vestram coercite, et agnoscite regem legibus, consuetudinibus, privilegiis et libertatibus datis, regia potestate praeesse, posse addere, posse minuere, mutare quamlibet, aequitate et ratione consulta, aut cum suis proceribus, sicut visum fuerit, temperare' (*ibid.*, p. 42).

[22] *Ibid.*, p. 21.

[23] For an innovative treatment of French ideas of empire at this time, see Chris Jones, *Eclipse of Empire? Perceptions of the Western Empire and its Rulers in Late Medieval France*, Cursor mundi, 1 (Turnhout: Brepols, 2007).

[24] See Dyson, *Three Royalist Tracts*, p. xxviii for forms of the title. All references are to Dyson's edition; all translations from Latin into English are my own.

balanced. It expressly set out to argue according to philosophical, theological, canon law and Roman law arguments. It is useful for modern historians because it serves as a compendium of theological and canonist authorities, whereas its use of philosophy is scant and of Roman law texts thin indeed.[25] Its date of composition cannot be demonstrated with certainty, although it was most likely produced between December 1301 and September 1303 during the second dispute, that is, after the publication of the two royal forgeries aimed at discrediting Boniface and before the events at Anagni. However, Karl Ubl has persuasively argued that it was produced to support the royal side in condemning the forgery, *Deum time*, in the process of calling the form of Estates General in April 1302.[26]

From its outset, the tract set itself the task of solving two interrelated questions concerning power: whether spiritual and temporal power were distinct and separate, and whether the pope possessed full power over both spiritual and temporal matters, in such a way that secular rulers were subject to him in temporals. The bulk of the tract consisted of arguments with general application to the relationship between the papacy and secular rulers. Initially, the author sought to demonstrate that the two powers were distinct and that the pope had no lordship over temporal matters. Then, in order the better to understand the two initial questions, the author systematically addressed five points: that both temporal and spiritual power were instituted and ordained by God; that these two powers were distinct and divided; that God in instituting the spiritual power gave it no lordship over earthly things; that there were areas in which the temporal power was subject to the spiritual and others in which it was not; and that the King of France enjoyed liberty and exemption such that he recognized no superior in temporal matters. The even-tempered character of the tract is especially revealed in

---

[25] The only Roman law reference is to the Auth., 'Quomodo oporteat episcopos' (Coll., 1.6 = Nov., 6).

[26] Karl Ubl, 'Johannes Quidorts Weg zur Sozialphilosophie', *Francia – Forschungen zur westeuropäischen Geschichte*, 30, 1 (2003), 65.

this last section because most of the arguments are expressed in general terms not specific to the French monarchy.

What was notable about the *Quaestio in utramque partem* was the fundamental reason it put forward for the division and separation between the two powers. The author had a very clear perception that the root cause was that spiritual and temporal matters were different in kind: they belonged to different *genera*: 'Since therefore spiritual and temporal things are of different *genera*, it does not follow that he who has power in spirituals has it in temporals.'[27] This was a very strong argument based on the categorization of observed phenomena. It argued *from* the difference in kind of the objects of the two powers *to* the separation of the exercisers of power over these objects. It was an approach that was radically different from the hierocratic approach, which assumed a hierarchy of difference whereby inferiors were led back to their origin in God through layers of superiors, with temporal power being necessarily derived from spiritual power, which was of greater dignity. Indeed, the author rejected the characteristic hierocratic form of argument from macrocosm to microcosm. He set out to refute the Pseudo-Dionysian proposition that the government of the church on earth should mirror that of the church in heaven through having one ruler: the imperfection of this world dictated that no one person could rule both spiritual and temporal things.[28]

On one level, the author certainly elaborated his theme that the two powers were distinct, corresponding to the dual nature of human beings: the spiritual to the life of the soul and the temporal to that of the body.[29] But the distinction was not a total one. He was heavily influenced by a moderate dualist interpretation of canon law. He was, for instance, willing to accept that the pope could declare subjects freed from their oaths of allegiance to their rulers on the grounds of heresy, schism or contumacy against the Roman church.[30] He also accepted the standard claims of church

[27] 'Cum igitur spiritualia et temporalia sint res diversorum generum, non sequitur quod qui habet potestatem in spiritualibus habeat eam in temporalibus' (p. 110).
[28] Dyson, *Three Royalist Tracts*, pp. 84–6. [29] *Ibid.*, p. 66. [30] *Ibid.*, p. 106.

jurisdiction in cases of conflict of laws where a temporal case had spiritual connections, as in feudal cases by reason of sin or where an oath was involved, or in cases involving dowries.[31]

Overall, the author was conscious of the fuzzy edges between the spheres of spiritual and temporal power. But because the hierocratic viewpoint conceived of both temporal and spiritual power as being exercised within the church, understood as the Christian community, the author of the *Quaestio* felt he had to reply to the possible accusation that his approach would destroy unity, a core value in his opponents' discourse. He accepted the greater dignity of spiritual things but not the conclusion of the hierocrats that he who had power in greater things necessarily had it in lesser ones (in this case temporal matters), since they were of different *genera*. It was more that there was, within the church, a mutual dependence between the two powers, respecting their fundamental difference:

If however these two powers were completely distinct, in such a way that one was not dependent on the other, this duality would be an occasion of division. But there is a mutual dependence, because the temporal needs the spiritual because of the soul, whereas the spiritual needs the temporal on account of its use of temporal things.[32]

In that way unity was preserved: 'Thus the temporal power is somehow ordained to the spiritual in those things which pertain to spirituality itself, that is, in spiritual things. And this way multiplicity is reduced to unity.'[33] But ultimate unity lay in the headship of Christ, from whom both powers were derived, with the pope as his principal spiritual vicar and the secular ruler, whether king or emperor, head as regards the rulership of temporal affairs.[34] Christ

---

[31] *Ibid.*, pp. 76–80.

[32] 'Si autem istae duae potestates essent omnino distinctae, ita quod una non dependeret ex alia, ista dualitas esset occasio divisionis. Sed inter eas est mutua dependentia, quia temporalis indiget spirituali propter animam, spiritualis vero indiget temporali propter temporalium rerum usum' (*ibid.*, p. 100).

[33] 'Sic potestas temporalis quodammodo ordinatur ad spritualem in iis quae ad ipsam spiritualitatem pertinent, id est, in spiritualibus. Et per istum modum multitudo reducitur ad unitatem' (*ibid.*, p. 86).

[34] *Ibid.*, p. 88.

himself had not used temporal power or entrusted it to his vicar, the pope, whose plenitude of power applied only to spiritual things and was in any case not absolute, but full only in comparison to that of inferior prelates who were called to part of the care of souls.[35]

Christ's shunning of earthly power had a further consequence for St Peter, the other apostles and their successors:

> Christ forbade Peter, as much as the other apostles, lordship, power and jurisdiction in temporal things, when he enjoined extreme poverty upon them, saying 'Do not possess gold and silver, etc. [Matthew 10:9]' . . . Christ commanded the apostles to be distanced from earthly possessions and temporal lordship, because he wished them to be spiritual men.[36]

In recognizing the link between earthly power and possessions, between powerlessness and poverty, the author was taking up a position in the contemporary debate about poverty, centred on the conflicts within the Franciscan order. As we shall see, the interrelated themes of poverty and power played a crucial role in ecclesiastical controversy in the first half of the fourteenth century, and were in many ways the most fundamental issues facing the church. The author's insistence on extreme poverty for the clergy reflected the interpretation of the rigorist wing, the Spiritual Franciscans. For him, the two distinct *genera* of spiritual and temporal matters implied poverty and possessions respectively.

Another anonymous *quaestio*, traditionally known by its *incipit* as the *Rex pacificus* (The Peacemaker King), also provided a balanced pro-royal approach. It was a classic defence of the dualist thesis, being designed to demonstrate that the pope had no jurisdiction in temporal matters (other than that given him by a temporal ruler) and none over the French monarch in particular. Again we do not know for certain when it was written, but it must have been after August 1297, because it refers to the canonization of Louis IX, and

---

[35] *Ibid.*, p. 108.

[36] 'Christus, tam Petro quam caeteris apostolis, dominium, potestatem et iurisdictionem in temporalibus interdixit; cum eis extremam paupertatem indixit, dicens: "Nolite possidere aurum et argentum, etc. [Matthew 10:9]" . . . Elongationem a possessione terrena et dominio temporali praecepit Christus apostolis, volens eos spirituales esse' (*ibid.*, pp. 70–2).

quite possibly after December 1301, because of what appears to be a reference in it to the wording of the royal forgery *Deum time*. Karl Ubl considers that it was also produced as part of the pro-royal propaganda effort harnessed to condemn *Deum time*, by way of preparation for the form of Estates General of April 1302.[37]

The *Rex pacificus* was notable for its clear treatment of power understood as jurisdiction exercised in the government of this world. The author made use of organic imagery:

> And just as in the human body, the operations of the heart and the head are distinct, so also in the government of the world, jurisdictions are distinct, namely spiritual, which is represented by the head, and temporal, which is represented by the heart.[38]

These two jurisdictions were distinct: their relationship was not one of mutual dependence but of mutual defence for the good rule of the *respublica* in both spiritual and corporeal matters,[39] a co-operation which created unity.[40] Indeed, the author, overtly accepting the Augustinian view that true justice was only to be found where Christ was the ruler, held that he had two vicars:

> When the pope is said to be the vicar of Christ, I say that it is true in spiritual matters, but he truly has another vicar in temporal ones, namely, the temporal power, which since it is from God, as is said in Romans 13, can be said to be in God's place in temporal rule.[41]

---

[37] Ubl, 'Johannes Quidorts Weg', p. 65.

[38] 'Et sicut in corpore humano cordis et capitis sunt distinctae operationes, sic in regimine mundano distinctae sunt iurisdictiones, videlicet spiritualis, que repraesentatur in capite, et temporalis, quae repraesentatur in corde' (p. 22 – all references are to R.W. Dyson (ed.), *Quaestio de potestate papae (Rex pacificus)/An Enquiry into the Power of the Pope. A Critical Edition and Translation*, Texts and Studies in Religion, 83 (Lewiston, NY, Queenston, Lampeter: Edwin Mellen Press, 1999)); all translations from Latin into English are my own. For the use of head and heart imagery, see now Takashi Shogimen, '"Head or Heart?" revisited: physiology and political thought in the thirteenth and fourteenth centuries', *History of Political Thought*, 28, 2 (Summer 2007), 208–29.

[39] Dyson, *Quaestio de potestate papae*, p. 50   [40] *Ibid.*, p. 51.

[41] 'Sed quando dicitur papa est Christi vicarius, dico quod verum est in spiritualibus, sed bene habet alium vicarium in temporalibus, videlicet, potestatem temporalem: quae cum sit a Deo, sicut dicitur ad Rom. XIII, potest dici vices Dei gerere in regimine temporali' (*ibid.*, p. 48).

He who was greater in the church should exercise only a humble ministry in temporal matters.[42] Furthermore, since there were kings before priests in point of time, temporal power could not be derived from spiritual power because 'the cause is prior to that whose cause it is'.[43]

The writer of the *Rex pacificus* made no clear distinction between church and state. There was a fluidity in his usage of the terms *respublica* and *ecclesia*. He made a traditional distinction between two meanings of *ecclesia*:

And this should be understood by explaining the word, 'church', not in its general sense, as when we say that the church is called the congregation of the faithful, but in its special one, namely, in so far as the church is distinguished from the world, and clergy and ecclesiastical men from laymen and secular people.[44]

He argued in this way because he was producing a dualist argument about the exercise of power within the *ecclesia* in its wider sense. His sources of authority were the Bible and canon law. He was in essence opposing the papacy on its own ground as all exponents of the dualist view were. The merit of the *Rex pacificus* was clarity of expression, not originality of thought. What was required for a more effective denial of Boniface VIII's claims was a clearer distinction between the notions of church and state rather than an attempt simply to delineate the relative spheres of spiritual and temporal jurisdiction within the Christian community.

THE MAJOR TRACTS

The major tracts, which examined fundamental issues arising from this conflict, were produced within a short time-frame between 1302 and 1303. Of these, probably the first in date of composition was that

---

[42] *Ibid.*, p. 18.   [43] 'Causa prior est eo cuius est causa' (*ibid.*, p. 48).

[44] 'Et hoc intelligi debet accipiendo Ecclesiam non in generali, prout dicimus quod Ecclesia dicitur congregatio fidelium, sed secundum quod accipitur in speciali: scilicet prout Ecclesia distinguitur contra saeculum, et clerici et viri ecclesiastici contra laicos et saeculares' (*ibid.*, p. 29).

of Giles of Rome (Aegidius Romanus), *De ecclesiastica potestate* (On Ecclesiastical Power), of 1302. This work, 209 pages long in the modern edition, was the first systematic and truly extensive treatment of the nature of ecclesiastical and in particular papal power and its relation to secular rulers. It was a classic exposition of the papal hierocratic claims at their most extreme. The tract itself was developed out of a sermon which Giles delivered before the papal curia earlier in the year.[45] Giles wrote expressly to support the position taken by Boniface VIII and indeed dedicated his work to the pope, who made use of it in the construction of *Unam sanctam.*[46] Giles, an intellectual product of the University of Paris, was the leading member of the Augustinians there, having been made their first professor of theology. In 1291 he was made Prior-General of the order and in 1294 Boniface had made him Archbishop of Bourges, although he spent most of the rest of his life at the papal curia. His academic standing was of the highest rank. *De ecclesiastica potestate* was not, however, his only contribution to political thought: in 1277/9 he had produced his *De regimine principum* (On the Government of Princes), which was fundamentally different in approach: it was thoroughly this-worldly in tone, making heavy use of an ultimately Aristotelian assumption of the autonomy of the political order, and ignored questions of the relationship between temporal and spiritual power. There was no hint in the earlier work of the line he would take in this later work. Was this evidence of a profound inner contradiction or of a change of mind? The intellectual explanation is that there was no problem, because Giles in the two works was arguing in different ways and on different levels, the political first and subsequently the theological, a method familiar in the Parisian schools.

---

[45] See Concetta Luna, 'Un nuovo documento del conflitto fra Bonifacio VIII e Filippo il Bello: il discorso "De potestate domini papae" di Egidio Romano (con un'appendice su Borromeo di Bologna e la "Eger cui lenia")', Documenti e studi sulla tradizione filosofica medievale, *Rivista della Società Internazionale per lo Studio del Medioevo Latino*, 3, 1–2 (1992), 167–243.

[46] Karl Ubl maintains that Giles was writing in answer to the pro-royal arguments produced by way of preparation for the form of Estates General of April 1302: 'Johannes Quidorts Weg', p. 70.

The practical explanation is that the works were offered to different rulers, whose requirements needed this mental versatility on Giles's part: the *De regimine principum* had been composed as an advice-book for the future Philip IV of France, no less, and in its manuscript dissemination became the most influential example of the medieval mirror-of-princes genre.

Giles did not of course set out to say anything new in *De ecclesiastica potestate*, but in taking hierocratic ideas to their extreme, logical conclusions he reached formulations which did extend their scope and meaning. His fundamental presuppositions were hierarchical: the superiority of the spiritual over the temporal, of the soul over the body and of the clergy over the laity. The tract itself is difficult to follow because it is highly diffuse and repetitive, showing every sign of having been written in a rush. But the cumulative effect is to hammer home the thesis of papal power. The tract is both exhaustive and exhausting to read.

Giles's core argument stemmed from the proposition that lordship (*dominium*) understood as both power of jurisdiction and property rights existed justly only within the church in its wider sense as the Christian community. Just *dominium* was therefore the product of grace. Within the Christian community, the church in its narrower sense of the clergy was the medium by which grace was administered through the sacraments and sinners were reconciled. The church, understood as the clergy, was therefore the ultimate possessor of all jurisdiction and property. Giles went further: he equated the church with the pope, in whom all the powers of the church were ultimately focused and from whom all of them were derived. His overall thesis was therefore a radical exposition of papal power.

The sources of Giles's tract were wide-ranging, notably the Bible, canon law (and especially papal decretals), Peter Comestor's *Historia scholastica*, Aristotle, Augustine, Pseudo-Dionysius, Bernard of Clairvaux and Hugh of St Victor. Giles wove these authorities into his text, but in ways which often departed from their original meanings and contexts. He used authorities to support his own structure of reasoning; as he said, 'Because, perchance, authorities may not suffice for someone, we want to produce the reasons why no one could have just ownership (*dominium*) of anything, unless he were regenerated through the church'.[47] He referred, for instance, to Augustine's famous statements, 'Remove justice, and what are kingdoms but bands of robbers on a large scale?' and 'True justice is found only in that commonwealth whose founder and ruler is Christ', in support of his hierocratic argument, whereas Augustine himself in his mature thought reached the position that true justice could not be attained in this world and that justice should be removed from the definition of the state.[48] What we find in Giles is an example of that medieval *Augustinisme politique* which understood Augustine to have meant that the only truly just society was a Christian one (that is, the church in its wider sense), with Christian rulership the only just form.[49]

Giles made it abundantly clear that he collapsed the power of the church as a whole into that of the pope. From the beginning of the tract there was a concentration on the power of the pope, and the whole work can be seen as an analysis and justification of papal claims to plenitude of power (*plenitudo potestatis*). In the first chapter of Book One, Giles gave the most urgent possible justification for covering this topic. Ignorance of matters of faith and morals led to damnation, but it lay with the pope exercising his plenitude of power to define matters of faith and morals in an authoritative way.[50] The question of papal plenitude of power thus related to salvation itself. Giles also recognized that he must treat

---

[47] 'Quia forte alicui auctoritates non sufficiunt, volumus raciones adducere, quod nullus possit cum iusticia de aliqua re habere dominium, nisi sit regeneratus per ecclesiam' (2.7, p. 74 – all references are to Aegidius Romanus, *De ecclesiastica potestate*, ed. R. Scholz (repr. Aalen: Scientia Verlag, 1961)).

[48] 'Remota itaque iustitia quid sint regna nisi magna latrocinia?' (Augustine of Hippo, *De civitate dei*, 4.4, Corpus Christianorum, Series Latina, vol. XLVII (Turnhout: Brepols, 1955), p. 101); 'Vera autem iustitia non est nisi in ea re publica, cuius conditor rectorque Christus est' (*De civitate dei* 2.21, p. 55). See R.A. Markus, *Saeculum: History and Society in the Theology of St Augustine* (Cambridge University Press, 1970).

[49] See Joseph Canning, *A History of Medieval Political Thought, 300–1450* (London and New York: Routledge, 1996), pp. 42–3.

[50] Aegidius Romanus, *De ecclesiastica potestate*, 1.1, p. 5.

the pope's power over temporal matters: 'For this too is discerned as pertaining to good morals, so that the laity may learn also in temporal things, in which they are very hostile to clergy, to obey their superiors.'[51]

In defining the pope's plenitude of power, Giles set it within the limits of what was given to the church: 'In the supreme pontiff, however, there is plenitude of power not in every way, but in so far as there is power within the church, so that the whole of the power which is in the church is reserved to the supreme pontiff.'[52] This plenitude of power had two modes of operation. As definer of matters of faith and morals, the pope had the power to lay down moral laws as positive law for humanity, but had the capacity to go beyond these himself, because he was above the laws which he had made. Also, in what could appear a somewhat obscure definition, the pope could achieve without a second cause that which he could achieve with one.[53] This was on the surface an innocuous formulation, but viewed within the hierarchical context of Giles's world view it was pregnant with meaning. God of course was the archetype who could do by himself whatever he could do through his human agents. The pope could do the same within his sphere of operation. This meant that all jurisdictional power within the Christian community lay ultimately with the pope. Within the church understood more narrowly as an ecclesiastical body, all authority (such as that of a bishop) derived from the pope, while within the church understood in its widest sense as the body of believing Christians, the power of secular rulers was also derived from the supreme pontiff. In normal circumstances there was an undisturbed hierarchy of functions in which ecclesiastical and temporal authorities exercised their specific powers, but in an emergency, if the

---

[51] 'Nam et hoc ad bonos mores pertinere dignoscitur, ut discant laici eciam in temporalibus, in quibus oppido infesti sunt clericis, suis superioribus obedire' (*ibid.*, 1.1, p. 5).

[52] 'In summo autem pontifice est plenitudo potestatis non quocumque modo, sed quantum ad posse, quod est in ecclesia, ita quod totum posse, quod est in ecclesia, reservatur in summo pontifice' (*ibid.*, 3.9, p. 193).

[53] *Ibid.*, 3.10, p. 195.

good of the church demanded it, the pope could intervene and, if necessary, exercise powers directly which he normally delegated to others lower down the hierarchical ladder.

The tract discussed, at inordinate length, the relationship between spiritual and temporal power. The power of the pope was primary and universal, while that of the secular ruler was secondary and particular.[54] Giles expressed his argument in classic terms. He argued that priesthood was prior to kingship in time and greater than it in dignity, on the grounds that the spiritual power had instituted the earthly power and could judge it for its delinquencies, referring expressly to the authoritative statement of Hugh of St Victor.[55] He repeated and elaborated in a hierocratic manner Bernard of Clairvaux's expression of the two-swords analogy, thereby going beyond Bernard's own intentions. Giles said that the two swords mentioned in Luke (22:38) signified spiritual and temporal power; that both were in the ultimate possession of the pope, who conceded the use of the material sword to the temporal ruler but retained the right to command its use, command being superior to use.[56] Giles held that of the church's two swords, one was drawn (that of spiritual power), while the other was sheathed (the material sword held by right of command).[57] Behind this view lay a deep conviction of the superiority of spiritual things over temporal things. Giles reflected the deeply ingrained notion that the clergy should not

[54] See for instance *ibid.*, 2.6 (at length), pp. 60–70; and 3.11, pp. 200–6.
[55] *Ibid.*, 1.4, pp. 11–12; 1.5, pp. 14–15; 1.6, p. 22; 2.5, p. 55. See Hugh of St Victor, *De sacramentis christianae fidei*, 2.2.4, *PL*, vol. CLXXVI, col. 418: 'Quanto autem vita spiritualis dignior est quam terrena, et spiritus quam corpus, tanto spiritualis potestas terrenam sive saecularem potestatem honore, ac dignitate praecedit. Nam spiritualis potestas terrenam potestatem et instituere habet, ut sit, et iudicare habet si bona non fuerit. Ipsa vero a Deo primum instituta est, et cum deviat, a solo Deo judicari potest.'
[56] Aegidius Romanus, *De ecclesiastica potestate*, 2.5, pp. 56–8; 2.15, pp. 137–8.
[57] *Ibid.*, 2.5, p. 56. Giles referred to Bede at this point for the notion of the drawn and undrawn swords, but his interpretation in terms of the spiritual and the material sword is not in Bede: see Bede, *In Lucae evangelium expositio*, 6 (*PL* 92, cols. 601–2), quoted in Thomas Aquinas, *Catena aurea in quattuor evangelia, Expositio in Lucam*, 22, c. 10, ed. P. Angelicus Guariditi (Rome: Marietti), p. 291.

dirty their hands with involvement in secular affairs – that was not their job. But he did maintain that there were occasions on which the church, and the pope in particular, could exercise temporal power directly. Canon law gave a wealth of examples justifying papal intervention in temporal matters in certain cases (*'certis causis inspectis'*): these were listed and discussed at length by Giles.[58] More interestingly, he argued ingeniously that just as Christ could override the normal workings of nature by performing a miracle, his vicar, the pope, could also override the normal function of the secular ruler by a direct intervention of power in a temporal matter.[59] Giles believed that power in itself was something good and only its use could be bad (one of the reasons justifying papal intervention), but that all power derived ultimately from God, who could permit his people to suffer a bad ruler for their spiritual improvement, an Augustinian argument.[60]

But was there any limit to the pope's ultimate power in temporal matters? This was an old conundrum for any medieval juristic discussion of sovereign power. Giles said:

We shall distinguish the double power of the Supreme Pontiff, and his double jurisdiction in temporal matters: the one absolute, the other regulated, because, as the wise philosophers say, he who makes the law should observe it. If, therefore, the Supreme Pontiff, according to his absolute power, is otherwise without bridle and halter, he should impose on himself a bridle and halter, through himself observing his legislation and law.[61]

This has echoes of the theme of the ruler's absolute and ordained power, a well-worked trope of both jurists and theologians from the

---

[58] Aegidius Romanus, *De ecclesiastica potestate*, 3.5–3.8, pp. 168–90.

[59] *Ibid.*, 3.9, pp. 190–1.

[60] *Ibid.*, 2.9, p. 83. See 3.7, pp. 179–85 for details of grounds for papal intervention in canon law.

[61] 'Distinguemus duplicem potestatem summi pontificis et duplicem eius iurisdiccionem in temporalibus rebus: unam absolutam et aliam regulatam, quia, ut tradiderunt sapientes philosophi, legis positivus debet esse legis observativus. Si ergo summus pontifex secundum suum posse absolutum est alias sine freno et sine capistro, ipse tamen debet sibi frenum et capistrum imponere, in se ipso observando leges et iura' (*ibid.*, 3.7, p. 181).

mid-thirteenth century. In juristic scholarship, the discussion
centred upon the possible conflict between the emperor's status as
being 'freed from the laws' (*legibus solutus*), that is, from human
ones, and the notion that it was fitting for him to observe the laws
which depended on his sovereign power for their validity.[62]

In sum, Giles held that the pope, as the 'fount of power' (*fons
potestatis*), had the most perfect human power.[63] In a highly revealing
passage right at the end of his tract, he openly acknowledged the
emotional message underlying his analysis of the church's and in
particular the pope's power:

> Let us all equally hear the purpose of my discourse. Fear the church and
> observe its commandments. This means every man; that is, every man is
> directed to this. Indeed, the church is to be feared and its commandments
> observed, or the Supreme Pontiff, who occupies the apex of the church and
> who can be said to be the church, is to be feared and his commandments
> observed, because his power is spiritual, heavenly and divine, and is without
> weight, number or measure.[64]

This shows just how far Giles had gone (like the papacy itself) in
seeing the church, and the pope in particular, in terms of the
possession and exercise of power.

But it was in his treatment of *dominium* in the sense of property
rights that Giles made his most extreme and truly striking statements,
discussing the whole question at very great length, notably in Book II.
He argued that all right to property came through the church, because
regeneration through the church's sacraments of baptism (the remedy
for original sin) and penance (that for actual sin) was necessary for

---

[62] See Canning, *A History of Medieval Political Thought*, pp. 118, 167; and Kenneth
Pennington, *The Prince and the Law, 1200–1600* (Berkeley, Los Angeles, Oxford:
University of California Press, 1993), pp. 54–75.

[63] Aegidius Romanus, *De ecclesiastica potestate*, 3.10, p. 197.

[64] 'Finem ergo loquendi omnes pariter audiamus: Ecclesiam time et mandata eius
observa, hoc est enim omnis homo, idest ad hoc ordinatur omnis homo. Ecclesia
quidem est timenda et mandata eius sunt observanda, sive summus pontifex, qui
tenet apicem ecclesie et qui potest dici ecclesia, est timendus et sua mandata sunt
observanda, quia potestas eius est spiritualis, celestis et divina, et est sine pondere,
numero et mensura' (*ibid.*, 3.12, p. 209).

just possession or ownership.[65] This led him to make the remarkable statement that: 'The church is more lord of your possessions than you are yourself.'[66] Dispossession on the grounds of mortal sin was therefore justified.[67] Excommunication would also have the same effect, which, he pointed out, would not be the case if the church were not the lord and mistress of all temporal goods.[68] Most shockingly of all, Giles hit at the centre of the structure of societal property relationships by maintaining that the church had ultimate control over inheritances, saying that one did not justly inherit simply by the will of one's carnal father. An heir's state of mortal sin could invalidate the possession of an inheritance.[69] It is difficult to believe that Giles expected to be taken seriously in reality; maybe he was just trying to make a point. What he was doing was to develop the hierocratic argument to its logical extreme.

When it came to the question of actual possession of property by the church as opposed to an ultimate form of lordship in the Christian community, Giles was more circumspect. He was ambivalent about the clergy's possession of wealth. He made it clear that the clergy should not make the accumulation of wealth their main aim, because possessions would tend to impose anxiety on them and distract them from their spiritual mission. The clergy, while retaining ownership and possession of temporal goods, should delegate the actual administration and care of the church's property to others. For both clergy and laity, temporal goods had to be ordered to a spiritual end.[70] These statements by Giles should be seen in the context of the early fourteenth-century debate about poverty and property. He was acutely aware of the recommendations to poverty in the New Testament. He accepted that to have nothing of one's own pertained to perfection, but that that was a work of supererogation, as in the case of the rich young man in the

---

[65] *Ibid.*, 2.8, p. 78.
[66] 'Magis itaque erit ecclesia domina possessionis tue, quam tu ipse' (*ibid.*, 2.7, p. 74).
[67] *Ibid.*, 2.7, p. 74. [68] *Ibid.*, 2.12, p. 108.
[69] *Ibid.*, 2.8, pp. 79–80. [70] *Ibid.*, 2.3, p. 44.

Gospels. For Giles, however, members of religious orders vowed to poverty retained this perfection if they held possessions as property of a church.[71] He maintained that the condition of the church had changed over time. In its first age, temporal possessions had been prohibited, but direct divine support given; in its second, possessions were conceded and God's hand somewhat removed. Nowadays, the church lived in a different age:

> In this third age, therefore, the church is endowed with both, because it rejoices in both the support of temporal possessions and divine help, so that, governing itself, it can maintain its standing. For in the first place the church had its beginning and then its growth; now however it has perfection and standing, on account of which, so that it may preserve its standing, it needs both divine help, lest it suffer shipwreck, and the support of temporal possessions, lest it be held in low esteem by laymen.[72]

This reflects Giles's main purpose in writing: to justify and, through his scholarship, vindicate the rights claimed by the church. He thus exactly expressed the aims of Boniface VIII, which is why Giles was recognized by the pope as his greatest intellectual support. Both men were demanding that the laity show proper respect for the divinely created rights of the church and the papacy in particular. Giles was defending the church's rights to jurisdiction and property, that is, its power in this world, which he considered to be the underpinning necessary to sustain its spiritual mission.

Another tract, *De regimine christiano* (On Christian Government), also written in 1302 (or slightly later), was produced by Giles's Augustinian colleague at Paris, James of Viterbo. This too supported the hierocratic claims of the papacy and was dedicated to Boniface VIII. It was a very extensive and detailed work divided into two parts: the first considered the nature of the church and the

---

[71] *Ibid.*, 2.1, p. 38.

[72] 'In hoc ergo tercio tempore utroque est ecclesia dotata, quia gaudet et temporalium subsidio et divino auxilio, ut se possit in suo statu regere et conservare. Habuit enim prius ecclesia inicium, postea incrementum; nunc autem habet perfeccionem et statum: propter quod, ut in statu huiusmodi se conservet, et indiget divino auxilio, ne naufragium paciatur, et temporalium subsidio, ne a laicis vilipendatur' (*ibid.*, 2.3, p. 48). See also 2.2, p. 38.

lengthier second expressly addressed the question of power within the church and the relationship between spiritual and temporal power. The tone of the piece was level-headed and it was well structured, being a measured, scholastic treatment, making a notable contribution to medieval ecclesiology. James's loyalty was rewarded: having already supported Boniface's position with his tract *De renunciatione papae* (On the Resignation of the Pope) concerning the resignation of Celestine V, he was made Archbishop of Benevento in September 1302 and named Archbishop of Naples in December of the same year.[73]

James understood the church to be a community, but one of grace rather than nature. In order to describe this community more accurately, he used traditional imagery which differentiated between three kinds in ascending order of magnitude: the house, the city and the kingdom. In so doing he referred expressly to Augustine and gave biblical citations for applying all three to the church. But the next step he took showed a more radical approach:

And although the church is rightly named by these three terms signifying community, it is however more properly called a kingdom (*regnum*): because the church contains a great multitude collected from diverse peoples and nations, and diffused and spread throughout the whole world; because in the ecclesiastical community there is found everything which suffices for the salvation of men and the spiritual life; because it was instituted for the common good of all men; and because, like a kingdom, it contains within itself very many interconnected congregations of an increasing scale of magnitude, like provinces, dioceses, parishes and colleges.[74]

[73] See E. Ypma, 'Recherches sur la carrière scolaire et la bibliothèque de Jacques de Viterbe †1308', *Augustiniana*, 24 (1974), 247–82.

[74] 'Et licet hiis tribus nominibus communitatem designantibus, recte nominetur ecclesia, magis tamen proprie regnum vocatur; [tum] quia ecclesia magnam multitudinem comprehendit, ex diversis populis et nationibus collectam, et toto orbe terrarum diffusam et dilatatam; tum quia in ecclesiastica communitate, omnia, que hominum saluti et spirituali vite sufficiunt, reperiuntur; tum quia propter omnium hominum commune bonum instituta est; tum quia, ad instar regni, intra se continet congregationes plurimas ad invicem ordinatas ac se excedentes, ut provincias, dyoceses, parrochias et collegia' (1.1, pp. 94–5 – all references are to James of Viterbo, *De regimine christiano*, in *Le plus ancien traité de l'Eglise, Jacque de Viterbe, De regimine christiano (1301–2), Etudes des sources et*

James was applying political criteria which owed much to Aristotle: magnitude, self-sufficiency and the end of the common good. He was transposing characteristics of the greatest natural community to that of grace, the better to comprehend the church as being one made up of human beings. His definition of the church as a *regnum* prepared the way for his main concentration on its government (*regimen*), through the exercise of power (*potestas*), located ultimately in the hands of its king (*rex*) – the pope.

James's approach differed from that of Giles of Rome's *De ecclesiastica potestate*. Whereas Giles in that tract considered that only Christian rulership had validity, James accepted that man's life in community was the product of the natural order:

> The institution of these communities or societies proceeded from the natural inclination itself of men, as the Philosopher shows in the first book of the *Politics*. For man is by nature a social animal and one living in a multitude, which results from natural necessity, in that one man cannot live in self-sufficiency on his own, but needs help from another.[75]

In explaining the relationship between natural and Christian rulership, James pursued what he called a 'middle way' (*via media*):

> The institution of temporal power, materially and in its origin, has its existence from the natural inclination of men, and thereby, from God, insofar as the work of nature is the work of God; as regards its perfection, however, and form, it has existence from the spiritual power which is derived from God in a special way. For grace does not do away with nature but perfects and forms it. Similarly, that which is of grace does not do away with that which is of nature, but forms and perfects it. Wherefore, because the spiritual power looks to grace, and the temporal to nature, the spiritual does not thereby exclude the temporal but forms and perfects it. Indeed, every human power is imperfect and unformed, unless it be formed and perfected by the

---

édition critique, critical text with an introduction by H.-X. Arquillière (Paris: Gabriel Beauchesne, 1926)).

[75] 'Harum autem communitatum seu societatum institutio ex ipsa hominum naturali inclinatione processit, ut Philosophus ostendit primo Polit. Homo enim naturaliter est animal sociale et in multitudine vivens, quod ex naturali necessitate provenit, eo quod unus homo non potest sufficienter vivere per seipsum sed indiget ab alio adjuvari' (*ibid.*, 1.1. p. 91).

spiritual. This formation however is by approbation and ratification. Human power, therefore, which exists amongst the infidels, even though it is the product of human inclination, and thereby legitimate, is nevertheless unformed, because it has not been approved and ratified by the spiritual. And similarly, that power which exists amongst the faithful, is not perfected and formed, until it shall have been approved and ratified by the spiritual.[76]

He went on to make it clear that this perfection and formation were through the process of royal unction performed by the spiritual power.[77]

James was clearly applying Aquinas's statement – that grace perfected nature but did not do away with it – to the relationship between temporal and spiritual power (a step which Aquinas did not take himself).[78] Different rules therefore applied to Christian rulership. Rulership itself was natural, indeed necessary, to man in his social life,[79] but 'that a believer should be over other believers is from divine law, which arises from grace'.[80] The regimen of grace brought in the spiritual power which both instituted and could command and judge the Christian temporal one.[81] Indeed, in a Christian community (the church in its wider sense), temporal rulership, although it was immediately concerned with secular

---

[76] 'Institutio potestatis temporalis materialiter et inchoative habet esse a naturali hominum inclinatione, ac per hoc, a Deo in quantum opus nature est opus Dei; perfective autem et formaliter habet esse a potestate spirituali, que a Deo speciali modo derivatur. Nam gratia non tollit naturam sed perficit eam et format; et similiter id, quod est gratie, non tollit id, quod est nature; sed id format et perficit. Unde quia potestas spiritualis gratiam respicit, temporalis vero naturam: ideo spiritualis temporalem non excludit sed eam format et perficit. Imperfecta quidem et informis est omnis humana potestas, nisi per spiritualem formetur et perficiatur. Hec autem formatio est approbatio et ratificatio. Unde potestas humana, que est apud infideles, quantumcumque sit ex inclinatione nature, ac per hoc legitima, tamen informis est: quia per spiritualem non est approbata et ratificata. Et similiter illa, que est apud fideles perfecta et formata non est, donec per spiritualem fuerit approbata et ratificata' (*ibid.*, 2.7, p. 232).

[77] *Ibid.*, 2.7, p. 233. [78] See *ST*, 1a, 8.2.

[79] James of Viterbo, *De regimine christiano*, 2.10, pp. 295 and 303.

[80] 'Quod autem homo fidelis sit super homines fideles est ex iure divino, quod a gratia oritur' (*ibid.*, 2.7, p. 233).

[81] *Ibid.*, 2.7, pp. 233–6; 2.10, p. 285.

matters, ultimately served the same spiritual ends as did the spiritual power: 'Although the proximate end of temporal power is other than the end of the spiritual, their ultimate end is however the same: namely, supernatural beatitude of which the spiritual power has immediate care; and thus temporal power, if it is exercised rightly, is said to be in some way spiritual.'[82]

James therefore showed how Aristotelian naturalistic notions of the natural order of government and community could be harnessed to a hierocratic conception through extending the application of Aquinas's doctrine of grace and nature in order to provide a deepened pro-papal understanding of Hugh of St Victor's contention that the church instituted the temporal power.[83] It was a considerable achievement on James's part to establish this link between the naturalistic political order and that of Christian rulership. Giles of Rome had not sought to integrate his thoroughly naturalistic approach in his *De regimine principum* with his hierocratic approach in *De ecclesiastica potestate*; Aquinas's treatment of the relationship between temporal and spiritual power was skimpy and, apparently, of little interest to him.[84] Given the prevalence in intellectual circles of naturalistic Aristotelian political concepts and the existence in fact of monarchs claiming to rule by the grace of God, James was addressing a crucial contemporary question.

But, surely, James's most important contribution was to the theory of power in itself, irrespective of who exercised it. He followed the established view which distinguished between two powers of bishops and priests: that of orders and that of jurisdiction – the *potestas ordinis* was sacramental, while the *potestas iurisdictionis* was concerned with judging and ruling. He then had an insight. He held that the power

---

[82] 'Licet finis proximus temporalis potestatis sit alius a fine spiritualis, tamen finis ultimus idem est: scilicet beatitudo supernaturalis, de qua immediate curam habet spiritualis potestas; et ideo temporalis potestas, si recta sit, dicitur aliquo modo spiritualis' (*ibid.*, 2.8, p. 257).

[83] *Ibid.*, 2.7, p. 231.

[84] See Joseph Canning, 'Aquinas', in David Boucher and Paul Kelly (eds.), *Political Thinkers from Socrates to the Present* (Oxford University Press, 2003), pp. 120–1.

of jurisdiction was by nature 'royal'.[85] Thus, bishops and priests possessed both priestly power (that of orders) and royal power (that of jurisdiction).[86] As such, to James's mind, there was a double (*duplex*) royal power of jurisdiction, possessed, on the one hand, by both bishops and priests, and, on the other, by kings.[87] He was therefore able to isolate this notion of power in itself, in the sense of ruling, without attaching it exclusively to either the temporal or the spiritual ruler. Royal power was in essence the same thing, whoever exercised it, priest or king. Power over what and by whom were secondary questions. He characterized jurisdiction as royal, because he was using the concept of *regnum* as the descriptor both of the church and of the civil community. It was thus his usage of the notion of *regnum* which facilitated his recognition of the nature of ruling power, which, as he said, was his main interest. Power in itself he saw as good, although it could be put to a good or a bad use.[88] He saw it as necessary to have one head in a community to direct it towards the common good.[89]

The head of the church was, of course, Christ, and on earth his vicar the pope, the *rex* of the *regnum ecclesiae*.[90] The pope received from Christ plenitude of power:

> The Vicar of Christ, however, is said to have plenitude of power, because the whole governing power which has been communicated by Christ to the church, priestly and royal, spiritual and temporal, is in the Supreme Pontiff, the Vicar of Christ. As much power has been communicated to the church as was useful for the salvation of the faithful; therefore, in the Vicar of Christ there is the whole of that power which is required for securing the salvation of men.[91]

---

[85] James of Viterbo, *De regimine christiano*, 2.3, p. 178.

[86] *Ibid.*, 2.4, pp. 187–200; 2.5, pp. 201–22.

[87] *Ibid.*, 2.6, pp. 223–8; 2.7, pp. 229–44.   [88] *Ibid.*, 2.10, p. 297.

[89] *Ibid.*, 2.5, p. 211; 2.10, p. 303.   [90] *Ibid.*, 1.1, p. 95.

[91] 'Verumtamen dicitur Christi vicarius habere plenitudinem potestatis: quia tota potentia gubernativa que a Christo communicata est ecclesie, sacerdotalis et regalis, spiritualis et temporalis, est in summo pontifice Christi vicario. Tanta vero potestas communicata est ecclesie quanta erat oportuna ad salutem fidelium; quare in vicario Christi tota illa potentia est, que ad hominum salutem procurandam requiritur' (*ibid.*, 2.9, p. 272).

The pope exercised power over the church militant, that is, all Christians on their pilgrim way in this world: papal *plenitudo potestatis* covered secular rulers within the context of the church in this wider sense – no one was excepted:

It is to be known that the power of the Supreme Pontiff and Vicar of Christ is called full, firstly, because no one belonging in any way to the church militant is excluded, but every man existing in the present church is subject to him; and secondly, because every power ordained by God and given to man for governing the faithful, whether spiritual or temporal, is contained in this power.[92]

Indeed, all power within the church was derived from that of the pope.[93] Temporal rulers' power was subject to the spiritual in both spiritual and temporal matters, with the result that the pope could depose them.[94] According to James's profoundly hierarchical understanding, the lesser temporal power pre-existed in the greater spiritual power.[95] This meant that in reality there was but one royal power which had two aspects, the spiritual and the temporal:

It can also be said that the spiritual royal power and the temporal are not two powers, but two parts of the one perfect royal power, of which one alone is in earthly kings and in an inferior manner, whereas both are in spiritual rulers and in a more excellent manner. Wherefore, in the prelates of the church and especially in the Supreme Pontiff there is royal power which is whole, perfect and full; amongst the princes of this world it exists in part and in a diminished form.[96]

---

[92] 'Sciendum est quod potentia summi pontificis et Christi vicarii plena dicitur, primo quia ab hac potentia nullus ad ecclesiam militantem qualitercumque pertinens excipitur; sed omnis homo in presenti ecclesia existens ei subicitur. Secundo, quia omnis potestas ad gubernationem fidelium a Deo ordinata et hominibus data, sive spiritualis sive temporalis, in hac potestate comprehenditur' (*ibid.*, 2.9, p. 273).

[93] *Ibid.*, 2.9, p. 273 – immediate continuation of the above passage.

[94] *Ibid.*, 2.10, p. 285.   [95] *Ibid.*, 2.8, p. 248.

[96] 'Potest etiam dici quod potestas regia spiritualis et temporalis non sunt due potentie, sed due partes unius regie potestatis perfecte, quarum una solum est in regibus terrenis et modo inferiori; in spiritualibus autem est utraque et modo excellentiori. Unde in prelatis ecclesie et precipue in summo prelato est potestas regia tota et perfecta et plena; in principibus autem seculi est secundum partem et diminuta' (*ibid.*, 2.10, pp. 288–9).

Therefore, in conferring the power of the keys on St Peter and in entrusting him with the care of his sheep, Christ gave him at the same time both spiritual and temporal power and jurisdiction.[97]

James's approach provided him with answers to stock objections to the exercise of temporal power by the papacy. To imagined opponents using the statement 'My kingdom is not of this world' (John 18:36), James replied that there were many things which Christ did not do but had the power to, and which his vicar may nonetheless do, the exercise of temporal power being a case in point.[98] His interpretation of the two-swords argument was a hierocratic rendering of St Bernard's statement in *De consideratione* that the spiritual power held both, directly exercising the spiritual and commanding the use of the temporal.[99] To the standard theocratic argument that the temporal power was instituted directly by God without any mediation by the spiritual, James responded with a concept of mediation by human agents: government and social life were the result of man's natural inclination; the perfect form of rulership required the mediation of the spiritual power.[100] To the apparent problem (from James's point of view) that the Donation of Constantine involved the exercise of human law over a matter for divine law, he responded that the emperor, in conceding an earthly kingdom together with imperial insignia and offices, had not conferred any authority on the pope but had shown reverence to the spiritual power and the subjection of the earthly to the heavenly kingdom. God had permitted this honour so that the office of pope should shine forth in greater splendour. Indeed, the Donation was an act of co-operation and service permitting the pope more easily to exercise, *de facto*, rights which he already possessed *de iure divino* but had been unable to use before the time of Constantine because of persecution by tyrants. The Donation made possible the pope's

---

[97] *Ibid.*, 2.10, p. 292.   [98] *Ibid.*, 2.10, pp. 290–2.

[99] *Ibid.*, 2.10, pp. 289–90. See Bernard of Clairvaux, *De consideratione*, 4.3.7, in *Opera omnia*, ed. J. Leclercq, H.M. Rochais and C.H. Talbot (Rome: Editiones Cistercienses, 1963), vol. III, p. 424.

[100] James of Viterbo, *De regimine christiano*, 2.10, p. 295.

direct involvement in temporal matters, for instance, during a
vacancy in the empire.[101]

For James, the church was not just a *regnum* but a true *respublica*
(commonwealth), because it was a unity and universal. To support
this view, he used a traditional Augustinian interpretation of Cicero's
definition of the people comprising a *res publica* – 'a multitude united
together by consent to law and the participation in a common
good'.[102] James concluded: 'According to this definition, no community is called a true *res publica*, except the ecclesiastical, because in
it alone exists true justice, true utility and true communion.'[103] The
unity of the church as a *regnum* derived from its having one ruler,
because that was the best form of government for a multitude – the
one which best secured the common good:

> For rulership or government is nothing other than the direction of the
> governed to an end which is a good of some kind. Unity however pertains
> to the nature of a good, as Boethius proves in Book III of *De consolatione*
> [On the Consolation of Philosophy], in this way – that just as everything
> desires the good, so it desires unity without which it cannot exist. Anything
> exists insofar as it is one. That, therefore, at which the intention of the
> governor of the multitude aims is rightly unity and the peace of the multitude
> in which unity consists the good and safety of any society.[104]

---

[101] *Ibid.*, 2.8, pp. 255–6.

[102] 'Populus autem est multitudinis cetus iuris consensu et utilitatis communione
sociatus' (*ibid.*, 2.4, p. 128) – see Cicero, *De republica*, ed. K. Ziegler (Leipzig:
B.G. Teubner, 1960), 1.25.39. For the difference between Augustine's final
interpretation of the implications of this passage and the medieval 'Augustinian'
interpretation of Augustine's discussion of it, see Canning, *History of Medieval
Political Thought*, pp. 41–3.

[103] 'Secundum hanc diffinitionem, nulla communitas dicitur vere res publica nisi
ecclesiastica, quia in ea sola est vera iustitia et vera utilitas et vera communio'
(James of Viterbo, *De regimine christiano*, 2.4, p. 128). See Augustine of Hippo,
De civitate dei, 2.21.

[104] 'Nam regimen sive gubernatio nichil est aliud quam directio gubernatorum ad
finem, qui est aliquod bonum. Unitas autem pertinet ad rationem boni, sicut
probat Boetius III. Libro *De consolatione*, per hoc quod sicut omnia desiderant
bonum, ita desiderant unitatem sine qua esse non possunt. Unumquodque enim
in tantum est in quantum unum est. Unde, illud ad quod tendit intentio
multitudinem gubernantis, recte est unitas et pax multitudinis, in qua unitate

The case of the pope, as the head and governor of the church on earth, was the pre-eminent example of the link between power and the common good, the end for which rulership existed.

Another pro-papal tract, *De potestate pape* (On the Power of the Pope), written by Henry of Cremona, a canonist at the papal court and later Bishop of Reggio in Emilia, deserves mention because of the notoriety which it achieved. It focused on demonstrating that the pope had temporal jurisdiction throughout the whole world. It was not long (thirteen pages in Richard Scholz's edition),[105] but it did provide a wide-ranging exposition of arguments, backed by a dense mass of authorities, mostly from the canon law and the Bible, in support of the papal position and refutation of stock objections. The tract was therefore a highly useful and concentrated source for those wishing to defend the pope. There is scholarly disagreement about when and where it was produced. Jürgen Miethke has argued that it was produced deep in the heart of the papacy, being a memorandum composed for a consistory in June 1302.[106] Karl Ubl has rejected Miethke's argument, maintaining that Henry of Cremona wrote his tract during his legation to Paris, when he engaged with pro-royal tracts in the debate over *Deum time* before the calling of the form of Estates General of April 1302.[107] Boniface VIII was specifically mentioned in the text, which was specifically aimed at his Ghibelline enemies, with those at Cremona being given special mention.[108] The tract was not overtly aimed at the French but knowledge of its contents spread very rapidly in Paris. One French-produced fifteenth-century manuscript of the work, now at Uppsala, states that it was delivered by Henry in a consistory before

---

consistit bonum et salus cuiuslibet societatis' (James of Viterbo, *De regimine christiano*, 2.5, p. 211).

[105] Henry of Cremona, *De potestate pape*, in Richard Scholz, *Die Publizistik zur Zeit Philipps des Schönen und Bonifaz' VIII.* (repr. Amsterdam: Editions Rodopi, 1969), pp. 459–71. All references are to this edition.

[106] See Miethke, *De potestate papae*, p. 85.

[107] Ubl, 'Johnnes Quidorts Weg', pp. 59–60, 65.

[108] Henry of Cremona, *De potestate pape*, p. 460.

Boniface in the presence of French ambassadors.[109] Ubl, however, does not consider this to be reliable evidence.[110]

Henry's approach was profoundly hierocratic. Out of the mass of arguments poured forth, certain merit particular attention. The Donation of Constantine, he maintained, merely recognized that the church thereby gained the exercise *de facto* of what it already possessed *de iure*, thus answering the objection that the Donation revealed an imperial source for papal power. Christ wished to come to the aid of the faith, which meant, in human terms, giving to the church that power which it had previously lacked – this he did through the medium of Constantine's donation, whereby the emperor renounced the empire and accepted that he held it from the church.[111] Henry clarified his meaning by referring to the much commented-on passage in Luke 14:15–24, where the giver of the feast, disappointed at the refusals of those whom he had first invited, instructed his servants to search the highways and hedge-rows and 'force all to come in' (*compellite omnes intrare*): this symbolized, according to Henry, that the early church, only having the role of inviting, possessed nothing, whereas the church of his own day had the power to compel. This passage showed that the church was going to have the temporal power which the emperors had lost through persecuting it and the popes in particular.[112] To the classic objection that Christ had said that his kingdom was not of this world, Henry replied that such was the case *de facto*, because Christ was not obeyed, but that *de iure* he was king of the world.[113] Henry felt secure in relying so much on canon law in addition to the Bible because he took the extreme position that 'the canons themselves have been dictated by the Holy Spirit'.[114] It is not surprising that there were similarities between parts of Henry's text and that of *Unam sanctam*, because he formed part of the intellectual

---

[109] See Miethke, *De potestate papae*, p. 86n229.
[110] Ubl, 'Johannes Quidorts Weg', pp. 59–60.
[111] Henry of Cremona, *De potestate pape*, pp. 467–8.
[112] *Ibid.*, p. 468.   [113] *Ibid.*, p. 470.
[114] 'Ipsi canones sunt per spiritum sanctum dictati' (*ibid.*, pp. 470–1).

milieu around Boniface. In particular, his arguments in favour of unity under one head found clear resonances in the later bull: that the church was one dove and one body with one head, Christ; that a body with two heads would be a monster; and that Christ's clothing was undivided.[115] But Henry's particular claim to fame was that his tract became the prime target of John of Paris's wrath against the papalists.

John of Paris (Jean Quidort), a Dominican at the University of Paris, wrote the tract *De regia potestate et papali* (On Royal and Papal Power). The scholarly consensus used to be that he wrote it some- time within the second half of 1302 and the first few weeks of 1303.[116] But Karl Ubl has produced very strong arguments that there were three successive redactions of the text. He claims that the first was written between February and April 1302 in response to a royal demand at the time of the debate over *Deum time*, and that shortly after the form of Estates General of April 1302, John reworked his tract to include polemic against Henry of Cremona and incorporated some suggestions from the *Rex pacificus*.[117] John was a supporter of the French crown in its conflict with Boniface VIII: for instance, he joined his fellow Dominicans of the Convent of St James in signing the petition of June 1303 requesting that the pope be tried before a general council of the church, a proposal agreed by that month's meeting of the three estates in Paris choreographed by the royal court. As a theologian, he was involved in several controversies, notably supporting Aquinas against his Franciscan opponents and, indeed, died in 1306 in the midst of an appeal to Pope Clement V against the decision made at Paris forbidding him to teach because

[115] *Ibid.*, pp. 469–70.

[116] See, however, Janet Coleman's divergent view that the text reflects Dominican arguments developed from the 1270s to the 1290s against Franciscan positions and cannot therefore be seen with any certainty as having been written in response to Boniface VIII's *Clericis laicos*, *Ausculta fili* or *Unam sanctam* (see Janet Coleman, 'The intellectual milieu of John of Paris, OP', in Jürgen Miethke (ed.), *Das Publikum politischer Theorie im 14. Jahrhundert* (Munich: Oldenbourg, 1992), pp. 173–206; and Janet Coleman, *A History of Political Thought. From the Middle Ages to the Renaissance* (Oxford: Blackwell, 2000), p. 121).

[117] Ubl, 'Johannes Quidorts Weg', pp. 52–3, 60, 65, 71–2.

of his idiosyncratic ideas on the nature of the Eucharist. His *De regia potestate et papali* was a scholastic work meant to be detached in nature and designed for general application – there were only a couple of references in it to the dispute between Philip and Boniface. The tract was moderate in tone and has been characterized as pursuing a *via media* between the extremes of papal and royal apologists.[118] Ubl rejects this interpretation, considering that John's tract was written to justify the royal position on the division between temporal and spiritual power, and the rejection of papal demands.[119] It is certain that John's aim was to protect the French monarchy against papal claims and to vindicate French sovereignty against both the pope and the emperor.

In this tract, John expressly and avowedly considered the question of power and was noteworthy because he addressed the problems of the nature of, and relationship between, temporal and spiritual power from both sides. This was the result of his scholastic method in exhaustively marshalling authorities for and against propositions, to provide biblical, juristic, historical and Aristotelian arguments which could be useful for the French royal position. His work had therefore to some extent the appearance of a mosaic of arguments, and paradoxically provided an excellent conspectus of the range of hierocratic ones.

At the heart of John's treatment of the relationship between temporal and spiritual power lay a recognition that human life had a dual end or purpose: a natural one in this world, achieved by the life of virtue, which itself was hierarchically ordered to a higher supernatural destiny, the enjoyment of the vision of God in heaven. Temporal government he saw as being primarily (but not exclusively) concerned with the natural dimension of man's existence, with spiritual power being primarily (but again not solely)

---

[118] See the classic treatment of Jean Rivière, *Le problème de l'Eglise et de l'Etat au temps de Philippe le Bel*, Etudes et documents 8 (Louvain: Spicilegium sacrum Lovaniense, 1926), pp. 281–300.

[119] Ubl, 'Johannes Quidorts Weg', p. 71. For a survey of John of Paris's political ideas, see, for instance, Monahan, *Consent, Coercion and Limit*, pp. 195–205.

concerned with what related to salvation. But he did not see the priesthood as being concerned with matters which were purely spiritual and other-worldly because the church existed as a body which needed to be governed, whereas secular rulers could not be considered in a purely naturalistic way because they governed subjects who were also Christians. The claims of temporal and spiritual power intersected at the level of government and jurisdiction, and it was here that John made his distinctive contributions.

Clearly, John was coming from a conventional position in working on the basis of a dual order of human life, and one which owed a lot to Aquinas; however, he went far beyond Aquinas in considering the relationship between the two powers, partly because this was the specific task he was undertaking and partly because of Thomas's relative lack of interest in the subject. John also benefited from a more considerable knowledge of canon law. Because John, unlike Aquinas, was writing in the context of a conflict, he set himself to master his opponents' arguments in order to refute them.

John began his work with an Aristotelian-Thomist definition: 'Kingship is the government of a perfect multitude ordained towards the common good by one man.'[120] Such government was derived from natural law and the *ius gentium* because man was by nature a civil or political and social animal.[121] He defined priesthood as being a power, but a spiritual and specifically sacramental one: 'Priesthood is a spiritual power conferred by Christ on the ministers of the church for dispensing the sacraments to the faithful.'[122] But what was the relationship between the two? God stood behind both powers, directly in the case of priestly power and ultimately in that of temporal power, in the sense that he had

---

[120] 'Regnum est regimen multitudinis perfectae ad commune bonum ordinatum ab uno' (ch. 1, p. 75) – all references are to the critical edition of John of Paris, *De regia potestate et papali*, in Fritz Bleienstein (ed.), *Johannes Quidort von Paris: Über königliche und päpstliche Gewalt (De regia potestate et papali). Textkritische Edition mit deutscher Übersetzung* (Stuttgart: Ernst Kless Verlag, 1969).

[121] *Ibid.*, ch. 1, pp. 75 and 77.

[122] 'Sacerdotium est spiritualis potestas ministris ecclesie a Christo collata ad dispensandum fidelibus sacramenta' (*ibid.*, ch. 2, p. 80).

implanted a natural instinct in men to live in community and create governments.[123] But his key argument was this: he admitted that the priesthood was greater in dignity than the secular power, whether king or emperor, because it was concerned with man's ultimate destiny in the next world, to which the virtuous life in this one (the concern of secular rulers) was but a prelude. But, he maintained, this did not mean that the secular power was derived from the spiritual: there was no causality, as from the higher to the lower – they existed in parallel. Indeed, each was the competent authority in its own sphere: the secular *princeps* was greater in temporal matters, whereas the priesthood was greater in spiritual ones.[124] This thesis gave an effective response to the hierocratic line of argument which relied on the notion that the hierarchical superiority of the priesthood necessarily involved an efficient causality whereby the lower secular power derived its very existence and legitimation from the higher spiritual power.

This argument was striking enough, but it was based on an idea of temporal and spiritual power as being different in kind. There remained an important area where this was not the case: that of jurisdiction. In his final three chapters (23–5) which wrestled with the topical question of whether a pope could resign, much debated by canonists and addressed by Giles of Rome in his *De renunciatione papae* (On the Resignation of a Pope), on which John much relied, he confronted the question of the nature of jurisdiction. He perceived very clearly that jurisdiction in itself remained essentially the same whether it was exercised by secular or spiritual powers. Spiritual power could not therefore be completely described as being sacramental; there was also a parallel spiritual power of jurisdiction which operated according to the same rules as temporal power. All jurisdiction, which of necessity involved a structure of command, belonged to the natural order of human life:

Those things which belong to jurisdiction are not above nature and the condition of [human] affairs, and above the human condition, because it is

---

[123] *Ibid.*, ch. 3, p. 82.   [124] *Ibid.*, ch. 5, p. 89.

not above the human condition that men should be in charge of men; rather it is natural somehow.[125]

This was said specifically about the pope's power of jurisdiction, the essence of the papal office, as opposed to his power of orders, which he shared with all bishops. Because jurisdiction was something natural, the choice of which individual should exercise it must lie with human beings. This applied to both temporal and spiritual jurisdiction. In the case of the pope, whereas the papal office itself was divinely instituted, the choice of which individual person should be pope lay with the cardinals.[126] Such consent could be withdrawn. The papacy existed for the good of the church as a whole. If an individual pope impeded the common good of the church, then the cardinals or a general council could depose him if he would not resign, as John made clear when refuting the argument that the papacy as the highest created power (*summa virtus creata*) in one person could not be removed by another created power:

> Although it is the highest power in one person, there is however an equal one to it or a greater in the college [of cardinals] or the whole church. Or it can be said that, by divine authority, he can be deposed by the college or even more by a general council whose consent is supposed and presumed for a deposition, when there is clear scandal and the head is incorrigible.[127]

Similarly, in the case of a king, John maintained that the ultimate, metaphysical source of royal power lay with God, but that the choice of king, whether in the individual or the dynasty, lay with the people.[128] The barons would be the means by which this election would be made, as, for instance, in the case of both the

---

[125] 'Ea quae sunt iurisdictionis non sunt super naturam et condicionem negotii et super conditionem hominum, quia non est super condicionem hominum quod homines praesint hominibus, immo naturale est aliquo modo' (*ibid.*, ch. 25, p. 209).

[126] *Ibid.*, ch. 25, p. 202.

[127] 'Licet sit summa virtus in persona, tamen est ei aequalis vel maior in collegio sive in tota ecclesia. Vel potest dici quod potest deponi a collegio vel magis a generali concilio auctoritate divina, cuius consensus supponitur et praesumitur ad deponendum ubi manifeste apparet scandalum et incorrigibilitas presidentis' (*ibid.*, ch. 25, p. 207).

[128] *Ibid.*, ch. 10, p. 113.

deposition of Childeric and the choice of Pepin.[129] Thus, temporal and spiritual jurisdiction differed not in kind but in their object: the kingdom or the church as a body which had to be governed.

However, there was another way in which temporal and spiritual jurisdictional power differed. John argued that by divine law there was one supreme ruler in spiritual matters instituted to settle disputes about the faith, lest the unity of the church be destroyed by conflict, whereas there existed no one universal temporal ruler, whether by divine or natural law.[130] In the secular sphere, the Christian faithful, through their divinely implanted natural instinct, had the right to set up a variety of different political communities and governments in order to live well under the diverse conditions of their lives.[131] John was clearly rejecting the notion of a universal emperorship, while retaining a universal spiritual role for the pope.

The arguments which John adduced to support his position were of different kinds. From a theological standpoint, all souls were essentially on the same level, because there was one human species, but bodies showed great diversity. The result was that secular power, but not spiritual power, must reflect variety.[132] The sheer scale of difference undermined any prospect of a universal political society:

There is thus no necessity for all the faithful to come together in some one political community but, according to the diversity of climate, language and condition of men, there can be diverse ways of life and diverse polities, and what is virtuous in one people is not virtuous in another.[133]

On the practical and empirical level, the spiritual power could impose its censures far and wide because they were verbal, whereas the physical power of the sword of secular authorities could not so easily be applied to those who were distant.[134] John also referred to

---

[129] *Ibid.*, ch. 14, pp. 145–6.   [130] *Ibid.*, ch. 3, pp. 83–4.

[131] *Ibid.*, ch. 3, p. 82.   [132] *Ibid.*, ch. 3, p. 82.

[133] 'Non sic autem fideles omnes necesse est convenire in aliqua una politia communi, sed possunt secundum diversitatem climatum et linguarum et condicionum hominum esse diversi modi vivendi et diversae politiae, et quod virtuosum est in una gente non est virtuosum in alia' (*ibid.*, ch. 3, p. 83).

[134] *Ibid.*, ch. 3, p. 82.

Aristotle's *Politics* as showing that the emergence of rulership in cities or regions was natural but that of imperial monarchy was not.[135] He bolstered his argument further by mentioning Augustine's view that the spread of the Roman Empire was the result of the desire to dominate, causing injury to others.[136]

On the fundamental question of the relationship between the ruler and property, John considered that there were both similarities and differences between the positions of the secular prince and the spiritual power. The determining principle of his approach was to distinguish between ownership (*dominium*) and jurisdiction.[137] From the prologue of his tract onwards he set out to demonstrate that the pope had no ownership or jurisdiction over the goods of laymen. Arguing in an established Dominican manner, he maintained that individuals' property was held by natural right through their own art, labour and industry. This meant that not only did the pope have no *dominium* over it, but that no secular ruler had either. An individual's property rights were therefore an area of freedom for him away from the claims of those in power. What the temporal prince, but not the pope, had over the goods of laymen was a power of jurisdiction. Where there was a difference, however, was in the goods of the church as such. The pope or prelates in no way owned these, but because ecclesiastical property was held collectively, dispensers were required to administer it. This left a role for one head of the church, the pope, as administrator of the church's possessions as a whole; prelates would fulfil this function at the diocesan level. This argument for one head did not apply to the temporal sphere because there was no such role for a universal administrator of temporal goods, since the goods of laymen were held individually. The clergy's individual, temporal goods were of

---

[135] *Ibid.*, ch. 3, p. 83. John gave no precise reference to the *Politics*.

[136] *Ibid.*, ch. 3, pp. 83–4. John referred to Augustine of Hippo, *De civitate dei*, 4. The most relevant chapter in Book IV (ch. 15) does not make this point directly but does comment that Rome was able to use the injustices of its neighbours to justify its expansive wars, a point which John noticed.

[137] *Ibid.*, ch. 8, p. 98.

course held on the same terms as those of laymen.[138] John's ideas about *dominium* and jurisdiction served as a riposte to the hierocratic argument of Giles of Rome, which through identifying *dominium* with both ownership of property and government attributed to the church ultimate power in both areas, encapsulated in the pope's *plenitudo potestatis*. According to John, Christ as man did not have jurisdiction over the goods of laymen and did not pass this on to St Peter.[139]

John's overall position on temporal and spiritual power was that there was no completely clear distinction between them, at least at the sub-sacramental level. The temporal power was not totally secular, nor was the ecclesiastical power entirely spiritual. The reason, of course, was that he was discussing a society which was in fact Christian. Through accepting that both temporal and spiritual jurisdiction co-existed at the public level, his thought contained the fuzzy edges of an incomplete demarcation between the two, a reflection of the situation of the time at which he wrote. His adoption of naturalistic political concepts did not lead him to produce a clear distinction between state and church; rather, he saw the church's own jurisdiction as itself natural. In a way, his thought remained quite old-fashioned in that he was clearly identifying the natural, political men who constructed communities and created their governments as 'faithful laymen' (*fideles laici*).[140] Further, he used the wider definition of church as the community of the faithful, in which the ecclesiastical judge presided in spiritual matters and the secular in temporal.[141] Moreover, in his response to the fundamental hierocratic argument that because the soul was superior to and ruled the body, the temporal power, having rule over bodies, derived from the spiritual as from a cause, John maintained in contrast that royal power was concerned with souls

---

[138] See *ibid.*, ch. 7, pp. 96–8; ch. 3, pp. 82–3. Janet Coleman has drawn especial attention to the importance of John's argument concerning the naturalness of property in, for instance, her *History of Political Thought*, pp. 118–33.
[139] See the lengthy discussion in chs. 8–10, pp. 98–117.   [140] *Ibid.*, ch. 3, p. 82.
[141] *Ibid.*, ch. 16, p. 154.

as well as bodies. On the face of it, this could seem like a traditional, theocratic view of kingship, but the justification which he provided referred to Aristotle:

The philosopher says in the *Ethics* that the intention of the legislator is to make men good and to lead them to virtue, and in the *Politics* he says that, just as the soul is better than the body, the legislator is better than the doctor, because the legislator has the care of souls, the doctor of bodies.[142]

In cases of extreme emergency the pope also had a claim on the possessions of believers for the good of the faith and to proclaim what was right in such circumstances.[143]

Similarly, John envisaged that there could be extreme situations when the temporal and spiritual powers could intervene drastically but indirectly in each other's affairs. The pope could encourage the people to depose a heretical ruler or one who ignored ecclesiastical censures – in which case the people would be deposing him directly and the pope 'accidentally' (*per accidens*). Likewise, the emperor could excommunicate indirectly a criminal or scandalous pope and depose him 'accidentally' through the medium of the college of cardinals; if that did not work, the emperor could put pressure on the people to depose the errant pontiff. John gave this justification for their mutual power of indirect intervention: 'They both have this power against the other, for both the pope and the emperor have universal and ubiquitous jurisdiction, although the former has spiritual and the latter temporal.'[144] The emperor could correct and punish a pope who was delinquent in temporal matters. John approved of the actions of Emperor Henry II in deposing two

---

[142] 'Dicit Philosophus in Ethicis, quod intentio legislatoris est homines facere bonos et inducere ad virtutem, et in Politicis dicit quod sicut anima melior est corpore, sic legislator melior est medico, quia legislator habet curam animarum, medicus corporum' (*ibid.*, ch. 17, p. 157). John gave no precise references to the *Ethics* and *Politics*.

[143] *Ibid.*, ch. 7, pp. 97–8.

[144] 'Et hoc quidem potest uterque in alterum, nam uterque papa et imperator universalem et ubique habet iurisdictionem, licet iste spiritualem et ille temporalem' (*ibid.*, ch. 13, p. 138).

papal claimants.[145] The cardinals had the right to call in the emperor as the secular arm to secure the deposition of a pope delinquent in spiritual matters.[146] In this section of his tract John was modifying his earlier expressed view that there was no possibility of universal temporal jurisdiction – no role for an emperor. It appears as an inconsistency in his thought. A remnant of this universalist view is also evident in ch. 10: 'The emperor is greater in temporals, not having a superior above him, just as the pope is in spirituals.'[147]

John's immediate aim of vindicating the French crown's independence of both the pope and the emperor was expressly addressed in ch. 21, which he devoted to the Donation of Constantine. His initial question was whether the pope had any authority by reason of it, especially over the kingdom of France. According to John, the pope gained no power from the Donation because it was invalid. To support this view, he adduced well-known Roman law arguments, primarily from the Gloss of Accursius. Furthermore, quite apart from the Donation, there had been no transfer of empire from the Greeks to the Germans at the time of Charlemagne. But, he went on, even if the Donation were valid, it would not apply to France, because the Franks were a free people who had never been subjected to the Romans. Even if one were to grant that France had once been part of the empire, through long prescription this was no longer the case. Not only this, the papacy had recognized saintly kings of France, most recently Louis IX. The kingdom of France was, for John, the prime example of the political arrangement which he favoured – a plurality of kingdoms as opposed to a universal empire. Indeed, justifying himself with references to the text of the Bible and the Gloss on it, he stressed that the Roman Empire had been founded on force and could therefore be removed by force or prescription. The Roman Empire had no more legitimacy than those which had preceded it

---

[145] *Ibid.*, ch. 13, p. 139.   [146] *Ibid.*, ch. 13, p. 140.

[147] 'Maior est imperator in temporalibus non habens super se superiorem sicut papa in spiritualibus' (*ibid.*, ch. 10, p. 106).

and could pass away like them. He was rejecting any divine providential view of the empire.[148]

John was contributing to a scholarly debate which addressed issues of enduring importance arising out of immediate crisis. Indeed, the disputes between Philip and Boniface provide us with the background for understanding so much about fourteenth-century ideas concerning the relationship between temporal and spiritual power. As a stimulus to political thought, shown in the tracts it generated, the conflict bore comparison with the Investiture Contest of the later eleventh and early twelfth centuries. But there was a telling contrast with the earlier dispute which, given the limited intellectual resources then available, had been conducted within a universe of discourse which was ultimately Augustinian. Writers participating in the Philip IV–Boniface VIII disputes made full use of a far wider range of authorities. In particular, both systematic and eclectic usage of ultimately Aristotelian as well as Augustinian arguments informed their creative treatments of issues of power and legitimate authority.

---

[148] *Ibid.*, ch. 21, pp. 185–91.

CHAPTER 2

Dante Alighieri: the approach of political philosophy

The tracts produced during the disputes between Philip IV and Boniface VIII were traditional in method in that they argued from authorities, mostly in a scholastic manner. In the aftermath of the conflict, a fresh approach to questions of power and legitimate authority appeared in the works of Dante Alighieri. In his political thought, Dante was proposing solutions to a prolonged political crisis which had partly ruined his own life. His highly original approach was philosophical and can be seen as a largely normative and evaluative response to an empirical problem, with its conclusions mainly derived from first principles and confirmed by historical examples. Overall he made innovative contributions to political philosophy through his method and the questions he considered. Primarily a poet, he was an amateur but well-informed student of philosophy, anxious to display his knowledge of authorities, but highly creative in his use of them.

The problems which Dante confronted were the political turmoil and fragmentation of Italy in the first two decades of the fourteenth century. He witnessed the strife within cities and the conflicts between them and with *signori*. He himself had been the victim of internal faction-fighting in his native Florence, having been exiled in 1302 as a member of the White Guelph faction by the Black Guelphs, who were supported by Boniface VIII. Dante was in exile for the rest of his life – the fundamental fact underlying all his subsequent

This chapter builds on and expands the content of a paper which I delivered at the University of Sheffield at a colloquium held in 2006 and which is to be published in Joseph Canning, Edmund King and Martial Staub (eds.), *Knowledge, Discipline and Power in the Middle Ages: Essays in Honour of David Luscombe* (Leiden: E.J. Brill, 2011).

writings. In political and religious terms he was an exile from Florence and from heaven. He was not a disinterested observer of politics but was personally involved, whether he liked it or not. Dante blamed Boniface in particular and the papacy in general for much of the unruly political condition of Italy, a condition which in itself contributed to the papal reluctance to return to the peninsula and its lengthening sojourn at Avignon. Dante's solution to Italy's problems was on the face of it a traditional one: the establishment of a strong Roman emperor. He became converted to this view after his exile from Florence, which he came to see as an evil city corrupted by wealth and riven with faction. He put high hopes in Henry VII of Luxemburg's expedition to Italy between 1310 and 1313, supporting him as he became increasingly involved in conflicts with the developing alliance between the papacy under Clement V and King Robert of Naples. But if the notion of an emperor was in itself far from new, Dante's method of argument to reach this position certainly was.

It could well be asked whether study of Dante's political thought is worthwhile, given that his main contention was to justify a universal form of emperorship. This view could appear to be of very little long-term relevance in terms of political theory and tied in to an historical moment in which it was itself an outdated idea. It is not Dante's advocacy of emperorship which is particularly interesting, but rather certain principles expressed in the course of his argument and the method he employed.

Dante's contribution to political thought is to be found firstly in his *Convivio* (Banquet) – a vernacular work of philosophical and literary consolation in exile and written in 1307. In just a few chapters (Book 4, chs. 4, 5, 6 and 9) he sketched in brief so many of the arguments which he developed later. Three of his *Epistolae* (Letters) contain important information about his political ideas: Letters V (to the rulers and peoples of Italy: September or October 1310), VI (to the Florentines: 31 March 1311) and VII (to Emperor Henry VII: 17 April 1311). He also expressed some of his political ideas in the *Divina Commedia* (Divine Comedy) itself, most notably in the survey of Roman history put into Justinian's mouth in *Paradiso*, VI. But by far his most extensive treatment of political thought is his tract *Monarchia*

(Monarchy), which is scholastic in form. It is impossible to demonstrate exactly when this was written. It could have been finished during or shortly after Henry VII's invasion. There is however a strong argument for a later date. At *Monarchia*, I.12, Dante referred to a passage from *Paradiso*, V, which modern scholars would not date before 1316. Although the authenticity of the cross-reference has in the past been doubted by some scholars, the balance of scholarly opinion now favours its genuineness.[1] An intriguing but unprovable argument has been advanced that Dante began *Monarchia* shortly after 31 March 1317. He was then in the service of Can Grande della Scala, *signore* of Verona. On that date Pope John XXII, in his bull *Si fratrum*, declared that all imperial vicariates had lapsed because the empire was vacant. The suggestion is that Dante was commissioned to write to prove the validity of Can Grande's vicariate on the grounds that the empire was not derived from the pope.[2]

Dante's approach in *Monarchia* is arresting from the start. He showed his originality by clearly setting out a question to be answered:

> Since, amongst other hidden and useful truths, a knowledge of temporal Monarchy would be most useful and lies very hidden and unattempted by all, because it does not lead to riches, my intention is to reveal it from its hiding-places, both that I may spend my wakeful nights usefully for the world, and also that I may be the first to win for my glory the honour of such a prize.[3]

---

[1] *Dante, Monarchia* (Latin text with introduction and English translation by Prue Shaw), Cambridge Medieval Classics, 4 (Cambridge University Press, 1995), pp. xxxviii–xli; *Dante's Monarchia* (English translation with an introduction and commentary by Richard Kay), Studies and Texts, 131 (Toronto: Pontifical Institute of Mediaeval Studies, 1998), pp. xxii–xxvi. For a rejection of the view that the reference to *Paradiso*, V, is significant for the dating of *Monarchia* and for the argument that *Monarchia* was probably written between 1312 and 1314, see George Holmes, '*Monarchia* and Dante's attitude to the popes', in John Woodhouse (ed.), *Dante and Governance* (Oxford: Clarendon Press, 1997), pp. 46–57.

[2] See Kay, *Dante's Monarchia*, pp. xxvi–xxx.

[3] 'Cumque inter alias veritates occultas et utiles, temporalis Monarchie notitia utilissima sit et maxime latens et, propter non se habere ad lucrum, ab omnibus intemptata, in proposito est hanc de suis enucleare latibulis, tum ut utiliter mundo pervigilem, tum etiam ut palmam tanti bravii primus in meam gloriam adipiscar' (*Mon.*, 1.1.5, pp. 2–4) – all references are to the Latin text of *Monarchia* in Shaw, *Dante, Monarchia*; the English translations are my own.

It is striking that Dante was excited by attempting something which he was sure no one else had tried to do. This self-confident and deliberate innovation was totally different from the traditionalist arguments from authorities which sought to hide originality (if there were any) under piles of other men's well-tried (and preferably old) intellectual garments. One is reminded, across the centuries, of Bodin's similar claim to be the first to define sovereignty. Dante was isolating the political concept of monarchy as a principle in itself. He rejected mere repetition of inherited arguments in favour of a fresh, individual contribution for the good of posterity.

Dante produced the following definition: 'Temporal monarchy, which they call "Empire", is a single principate both over all men [living] in time and in those things and over those things which are measured by time.'[4] He ordered his tract according to three questions which he set himself to answer to illuminate the topic of monarchy: whether monarchy was necessary for the wellbeing of the world; whether the Roman people had obtained the office of monarch by right; and whether the authority of the monarch derived directly from God or another, that is, the pope, God's minister or vicar.[5]

THE RIGHT AND WRONG USES OF KNOWLEDGE

In *Monarchia*, Dante addressed the fundamental problem of political thought: to show where legitimate authority lay. The method of argument which he employed was the most interesting and original aspect of his quest. The question of the right and wrong uses of knowledge lay at the core of his approach. What knowledge was relevant for speculation about politics? What forms of argument were admissible for sustaining arguments about political matters? In his attempt to demonstrate that the rule of the universal Roman

---

[4] 'Est ergo temporalis Monarchia, quam dicunt "Imperium", unicus principatus et super omnes in tempore vel in hiis et super hiis que tempore mensurantur' (*Mon.*, 1.2, 2, p. 4).

[5] *Ibid.*, 1.2.3, p. 4.

Emperor was necessary for the wellbeing of humanity, a rule independent of the papacy, Dante confronted a key question in late medieval political thought: did revelation in the form of Scripture provide sources relevant to political argument? Could propositions concerning the government of human society and the exercise of power within it be proved or disproved by reference to biblical texts? Was there any sense in which the Old and New Testaments were relevant outside moral and theological matters? If they were not, clearly a whole, venerable structure of political speculation would collapse.

Dante's overall position on which kinds of knowledge were relevant to politics, and the right and wrong uses of such knowledge, can be briefly summed up. The correct path was a normative approach consisting of logical deduction from first principles according to the rules of scholastic dialectic. The conclusions arrived at by this process were then confirmed empirically by reference to experience, which included appeals to historical knowledge – past experience. The Roman Emperor acted as guide to humanity in this world by the lights of philosophy.[6] The incorrect path was that of the allegorical interpretation of Scripture. Dante rejected the claims of the papacy to jurisdictional superiority over the emperor on the grounds that the popes were arguing illogically from texts which were not relevant to politics and the exercise of power in this world. In short, Dante accepted that Scripture could validly be interpreted allegorically, but denied that papal deductions from such allegories could provide valid proofs for papal jurisdictional claims. The pope's role was to interpret Scripture as mankind's guide for the next life, not its ruler in this one:

---

[6] Dante had foreshadowed this view in *Convivio*, 4.6. See the discussion in Peter Armour, *Dante's Griffin and the History of the World. A Study of the Earthly Paradise (Purgatorio, Cantos XXIX–XXXIII)* (Oxford: Clarendon Press, 1989), pp. 124–5. See also Bruno Nardi, *Dal 'Convivio' alla 'Commedia' (Sei saggi danteschi)*, Nuovi Studi Storici, 18 (Rome: Istituto Storico Italiano per il Medio Evo, repr. 1992), p. 91, and John Took, '"Diligite iustitiam qui iudicatis terram": justice and the just ruler in Dante', in Woodhouse, *Dante and Governance*, p. 144.

Man needed a double guide according to his double end: that is, the supreme Pontiff who, following Revelation, would lead the human race through to eternal life, and the Emperor who, following the writings of philosophy, would lead the human race to its temporal happiness.[7]

Dante's diminishing of the role of Scripture in political argument did not mean that he rejected God's role in human affairs – quite the reverse. He held that God stood behind nature but could only be known by his effects, as shown in Dante's use of the seal and wax image:

For nature is in the mind of the first mover, who is God, and then in the heavens, as in an instrument by means of which the likeness of eternal goodness is spread out into the fluidity of matter . . . The will of God is indeed invisible in itself and the invisible things of God 'are perceived and understood through things which have been made.' For while the seal is hidden, the wax bearing the impression of it (although the seal remains hidden) reveals clear knowledge of it. Nor is it strange, if the divine will must be sought through signs, since even that of humans, outside the person willing, is discerned only through signs.[8]

The electors' choice of the emperor was an expression of the divine will (they were 'proclaimers of divine providence'),[9] but this did not justify the popes in using illegitimate interpretations of Scripture to support their claims to control the emperor.

---

[7] 'Opus fuit homini duplici directivo secundum duplicem finem: scilicet summo Pontifice, qui secundum revelata humanum genus perduceret ad vitam eternam, et Imperatore, qui secundum phylosophica documenta genus humanum ad temporalem felicitatem dirigeret' (*Mon.*, 3.16, 10, p. 146).

[8] 'Est enim natura in mente primi motoris, qui Deus est; deinde in celo, tanquam in organo quo mediante similitudo bonitatis ecterne in fluitantem materiam explicatur . . . Voluntas quidem Dei per se invisibilis est; et invisibilia Dei "per ea que facta sunt intellecta conspiciuntur"; nam, occulto existente sigillo, cera impressa de illo quamvis occulto tradit notitiam manifestam. Nec mirum si divina voluntas per signa querenda est, cum etiam humana extra volentem non aliter quam per signa cernatur' (*ibid.*, 2.2.2–8, pp. 48 and 51). See the discussion in Gennaro Sasso, *Dante. L'imperatore e Aristotele*, Nuovi Studi Storici, 62 (Rome: Istituto Storico Italiano per il Medio Evo, 2002), p. 198.

[9] 'Denunciatores divine providentie' (*Mon.*, 3.16.13, p. 148).

THE RIGHT PATH

The first fifteen of the sixteen chapters of Book I of *Monarchia* consisted of an attempt to demonstrate the proposition that the rule of one man was necessary for universal peace, the means for achieving the happiness and wellbeing of humanity.[10] A range of deductive arguments from first principles was employed, including ones for unity under one leader.[11] One person must direct mankind to its one goal.[12] All parts of the human race were ordered to the ruler of the whole.[13] The microcosm of this world was related to the macrocosm, so that there should be one ruler on earth just as God ruled the universe.[14] Humanity most resembled God when it was under one ruler.[15] Central to Dante's approach was his understanding of man as an intellectual being: 'It is clear therefore that the ultimate potentiality of humanity itself is the intellectual potentiality or faculty.'[16] His contention was that the full intellectual capacity of the human race, the realization of the possible intellect of humanity, in thought and action could only be achieved under the rule of one monarch.[17]

Such arguments were purely theoretical and were at a philosophical level. But did they have any relation to the world of fact? For Dante, it was crucial that the findings of reason were confirmed by the empirical test of experience. He considered that the correctness of his theoretical arguments was even more firmly proved by the witness of past experience – the lessons of history.

---

[10] *Mon.*, 1.4.5–6, p. 12.
[11] For Dante's arguments from justice and freedom, see below, pp. 76–9.
[12] *Mon.*, 1.5, pp. 12–14.   [13] *Ibid.*, 1.6, p. 16.
[14] *Ibid.*, 1.7, pp. 16–18.   [15] *Ibid.*, 1.8, p. 18.
[16] 'Patet igitur quod ultimum de potentia ipsius humanitatis est potentia sive virtus intellectiva' (*ibid.*, 1.3.7, p. 8).
[17] *Ibid.*, 1.3.4–10, pp. 8–10; 4.1.1, p. 10; 1.5.9, p. 14. For medieval discussions of the Aristotelian notion of the possible or potential intellect, see, for instance, Norman Kretzmann, Anthony Kenny, Jan Pinborg and Eleonore Stump (eds.), *The Cambridge History of Later Medieval Philosophy, 1100–1600* (Cambridge University Press, 1982), pp. 595–601 and 613–15. For a discussion of Dante's usage of the concept, see, for instance, Kay, *Dante's Monarchia*, pp. 18–21.

The switch to this approach came in the final chapter of Book I. Having given such exhaustive treatment to his deductive arguments from first principles, he appealed to history, described as 'memorable experience' (*experientia memorabilis*), for confirmation. The historical fact he alluded to was the peaceful condition of the Roman Empire at the time of Christ's birth – the perfect monarchy.[18] This providential view of history was of course a traditional one within medieval historiography (but not one which the mature Augustine accepted). That Dante expressed this view was unremarkable. What was significant was the nature of his appeal to Scripture at this point. Here and elsewhere he treated Scripture as a valid source for historical proofs, providing information relevant to his empirical arguments. In terms of politics, Scripture for him performed the role of memorable sacred history. Scripture did not provide those philosophical principles from which political truths could be deduced. This last chapter of Book I served as a prologue to Book II, where he assembled a mass of empirical justifications for the Romans' possession of universal empire, drawing on Roman history, notably from the works of Latin poets and historians, and on Scripture as sacred history.[19]

Dante's most audacious argument was in the final chapter of Book II. He treated the atonement as a central event in human

---

[18] 'Rationibus omnibus supra positis experientia memorabilis attestatur: status videlicet illius mortalium quem Dei Filius, in salutem hominis hominem assumpturus, vel expectavit vel cum voluit ipse disposuit. Nam si a lapsu primorum parentum, qui diverticulum fuit totius nostre deviationis, dispositiones hominum et tempora recolamus, non inveniemus nisi sub divo Augusto monarcha, existente Monarchia perfecta, mundum undique fuisse quietum' (*Mon.*, 1.16.1, p. 42). For Dante's treatment of the Roman Empire, see the classic works of Alessandro Passerin d'Entrèves, *Dante as a Political Thinker* (Oxford: Clarendon Press, 1952), pp. 26–51, and Charles Till Davis, *Dante and the Idea of Rome* (Oxford: Clarendon Press, 1957), especially pp. 139–94. See also Charles Till Davis, 'Dante's vision of history', in *Dante's Italy and Other Essays* (Philadelphia: University of Pennsylvania Press, 1984), pp. 23–41.

[19] For Dante's providential interpretation of Roman history in Book II, see also Peter Armour, 'Dante and popular sovereignty', in Woodhouse, *Dante and Governance*, pp. 34–5.

history but he understood it in such a way that it justified the Roman Empire. He produced the extraordinary argument that for the atonement to be valid, Christ had to be condemned and punished by a judge appointed by legitimate, universal authority, namely the Emperor Tiberius:

And if the Roman Empire was not by right, the sin of Adam was not punished in Christ. This however is false . . . If therefore Christ had not suffered under a judge with ordinary jurisdiction, that penalty would not have been a punishment. And he could not have been a judge with ordinary jurisdiction, unless he had jurisdiction over the whole human race, since the whole human race was punished in the flesh of Christ who bore our sorrows, as the Prophet says. And Tiberius Caesar, whose vicar Pilate was, would not have had jurisdiction over the whole human race, unless the Roman Empire had been by right.[20]

This was a theologically idiosyncratic view to say the least: one which went against theological orthodoxy and was rapidly condemned by his opponents, as for instance Guido Vernani showed.[21] Dante of course considered that he had thereby produced an irrefutable argument in the emperor's favour, but in this he seemed

---

[20] 'Et si romanum Imperium de iure non fuit, peccatum Ade in Cristo non fuit punitum; hoc autem est falsum . . . Si ergo sub ordinario iudice Cristus passus non fuisset, illa pena punitio non fuisset. Et iudex ordinarius esse non poterat nisi supra totum humanum genus iurisdictionem habens, cum totum humanum genus in carne illa Cristi portantis dolores nostros, ut ait Propheta, puniretur. Et supra totum humanum genus Tyberius Cesar, cuius vicarius erat Pilatus, iurisdictionem non habuisset, nisi romanum Imperium de iure fuisset' (*Mon.*, 2.11.1–5, pp. 94–6).

[21] See Guido Vernani, *De reprobatione Monarchie composite a Dante Alighiero Florentino* (critical texts in Thomas Kaeppeli (ed.), *Der Dantegegner Guido Vernani, OP, von Rimini*, Quellen und Forschungen aus italienischen Archiven und Bibliotheken, 28 (1937–8), pp. 107–46, and Nevio Matteini, *Il più antico oppositore politico di Dante, Guido Vernani da Rimini: testo critico del 'De reprobatione monarchiae'*, Il pensiero medioevale; collana di storia della filosofia, series 1, 6 (Padua: CEDAM, 1958). See also Anthony K. Cassell, *The Monarchia Controversy. An Historical Study with Accompanying Translations of Dante Alighieri's Monarchia, Guido Vernani's Refutation of the 'Monarchia' Composed by Dante, and Pope John XXII's Bull Si fratrum* (Washington, DC: Catholic University of America Press, 2004), pp. 50–107 and 174–97.

to have been alone. In this use of the Bible as sacred history he was going out on a limb far beyond the traditional providential view.[22]

THE WRONG PATH

Dante set out to demonstrate that the papacy's arguments, whereby it claimed that the emperor derived his temporal power from the pope, were wrongly founded. He maintained that papal arguments were faulty because they were based on texts irrelevant to politics and government, that is, Scriptural passages with purely spiritual or emotional (rather than historical) significance, and because they were elaborated by an unsuitable method, that of allegorical interpretation suited to emotional or spiritual persuasion, rather than the dialectical approach applicable to politics.[23]

In rejecting the allegorical interpretation of Scripture, Dante was following an established tradition in medieval exegesis and one which went back at least to Augustine, who had maintained that allegory had only emotional and persuasive power and could not prove any theological point, for which a literal reading of Scripture was required.[24] Amongst Dante's contemporaries, John of Paris was notable for reiterating this point of view in his tract *De regia potestate et papali*.[25]

Dante addressed the papal arguments which had the greatest prominence in his day. From the times of Gregory VII and Innocent III, the papacy had used the sun–moon allegory to illustrate the emperor's subordination to the pope: the lesser light, the moon (representing the emperor), shone only by the reflection from the greater light, the sun (representing the pope). Dante sought to show logical inconsistencies in this interpretation – how could the two lights have this significance if they were created earlier in the days

---

[22] See, for instance, Jean Rivière, 'La dogme de la rédemption. Etudes critiques et documents', in *Bibliothèque de la Revue d'Histoire Ecclésiastique*, 5 (Louvain: Bureaux de la Revue, 1931), pp. 350–1.

[23] See *Mon.*, 3.4, pp. 106–12.

[24] The literal interpretation of Scripture was also identified with the historical.

[25] John of Paris, *De regia potestate et papali*, ch. 18, pp. 167–8.

of creation than man, since they were being understood to represent the emperor and the pope? He did admittedly score an own goal by arguing that the moon did have some light of its own – a mis-understanding of the causes of the faint light from the moon observable during a lunar eclipse.[26] However, he did not employ the imagery which he used in *Purgatorio*, in the Divine Comedy, where he referred to the 'two suns' of papal and imperial power – an image better suited to his argument.[27]

Dante had to consider the papal version of the two-swords theory, whereby one was understood to represent spiritual power and the other secular power, with the latter being derived from the former and exercised at the command of the pope. He favoured a literalist interpretation of the text of Luke, 'Here are two swords' (Luke 22:38), and sought to demonstrate that the papal argument was based on a false allegorical interpretation.[28] He maintained, following a tradition of biblical exegesis, that any figurative inter-pretation of the text would apply to the Pauline notion of the sword of the spirit:

> But if those words of Christ and Peter are to be understood figuratively, they are not to be made to mean what those people say but to relate to that sword of which Matthew thus writes, 'Do not therefore think that I came to send peace to earth; I did not come to send peace but the sword'.[29]

Peter, Dante considered, had a very straightforward understanding of Christ's words.

---

[26] For Dante's treatment of the sun–moon allegory, see *Mon.*, 3.4, pp. 106–12.

[27] *Purgatorio*, xvi, 107. See the discussion in E.H. Kantorowicz, 'Dante's "Two Suns"', in *Selected Studies* (New York: Augustin, 1965), pp. 325–38; Anthony K. Cassell, '"Luna est ecclesia": Dante and the "Two Great Lights"', *Dante Studies*, 119 (2001), 1–26. For the importance of *Purgatorio* as a source for Dante's political ideas, see John A. Scott, *Dante's Political Purgatory* (Philadelphia: University of Pennsylvania Press, 1996).

[28] *Mon.*, 3.9, pp. 122–6.

[29] 'Quod si verba illa Cristi et Petri typice sunt accipienda, non ad hoc quod dicunt isti trahenda sunt, sed referenda sunt ad sensum illius gladii de quo scribit Matheus sic: "Nolite ergo arbitrari quia veni mictere pacem in terram: non veni pacem mictere, sed gladium"' (*ibid.*, 3.9.18, p. 126).

However, in his discussion of the gifts of the Magi in Matthew 2:1–13, there may have appeared to be some softening of Dante's position on the allegorical interpretation of Scripture. He accepted both the literal understanding of the gifts of frankincense and gold and also the allegorical interpretation whereby these signified that Christ was lord of temporal and spiritual things. But he explicitly rejected the pro-papal inference from this allegory that Christ's vicar also thereby had authority over both. He argued that this approach used a false syllogism: 'God is the lord of spiritual and temporal things; the supreme Pontiff is God's vicar; therefore he is lord of spiritual and temporal things.'[30] The fault in the argument according to him was that the term 'God' was not the same as 'God's vicar'. St Peter's successors did not have divine authority: the allegorical interpretation could not apply to the powers of the pope.

Dante also considered the fundamental proof-text of the papal position in Matthew 16:19 – 'Whatever you shall bind on earth shall be bound also in heaven; and whatever you shall loose on earth shall be loosed also in heaven.' Gregory VII, and after him Innocent III, interpreted the word 'whatever' as justifying an extremely wide-ranging application of papal power. Dante sought to show logical flaws in the papal argument by showing that 'whatever' could not mean, literally, 'whatever':

And thus the universal sign which is contained in 'whatever' is limited in its applicability by the office of the keys of the kingdom of heaven. If it is understood this way, this proposition is true, but not so absolutely, as is clear.[31]

The office of the keys did not contain the power to bind or loose the laws of the empire.

He had to address the Donation of Constantine because of the use which was made of it by his pro-papal opponents. He attempted to reveal logical faults in their position and also employed a well-known

---

[30] 'Deus est dominus spiritualium et temporalium; summus Pontifex est vicarius Dei; ergo est dominus spiritualium et temporalium' (*ibid.*, 3.7.2, p. 116).
[31] 'Et sic signum universale quod includitur in "quodcunque" contrahitur in sua distributione ab offitio clavium regni celorum: et sic assumendo, vera est illa propositio; absolute vero non, ut patet' (*ibid.*, 3.8.10, p. 120).

Roman law argument to show that the Donation was legally invalid. He maintained that Constantine was not in a position to give the Donation to the church, nor was the church in one to receive it. The emperor would thereby have been alienating the empire, which would have gone against the duties of his office; the church would have been infringing the injunction of Christ that it should not have worldly possessions:

> But the church was entirely unsuited to receiving temporal possessions through an express prohibitive command, as we have thus in Matthew: 'Do not possess gold or silver, nor copper coins in your money-belts, nor wallet for your journey.'[32]

Any imperial gifts to the church must not diminish imperial ownership over them and would place the church in the position merely of their administrator, not their possessor, a role especially for the good of the poor.

All the above topics were to be expected in a tract by an author attacking the papal interpretation of the relationship between spiritual and temporal power. There was, however, another argument produced by Dante which attacked the core of the hierocratic position in an ingenious fashion. Central to the hierocratic interpretation was a *reductio ad unum* – an argument from unity. All power must ultimately be derived from one source – on earth, the pope (who derived his power from God). Dante argued that the pope and the emperor, as individual men, shared a common humanity. But the offices of pope and of emperor were essentially accidental attributes of both of them. He accused the papacy of making the logical error of basing its *reductio ad unum* on these accidental qualities (an argument *per accidens*). A true *reductio ad unum* in the cases of the emperor and the pope would apply to their common nature as human beings – the relationship of imperial to papal office would not be at issue. But if their offices were considered, then this

---

[32] 'Sed Ecclesia omnino indisposita erat ad temporalia recipienda per preceptum prohibitivum expressum, ut habemus per Matheum sic: "Nolite possidere aurum, neque argentum, necque pecuniam in zonis vestris, non peram in via"' (*ibid.*, 3.10.14, p. 130).

reduction would be to a principle of authority outside themselves (such as God) to which papal and imperial authority were relative.[33]

Dante, as a believing Christian, accepted the intrinsic superiority of the spiritual over the temporal, but in such a way that the authority of the emperor in the earthly paradise of this life was not diminished by that of the pope, the guide towards the heavenly paradise of the next life. The emperor retained his autonomy: both powers existed in parallel. However, Dante held that the power of the emperor would be increased by co-operation with the spiritual grace bestowed by the pope and that temporal power would be made more effective thereby. This is made clear in *Monarchia*, 3.4.18–20:

As regards its existence, in no way does the moon depend on the sun . . . But as regards its better and more effective operation, it does receive something from the sun, that is abundance of light, and having received this, it operates more effectively. Thus therefore I say that temporal rulership does not receive its existence from the spiritual, nor its power which is its authority, nor even its operation as such; but it well receives from it that by which it may operate more effectively through the light of grace which in heaven and on earth the blessing of the supreme Pontiff infuses into it.[34]

This argument was reiterated in the famous final paragraph of the whole text where Dante reviewed his achievement in having answered the three questions he had set himself at the beginning of his tract: whether the office of emperor was necessary for the wellbeing of the world; whether the Roman people had obtained that empire by right; and whether the authority of the emperor was derived immediately from God or from another. He said:

---

[33] *Ibid.*, 3.12, pp. 132–6. For a discussion of Dante's argument, see Giovanni Di Giannatale, 'Papa e imperatore in "Monarchia III, 12"', *L'Alighieri*, 22, 2 (1981), 46–60.

[34] 'Quantum est ad esse, nullo modo luna dependet a sole . . . Sed quantum ad melius et virtuosius operandum, recipit aliquid a sole, quia lucem habundantem: qua recepta, virtuosius operatur. Sic ergo dico quod regimen temporale non recipit esse a spirituali, nec virtutem que est eius auctoritas, nec etiam operationem simpliciter; sed bene ab eo recipit ut virtuosius operetur per lucem gratie quam in celo et in terra benedictio summi Pontificis infundit illi' (*Mon.*, 3.4.18–20, p. 112). See Sabrina Ferrara, 'Dante, Cino, il sole e la luna', *L'Alighieri. Rassegna dantesca*, n.s., 25 (2002), 27–47.

The truth of this last question is not to be understood so strictly that the Roman Prince is not in some way subordinate to the Roman Pontiff, since this mortal happiness is in some way ordered to immortal happiness. Let Caesar therefore show that reverence to Peter which a first-born son should show to his father, so that illuminated by the light of paternal grace he may more effectively light up the orb of the world, over which he has been placed by Him, who is the governor of all things spiritual and temporal.[35]

What we find in Dante is a version of the same argument which John of Paris had employed and which was entirely destructive of the hierocratic position.[36] The hierocratic argument assumed that the universe was hierarchically ordered and that what was inferior was derived from what was superior. The temporal power was inferior to the spiritual and must therefore derive its power from it. The superior could in turn revoke that delegated power of the inferior. Dante, like John of Paris, pointed out that just because the pope was the spiritual superior of the emperor, it did not follow that the temporal power of the emperor was derived from the pope. Temporal and spiritual power were different in kind, although spiritual power had greater dignity absolutely. For Dante, the ultimate source of imperial authority was God, but not through the agency of the church; rather, through the choice of the princely electors. God stood behind nature: he was the force driving the macrocosm which the microcosm of this world, this cockpit or threshing-floor, reflected. As he said: 'This is the target at which the protector of the world, who is called the Roman Prince, should aim, that there should be freedom with peace in this threshing-floor of mortals.'[37]

---

[35] 'Que quidem veritas ultime questionis non sic stricte recipienda est, ut romanus Princeps in aliquo romano Pontifici non subiaceat, cum mortalis ista felicitas quodammodo ad inmortalem felicitatem ordinetur. Illa igitur reverentia Cesar utatur ad Petrum qua primogenitus filius debet uti ad patrem: ut luce paterne gratie illustratus virtuosius orbem terre irradiet, cui ab Illo solo prefectus est, qui est omnium spiritualium et temporalium gubernator' (*Mon.*, 3.16.17–18, p. 148).

[36] See John of Paris, *De regia potestate et papali*, 5, pp. 88–9. See above, p. 52.

[37] 'Hoc est illud signum ad quod maxime debet intendere curator orbis, qui dicitur romanus Princeps, ut scilicet in areola ista mortalium libere cum pace vivatur' (*Mon.*, 3.16.11, p. 146). See also *Paradiso*, xxii, 151.

Dante also had to confront juristic arguments to some extent because of the way in which the papacy elaborated its claims in terms of canon law. As we have seen in the case of the Donation of Constantine, he showed some knowledge of juristic argument, but there was no question of a detailed refutation of canonist pro-papal positions. Dante sought to destroy canonists' arguments on the grounds of the method they employed. To do so, he followed the usual criticism which the theologians and philosophers levelled against the jurists, by accusing them of using a narrative method rather than a dialectical one, which was that apposite to political questions: the jurists argued in an entirely circular way in terms of legal texts. For instance, the popes made claims in decretals and the canonists argued exclusively in terms of these decretals rather than normatively from first principles and empirically from experience. Dante was not seeking to denigrate papal decretals as such (indeed, he said he venerated them) but to castigate improper conclusions drawn from them.[38]

What is striking about Dante's approach is that he sought to disprove papal positions on the grounds that the arguments employed were illogical or inapposite. It was a thoroughly intellectual approach suited to his understanding of man as an intellectual being. His argument in favour of one emperor for humanity derived from his notion of the shared intellectual capability of humanity. The governmental claims of the papacy, because they were illogical and undermined the correct order for ruling this world, were illegitimate. Dante indeed recognized that there existed a multiplicity of rulers and governments, but they should submit to the overall guidance of the emperor; if they did not, as he recognized was the case, the correct order would be undermined and peace destroyed. Lesser rulers could deal with regulation through laws they made suited to local conditions; the emperor's role was to lay down general guidelines – a relationship like that between the theoretical and the practical intellects.[39] For, Dante relevant knowledge, correctly

---

[38] See, for instance, *Mon.*, 3.3.9, p. 104.   [39] See *ibid.*, 1.14, pp. 36–8.

interpreted, demonstrated the legitimacy of the empire, a legitimacy which historical experience confirmed.

In the course of establishing where legitimate and illegitimate authority lay, Dante also addressed the questions of the positive and negative uses of power. The role of the emperor was to employ his unique power in a positive way by putting justice into effect. Indeed, his power was necessary for this to be achieved. Only he could settle disputes between rulers and bring about peace, the precondition for human fulfilment.[40] Dante summed up his position thus:

> Justice is at its most powerful in the world when it resides in a subject who has the greatest level of will and power. The Monarch alone is of this kind. Therefore justice is at its most powerful in the world when it resides in the Monarch alone.[41]

The emperor, as philosopher-ruler, had the power to understand moral norms and put them into action. This approach, fundamental to the *Monarchia*, was foreshadowed in the *Convivio*. There, Dante advocated the combination of the philosophy of Aristotle and the power of the emperor:

> [Philosophical] authority does not detract from imperial. Rather the latter without the former is dangerous and the former without the latter is as if weak, not of itself but because people are disorderly. So when the one is combined with the other, they are most useful and full of strength . . . Join philosophical with imperial authority to rule well and perfectly.[42]

---

[40] See *ibid.*, 1.10, pp. 20–2.

[41] 'Iustitia potissima est in mundo quando volentissimo et potentissimo subiecto inest; huiusmodi solus Monarcha est: ergo soli Monarche insistens iustitia in mundo potissima est' (*ibid.*, 1.11.8, p. 26).

[42] 'E non repugna [la filosofica] autoritade alla imperiale; ma quella sanza questa è pericolosa, e questa sanza quella è quasi debile, non per sé ma per la disordinanza della gente: sì che l'una coll'altra congiunta utilissime e pienissime sono d'ogni vigore . . . Congiungasi la filosofica autoritade colla imperiale, a bene e perfettamente reggere' (*Convivio*, 4.4.17–18, pp. 298–9).

Dante applied to the emperor the image of the 'rider of the human will' (*lo cavalcatore della umana voluntade*): without an emperor, Italy was like a horse without a rider, a simile developed at length in *Purgatorio*.[43] In *Monarchia* he saw concord as depending on the unity of human wills; the ideal state of mankind therefore required that one will, that of the monarch, should direct all the others to one goal.[44]

But it could be objected that the Roman Empire was built on force, the negative aspect of power; indeed, this was the contention of the Neapolitan school of jurists. Marinus da Caramanico (d. 1288), for instance, had maintained that the Roman Empire, because it was founded on force, had a *de facto* rather than *de iure* existence.[45] In *Convivio* Dante, directly confronting such objectors as 'cavillers', argued that the ends justified the means. The Roman Empire was not principally obtained by force but by divine reason: 'Force was not, then, the moving cause, as the caviller believed, but was the instrumental cause . . . and thus, not force, but reason, indeed divine reason, must be considered the source of the Roman Empire.'[46] In *Monarchia* Dante's extensive justification of Rome's wars in terms of providential history put flesh on the bones of this argument. Furthermore, in Book II he argued from evidence in Latin literature that Rome's wars in setting up and defending its empire and allies were justified because they aimed at the public good: the Romans, the most noble of peoples, acted out of a desire for service, not lust for domination.[47] He also used an argument from nature to show that it was actually just that some peoples should be ruled by others, even if force had to be used to bring this about:

---

[43] *Ibid.*, 9.10, p. 317; *Purgatorio*, 6, 88–96.　　[44] *Mon.*, 1.15, 8–10, pp. 40–2.

[45] Marinus da Caramanico, *Super libro constitutionum*, *Proem*, 17, in F. Calasso, *I Glossatori e la teoria della sovranità*, 3rd edn (Milan: Giuffré, 1957), pp. 196–7.

[46] 'La forza dunque non fu cagione movente, sì come credeva chi gavillava, ma fu cagione instrumentale . . . e così non forza, ma ragione, e ragione ancora divina, conviene essere stata principio dello romano imperio' (*Convivio*, 4.4.12, pp. 280–1).

[47] See *Mon.*, 2.5, pp. 60–70; 2.3, pp. 52–8.

We see that not just certain individuals, but certain peoples are born fitted to rule, and certain others to be subject and to serve, as Aristotle affirms in the *Politics* [*Pol.*, 1.5, 1254a 21–3]; and, as he says, it is not only expedient but also just that such people should be ruled, even if they are forced into this. If this is the way things are, there is no doubt that nature ordained a place and a race to exercise universal rule in the world: otherwise she would have failed in her provisions, which is impossible. From what has been said above and what will be said below it is clear enough which place that was and which race: it was Rome and her citizens, that is to say her people.[48]

This is immediately followed in the text by the culmination of Dante's argument, the quotation from Virgil, *Aeneid*, VI: the arts of Rome shall be 'to spare subjects and to subdue the proud'.[49] For those with a classical education, these words had such resonance as encapsulating the civilizing mission of Rome. But one had to have already bought into the myth of Rome to be convinced by them.

DANTE'S INSIGHT

For Dante, the emperor's legitimate authority was ultimately justified by its fruits – happiness in this life: the *vita felice* as he sublimely called it in the *Convivio*: 'The root and foundation of imperial majesty, according to the truth, is the necessity for humans to live a civil life, which is directed to one end, that is a happy life.'[50] This was an application of Aristotelian ideas.

Dante believed that freedom was most conducive to happiness in this life and that this was best achieved under the rule of one man:

---

[48] 'Propter quod videmus quod quidam non solum singulares homines, quinetiam populi, apti nati sunt ad principari, quidam alii ad sibici atque ministrare, ut Phylosophus astruit in hiis que *De politicis*: et talibus, ut ipse dicit, non solum regi est expediens, sed etiam iustum, etiamsi ad hoc cogantur. Que si ita se habent, non dubium est quin natura locum et gentem disposuerit in mundo ad universaliter principandum: aliter sibi defecisset, quod est impossibile. Quis autem fuerit locus et que gens, per dicta superius et per dicenda inferius satis est manifestum quod fuerit Roma, et cives eius sive populus' (*ibid.*, 2.67–8, p. 72).

[49] 'Parcere subiectis et debellare superbos' (*Aeneid*, VI, 853), at *Mon.*, 2.6.9, p. 74.

[50] 'Lo fondamento radicale della imperiale maiestade, secondo lo vero, è la necessità della umana civilitade, che a uno fine è ordinata, cioè a vita felice' (*Convivio*, 4.4.1, p. 275).

It can be clear that this freedom (or this principle of the whole of our freedom) is the greatest gift conferred by God on human nature, as I have already said in the *Paradiso* of the *Commedia* – because through it we are happy here as men, through it we are happy elsewhere as gods. If this is so, who will there be who will not say that the human race is in the best state, when it could use this principle most fully? But living under a Monarch it is most fully free.[51]

Freedom, justice and peace existed side-by-side under imperial rule. Mankind was happiest under the reign of the Emperor Augustus.[52]

In the final chapter of *Monarchia*, Dante explained the purpose of human life in terms of happiness:

Unerring providence therefore set two goals for man to aim at: that is the happiness of this life which consists in the operation of our own powers and is symbolized by the earthly paradise, and the happiness of eternal life, which consists in the enjoyment of the divine vision (to which our own powers cannot ascend, unless aided by divine light) and which is signified by the heavenly paradise.[53]

The emperor was the guide for this life and the pope for the next life.[54] The vice which above all ruined human happiness was greed, the theme which ran throughout Dante's works: cupidity was a destructive passion which destroyed human society. The emperor could rule justly because as universal ruler he had nothing left to

---

[51] 'Manifestum esse potest quod hec libertas sive principium hoc totius nostre libertatis est maximum donum humane nature a Deo collatum – sicut in Paradiso Comedie iam dixi – quia per ipsum hic felicitamur ut homines, per ipsum alibi felicitamur ut dii. Quod si ita est, quis erit qui humanum genus optime se habere non dicat, cum potissime hoc principio possit uti? Sed existens sub Monarcha est potissime liberum' (*Mon.*, 1.12.6–8, p. 30). This is the passage crucial for dating *Monarchia* (see above, p. 62).

[52] *Mon.*, 1.16.1–2, p. 42.

[53] 'Duos igitur fines providentia illa inerrabilis homini proposuit intendendos: beatitudinem scilicet huius vite, que in operatione proprie virtutis consistit et per terrestrem paradisum figuratur; et beatitudinem vite ecterne, que [qui *ed. Shaw*] consistit in fruitione divini aspectus ad quam propria virtus ascendere non potest, nisi lumine divino adiuta, que paradisum celestem intelligi datur' (*Mon.*, 3.16, pp. 144–6).

[54] See above, pp. 64–5.

covet.[55] Cupidity and factions were the vices of republics, of Florence above all. The liberty of Florence, which had rebelled against Henry VII, was therefore a false one.[56] Dante proposed a universal solution to the problem of where legitimate political authority lay, but it was Italy which he had in the forefront of his mind, his beleaguered homeland, whose happiness had been destroyed by the noxious combination of the selfishness of the city-republics and the illegitimate political claims of the popes. For him, the Roman emperor was by right both lord of the world and the only legitimate candidate for sole ruler of Italy.

Dante had produced a unique and somewhat idiosyncratic response to the political crisis which dominated his life. His political thought was both a philosophical response and intended as a real solution to the problem, a solution justified at both the theoretical and empirical levels. He defended the legitimate authority of universal empire, because of the core values that he held as a philosopher and a poet: his commitment to a common and therefore universal humanity – what it meant to be a human being. This human potential could only be realized in this life by living under one emperor. Was his solution realistic? Dante thought it was.

---

[55] *Mon.*, I.11.11–12, p. 26.
[56] See *Epistola*, VI, especially 2 (p. 552) and 5–6 (pp. 556–60).

CHAPTER 3

Marsilius of Padua

The intention of this chapter is to consolidate a new interpretation of the political thought of Marsilius of Padua (*c*.1275/80–1343), by giving priority to his treatment of questions of power and legitimate authority.[1] Marsilius, like Dante, also argued from first principles and was even more driven to write by his experience of contemporary politics. His prime concern was to uncover the sources of strife and to show how peace could be achieved. To this end he sought to demonstrate where legitimate authority lay and (above all) where it did not. These two interrelated questions are the key to unravelling his political thought and address his express reasons for writing.

Marsilius was the product of two intellectual milieux: those of Padua and the University of Paris, where he was rector in 1313. At Padua his professional training was in medicine and at Paris his institutional home was the Faculty of Arts. His main political work, *Defensor pacis* (Defender of Peace) (completed at Paris on 24 June 1324), was a massive undertaking – the modern critical edition of Richard Scholz, for instance, amounts to 613 pages.[2] But he also wrote two short works: *De translatione imperii* (On the Translation of the Empire), composed at Paris, 1324–6(?), and the *Defensor minor* (Lesser Defender), produced at the court of Lewis IV of Bavaria at Munich between 1339 and 1341, together with two short tracts on whether the marriage between Margaret Maultasch, Countess

---

[1] Marsilius was born in Padua; his death was recorded in a *collatio* of Pope Clement VI (10 April 1343) and may well have taken place in 1342.

[2] Marsilius von Padua, *Defensor pacis*, ed. R. Scholz, in *M.G.H.*, *Fontes iuris Germanici antiqui* (Hanover: Hahnsche Buchhandlung, 1932).

of Tyrol and Carinthia, and the emperor's son would be legal, tracts which were incorporated as the final four chapters of the manuscript of the *Defensor minor*.[3]

The modern scholarly interpretation of Marsilius has been and remains deeply contested. The disagreements are partly the result of different disciplinary approaches: historians have tended to understand his works in ways different from those followed by political theorists and philosophers. This is especially so if Marsilius's texts are understood in their original historical context both in terms of events and use of language. But both historical and philosophical interpretations of texts have their own merits. Even if one is determined to follow a strictly historical approach, philosophical problems suggested by the text do present themselves to one's mind. There is a place for both approaches; they are not necessarily mutually exclusive.

Marsilius has gained the reputation of being the most radical political thinker of the Middle Ages, but this is in part the result of an unhistorical political science approach to his writings. However, the differences in interpretation also reflect the differences in Marsilius's own approach in Discourse One and Discourse Two of the *Defensor pacis*. Discourse One set forth a general political theory which was derived from first principles and which established the criteria for determining where legitimate authority lay and where it did not. Discourse Two used history and Scripture to demolish papal claims to plenitude of power, which Marsilius saw as destroying peace: this was his main aim in writing. Discourse One was fundamental to his thought in providing a model political structure of general

[3] See *Marsile de Padoue. Oeuvres mineures: Defensor minor, De translatione imperii*, Latin text (ed. and trans. into French by C. Jeudy and J. Quillet) (Paris: Editions du Centre National de la Recherche Scientifique, 1979) – the edition in which the Latin text of *Defensor minor* amounts to sixty-nine pages and that of *De translatione imperii* to thirty pages; the two marriage tracts were written in 1341–2. There also exists a series of *Questiones super metaphysicam* attributed to Marsilius and Jean of Jandun, his associate at Paris: see R. Lambertini and A. Tabarroni, 'Le *Quaestiones super metaphysicam* attribuite a Giovanni di Jandun. Osservazioni e problemi', *Medioevo*, 10 (1984), 41–64.

application, a necessary preparation for his elaboration in Discourse Two of a theological-historical destruction of the papal position. The political theory of Discourse One, when remembered in reading Discourse Two, explained why papal plenitude of power had no legitimacy. There is also the question of the relationship between the *Defensor pacis* and the later and clearly pro-imperial *Defensor minor*.

The decision to give first place to Marsilius's treatment of power has resulted from exploring the research question of where he located legitimate authority and reflects his own obsession with what he saw as the realities of the misuse of power by the papacy. This approach, reflecting his priority, has been largely neglected by previous scholarship. I have begun to argue this thesis in two earlier articles.[4] Of course, all interpreters of Marsilius, whatever their angle of approach to his works, have considered his treatment of power and coercion: it cannot be avoided. Gewirth, for instance, wrote that 'the force of Marsilius' ecclesiastic ideas is to be found equally in his solution of the problems of political power as such: those problems receive at his hands a consistent and striking treatment from a fresh point of view',[5] but did not follow up this insight systematically. Lagarde, for instance, in his treatment of the *Defensor pacis*, provided an excellent survey of the importance of the principate, the instrument of coercion within the political community.[6] This is not to deny the importance of consent in Marsilius's political theory – this has been much stressed in interpretations of his works. But it is a question of determining what his main focus was. My contention is that Marsilius argued above all that peace and tranquillity were achieved and

---

[4] Joseph Canning, 'The role of power in the political thought of Marsilius of Padua', *History of Political Thought*, 20, 1 (Spring 1999), 21–34; Canning, 'Power and powerlessness in the political thought of Marsilius of Padua', in Gerson Moreno-Riaño (ed.), *The World of Marsilius of Padua*, Disputatio, 5 (Turnhout: Brepols, 2006), pp. 211–25.

[5] Alan Gewirth, *Marsilius of Padua*, vol. I: *Marsilius of Padua and Medieval Political Philosophy* (New York: Columbia University Press, 1951), p. 9.

[6] Georges de Lagarde, *La naissance de l'esprit laïque au déclin du moyen âge*, vol. III: *Le Defensor pacis* (Paris and Louvain: Nauwelaerts, 1970), pp. 113–23.

preserved by the legitimate exercise of power. The defender of peace had the power to protect it. My approach locates Marsilius's thesis in its historical context: the political reality which so concerned him and which he hoped to help to change.

PREVIOUS INTERPRETATIONS OF MARSILIUS´S THOUGHT

The most recent detailed surveys of the differing interpretations of Marsilius's works have been produced by Cary J. Nederman and George Garnett.[7] Three main approaches are at issue: the republican, the imperial and (within the imperial) the providential-historical.

The republican interpretation maintains that Marsilius elaborated a thesis of popular sovereignty with the communal regime of the city-republic of his native Padua in mind. Nicolai Rubinstein, for instance, stressed the importance of this republican context, although he took due account of the imperial aspects in Marsilius's thought, holding that even in the overtly pro-imperial *Defensor minor*, 'Marsilius remained loyal to his fundamental premises'.[8] Quentin Skinner (in *The Foundations of Modern Political Thought* at any rate), while discussing the scholastic thesis of republican liberty, developed Rubinstein's approach, presenting the Paduan as a republican advocate of popular sovereignty.[9] Marsilius's thought can appear to be like this, if one focuses just on the *Defensor pacis* and concentrates on Discourse One.[10] The model for the structure of government which he set out there can be read this way. He identified the people or corporation of citizens as the human legislator:

[7] Cary J. Nederman, 'Marsiglio of Padua studies today – and tomorrow', in Moreno-Riaño, *World of Marsilius*, pp. 11–25; George Garnett, *Marsilius of Padua's 'The Truth of History'* (Oxford University Press, 2006), pp. 1–14.
[8] Nicolai Rubinstein, 'Marsilius and Italian political thought of his time', in John Hale, Roger Highfield and Beryl Smalley (eds.), *Europe in the Late Middle Ages* (London: Faber, 1965), p. 75.
[9] Skinner, *Foundations*, vol. I: *The Renaissance*, pp. 60–5.
[10] For a republican interpretation of Discourse One, see also Gewirth, *Marsilius of Padua*, vol. I, pp. 167–225.

Let us say according to the truth and advice of Aristotle, Politics 3, chapter 6, that the legislator or first and effective cause of the law is the people or the corporate body of citizens or its weightier part, through its election or will in a general congregation of the citizens through an express statement commanding or determining that something be done or omitted concerning human civil acts under temporal pain or punishment.[11]

Furthermore, the human legislator in turn instituted the principate or princely part:

Let us say according to the truth and opinion of Aristotle, Politics 3, chapter 6, that the power to make or institute the principate or to elect it belongs to the legislator or the corporate body of citizens, just as we said legislation belongs to the same in chapter 12 of this book.[12]

It is fundamental to the republican interpretation to maintain that Marsilius was producing an argument from consent. On the whole, the approach of political scientists has been to privilege Discourse One and to view Marsilius as a contributor to the development of notions of republicanism. If one is asking specifically political science questions, then the language and arguments of Discourse One readily lend themselves to providing apparently suitable answers. Nederman, primarily a political scientist, in his discussion of Discourse One has been a notable exponent of the consent

---

[11] *DP* 1.12.3, p. 63: 'Nos autem dicamus secundum veritatem atque consilium Aristotelis 3° Politice, capitulo 6°, legislatorem seu causam legis effectivam primam et propriam esse populum seu civium universitatem aut eius valenciorem partem, per suam eleccionem seu voluntatem in generali civium congrecacione per sermonem expressam precipientem seu determinantem aliquid fieri vel omitti circa civiles actus humanos sub pena vel supplicio temporali.' All translations from the *Defensor pacis* are my own. However, for a translation of the whole work, see Marsilius of Padua, *The Defender of the Peace*, ed. and trans. Annabel Brett, Cambridge Texts in the History of Political Thought (Cambridge University Press, 2005).

[12] *DP* 1.15.2, p. 85: 'Dicamus secundum veritatem et sentenciam Aristotelis 3° Politice, capitulo 6°, potestatem factivam institucionis principatus seu eleccionis ipsius ad legislatorem seu civium universitatem, quemadmodum ad eandem legumlacionem diximus pertinere 12° huius.' I have adopted Brett's rendering of *principatus* as principate (see her discussion at Marsilius of Padua, *The Defender of the Peace*, pp. xlvii–xlviii). See also Annabel Brett, 'Issues in translating the *Defensor pacis*', in Moreno-Riaño, *World of Marsilius*, pp. 91–108.

interpretation. But his nuanced approach has not led him into a republican reading of Marsilius; rather, he has expressly sought to combine historical with philosophical methods.[13] Discourse Two and Three, and the *Defensor minor* best reveal their secrets to the historian. Rubinstein and Skinner, of course, did approach Marsilius as historians, and Rubinstein did address the non-republican aspects of his thought, but they privileged the republican context in his arguments.

However, it is worth noting that Marsilius himself did not describe such cities as *respublicae*: he used terms such as *civitas*, *civilitas* and *civilis communicatio*. The couple of passages in which he used the term *respublica* had completely different connotations. In the *Defensor minor* he referred to money which might have been spent on pilgrimage but was spent instead 'to defend the *respublica*, when necessity threatens it' and (in the context of pilgrimage) to 'an expedition beyond the seas with the said intention of helping the *respublica*'.[14] In the *De translatione imperii* he said of Julius Caesar: 'He was not emperor but violator of the *respublica* and rather its usurper.'[15]

The pro-imperial interpretation of Marsilius's thought can seem the polar opposite of the republican: that both are possible reflects a certain indeterminacy in Marsilius's texts. The *Defensor pacis* was dedicated to Lewis IV of Bavaria, whose claim to the Roman emperorship Marsilius supported.[16] At *DP* 1.19.12, Marsilius expressly

---

[13] See Cary J. Nederman, *Community and Consent: The Secular Political Theory of Marsiglio of Padua's Defensor pacis* (Lanham, MD: Rowman & Littlefield, 1995), especially p. 2.

[14] *DM* 7.4: 'Propter rempublicam defendendam, cum necessitas sibi imminetur' (p. 216); 'ultramarinus transitus intentione iam dicta, videlicet reipublicae iuvandae' (pp. 217–18). All translations from *Defensor minor* and *De translatione imperii* are my own. However, for an English translation of the complete texts, see *Marsilius of Padua. Writings on the Empire. Defensor minor and De translatione imperii*, ed. and trans. Cary J. Nederman, Cambridge Texts in the History of Political Thought (Cambridge University Press, 1993).

[15] *De translatione*, 2, p. 380: 'Non fuit imperator, sed rei publicae violator et illius potius usurpator.'

[16] *DP* 1.1.6, p. 8.

attributed the ills of Italy to the absence of imperial power brought about by the exercise of papal pretensions to plenitude of power.[17] In the pro-imperial *Defensor minor*, Marsilius explained the origin of the Roman emperorship with direct reference to his model for the establishment of rulership, as expounded in *DP* 1.12.3:

The supreme human legislator, above all since the time of Christ up to the present day . . . was, is and will be that of the corporation of men, who should be subject to the coercive precepts of the law, or the weightier part thereof, in each region or province. And because this power or authority was through the corporation of provinces (or its weightier part) transferred to the Roman people on account of its preeminent virtue, the Roman people had and has the authority to make laws for all the provinces of the world, and if this people transferred to its prince the authority of making law, it must be said similarly that their prince has the power of this kind; and their authority or power to make laws (that is the Roman people's and its prince's) should last and are reasonably to last until they should be revoked, in the case of the Roman people by the corporation of provinces and in that of the Roman prince by the Roman people. And we understand that such powers are duly revoked and to be revoked, when the corporation of provinces through itself or through representatives or the Roman people shall have been duly congregated and shall have made a deliberation concerning revocation, or their weightier part, as we said and demonstrated in the 12th chapter of Discourse I of the *Defensor pacis*.[18]

---

[17] *Ibid.*, 1.19.12, p. 135.

[18] *DM* 12.1, p. 254: 'Supremus legislator humanus praesertim a tempore Christi usque in praesens tempus, et ante fortassis per aliqua tempora, fuit et est et esse debet universitatis hominum, qui coactivis legis praeceptis subesse debent, aut ipsorum valentior pars, in singulis regionibus atque provinciis. Et quoniam haec potestas sive auctoritas per universitatem provinciarum, aut ipsorum valentiorem partem, translata fuit in Romanum populum, propter excedentem virtutem ipsius, Romanus populus auctoritatem habuit et habet ferendi leges super universas mundi provincias, et si populus hic auctoritatem leges ferendi in suum principem transtulit, dicendum similiter ipsorum principem habere huiusmodi potestatem, quorum si quidem auctoritas seu potestas leges ferendi (scilicet Romani populi et principis sui) tam diu durare debet et duratura est rationabiliter, quamdiu ab eisdem per universitatem provinciarum a Romano populo vel per Romanum populum ab eius principe fuerint revocatae. Et intendimus debite revocatas aut revocandas esse tales potestates, cum provinciarum universitas per se vel per syndicos vel Romanus populus debite fuerint congregati, et talem deliberationem de revocando fecerint, aut eorum valentior pars, quemadmodum diximus et monstravimus 12 primae.'

On this basis, Marsilius was able to identify the human legislator with the emperor: 'According to human law there is a legislator, that is the corporation of citizens or its weightier part, or the supreme prince of the Romans called the emperor.'[19] This process of identification had been foreshadowed in Discourse Two of the *Defensor pacis*, where he referred to the human legislator or he who holds the principate by its authority and accepted that the legislator could be one or many.[20] The pro-imperial interpretation has been argued at length by Michael Wilks, Georges de Lagarde and Jeannine Quillet.[21] Janet Coleman also gives due weight to Marsilius's treatment of empire.[22] In her sophisticated and nuanced introduction to her translation of the *Defensor pacis*, Annabel Brett argues that, in Discourse Two, Marsilius was building an argument that tranquillity could only be achieved if the emperor was restored to his position as supreme civic legislator in spiritual as well as temporal matters.[23]

The third approach (which may be termed the providential-historical approach) has recently been elaborated by George Garnett.[24] He addresses above all the *Defensor pacis* – his approach is very much that of an historian seeking to understand the text in its original historical context. His assessment of Marsilius's text is focused on the reaction of contemporaries and near-contemporaries. Garnett considers that this is the prime way of determining the true importance

---

[19] 'Est etiam similiter secundum legem humanam legislator, ut civium universitas aut eius pars valentior, vel Romanus princeps summus imperator vocatus' (*ibid.*, 13.9, p. 280).

[20] See *DP* 2.17.9, p. 363, where he says that no priest or bishop can co-operate with promotion to ecclesiastical office 'absque legislatoris humani vel ipsius auctoritate principantis licentia'; see also *DP* 2.18.8, p. 384; 2.20.2, p. 393; 2.21.1–8, pp. 402–10.

[21] See Michael J. Wilks, *The Problem of Sovereignty in the Later Middle Ages. The Papal Monarchy with Augustinus Triumphus and the Publicists*, Cambridge Studies in Medieval Life and Thought, second series, 9 (Cambridge University Press, 1963), pp. 109–17; Jeannine Quillet, *La philosophie politique de Marsile de Padoue* (Paris: Vrin, 1970); de Lagarde, *La naissance de l'esprit laïque*, vol. III, pp. 93, 154–5 and 268.

[22] Coleman, *History of Political Thought*, pp. 134–68.

[23] Marsilius of Padua, *The Defender of the Peace*, pp. xxviii–xxxi.

[24] Garnett, *Marsilius of Padua's 'The Truth of History'*. See Joseph Canning's review of this in *EHR*, 125, 512 (February 2010), 158–61.

of what Marsilius wrote. His contention is that modern writers have concentrated on Discourse One and have seen this as a radical contribution to political theory (especially republican) precisely because they have approached the text from the point of view of political theorists. But, he maintains, if one examines the reactions of contemporaries, it is clear that it was the attack on papal plenitude of power in Discourse Two which attracted all their attention. It was Marsilius's assault on the papacy which made him notorious in his own lifetime.[25] Garnett therefore considers that privileging Discourse One is a mistake and that the crux and main message of the *Defensor pacis* lies in Discourse Two. But he considers that there is a further sense in which an historical interpretation is the correct one. His view is that the key to understanding the text lies in Marsilius's providential view of history and that this key has been neglected. It is in these areas that Garnett's claim to originality lies.

Where Garnett definitely does produce an important new interpretation is in his examination of the way in which Marsilius himself used an historical approach. In applying a providential view of history, Marsilius was, of course, arguing in a traditional manner. But Garnett argues that his author was interpreting that view in a unique way. The historical process of perfection involved the Christianization of the empire, but, according to Garnett, Marsilius identified a necessary flaw in this process, a paradox in providential history – that as the corporation of the faithful (*universitas fidelium*) became elided with the corporation of the citizens (*universitas civium*), the clergy became increasingly unsuited to their role. Constantine made a terrible mistake with his Donation, which had culminated in the apocalyptic struggle between Pope John XXII and Emperor Lewis IV in Marsilius's own day.

These are the main lines of interpretation of Marsilius's political thought. But attention should also be drawn to the wide-ranging treatment of his works in a general history of medieval political

---

[25] See also Thomas Turley, 'The impact of Marsilius: papalist responses to the *Defensor pacis*', in Moreno-Riaño, *World of Marsilius*, pp. 47–64.

thought. Antony Black has given detailed attention to Marsilius's ideas in their historical context, stressing his justification of a wide range of forms of civil authority in self-determining states, together with a refutation of the claims of the clergy.[26] But Black's latest contribution is a challenging comparison of Marsilius's political ideas with those of Moslem writers.[27] Conal Condren has emphasized that ambiguity in Marsilius's writings was designed to give them the widest possible application and audience.[28]

THE HISTORICAL CONTEXT OF MARSILIUS'S WORKS

An understanding of the precise context in which Marsilius wrote is crucial for an historical understanding of his work. But here difficulties arise because we know relatively few details of his life. Marsilius did indeed grow up in a Padua which was still an independent republic. But the *Defensor pacis* was actually written during Padua's period of transition from a republican to signorial regimes, albeit ones in which, as was usual in north Italy, communal constitutional forms were retained. In July 1318 the city's Consiglio Maggiore made Giacomo da Carrara its *signore* by transferring to him all the power of the people and commune of Padua.[29] In January 1320 Frederick of Austria was made *signore* and the next few years witnessed a series of German vicars. Then in 1327 Marsiglio da Carrara became *signore* of the city, being elected 'captain, protector and general defender of Padua' in September 1328, to be followed

---

[26] Black, *Political Thought*, pp. 58–71, 123–6.

[27] See Antony Black, *The West and Islam. Religion and Political Thought in World History* (Oxford University Press, 2008), pp. 51–9.

[28] See Conal Condren, 'Marsilius of Padua's argument from authority: a survey of its significance in the *Defensor pacis*', *Political Theory*, 5 (May 1977), 214; Condren, *The Status and Appraisal of Classic Texts* (Princeton University Press, 1985), pp. 195–6, 264, 269. For criticism of Condren's approach, see James M. Blythe, *Ideal Government and the Mixed Constitution in the Middle Ages* (Princeton University Press, 1992), pp. 199–201.

[29] 'Et ei et in eum omne imperium et omnis potestas Populi et Communis Padue concessa et translata sint': see Benjamin G. Kohl, *Padua under the Carrara, 1318–1405* (Baltimore, MD: Johns Hopkins University Press, 1998), p. 40.

by Can Grande della Scala himself, who accepted the lordship of Padua in 1328 and made Marsiglio his vicar: in both cases the grant of authority was made by the Consiglio Maggiore. In November 1328 Can Grande was made imperial vicar by Lewis IV. Furthermore, Marsilius of Padua himself served *signori*: in 1319 he was a member of an embassy sent by the leaders of the Ghibelline League, Matteo Visconti of Milan and Can Grande della Scala, to offer to Charles de la Marche, the future King Charles IV of France, the leadership of the League, an offer which was refused.[30]

The wider context was the conflict between Pope John XXII and Lewis IV. After the death of Henry VII, a disputed election had occurred in Germany and both Lewis and Frederick of Austria claimed to have been elected King of the Romans with the expectation of being made Roman Emperor. John XXII maintained that the Empire was vacant, because he recognized neither candidate, and consequently claimed that he himself exercised imperial authority in north Italy (the *regnum italicum*) on the grounds that the pope instituted the emperor. After Lewis's defeat of Frederick at the battle of Mühldorf in 1322, the crisis deepened. As Lewis increasingly intervened in the affairs of north Italy, open conflict between him and John broke out in 1323, culminating in a papal excommunication in March 1324. This remained in force after John's death in 1334, during the pontificates of Benedict XII and Clement VI, until Lewis's death in 1347.

From an imperial point of view, the papacy would be seen as posing a threat to peace in the *regnum italicum* with whose wellbeing Marsilius was primarily concerned in writing the *Defensor pacis*. Thereafter his involvement with Lewis IV deepened. He left Paris with John of Jandun in 1325 and went to join Lewis's court at Nuremberg. Marsilius accompanied Lewis on his expedition to Italy in 1327–8, although there is no evidence that he received the title of vicar in spirituals. It is likely but not certain that he was involved in the ceremony in January 1328 in Rome at which Sciarra Colonna,

---

[30] C.W. Previte-Orton, 'Marsilius of Padua and the Visconti', *EHR*, 44, 173 (April 1929), 278–9.

representing the Roman people, crowned Lewis Emperor and certain deposed bishops consecrated him – an innovative and fabricated ceremony which sought to bypass papal coronation. This unique event did closely reflect Marsilius's ideas concerning the source of imperial power, as did the deposition sentence passed on John XXII in April 1328 and the institution of Lewis's antipope, Nicholas V, the next month. Marsilius returned to Germany in 1329 and remained in imperial service at Munich, although he may well have fallen out of favour somewhat: as a notorious heretic, he would have been an embarrassment to Lewis in his repeated attempts to persuade the papacy to lift his excommunication. This was the world in which Marsilius wrote the *Defensor minor*. In a *collatio* of April 1343, Pope Clement VI reported that he was dead.[31]

MARSILIUS'S GENERAL POLITICAL MODEL

Marsilius provided a model for a structure of government of general application based on fundamental principles but produced for a specific purpose in a specific context. He sought to elaborate a model for the nature and government of political society, whereby papal claims to jurisdiction would be excluded. As is already clear, this was the model set out in Discourse One of the *Defensor pacis* and referred back to in *Defensor minor*: the *populus* or *universitas civium* as the *legislator humanus* appointed the ruling part, the *pars principans* or *principatus*. Marsilius set forth a political structure expressed in purely human and this-worldly terms, although he assumed that the citizen-body would be Christian. God was not excluded but remained in the background as the remote cause (*causa remota*) of political societies and government set-up, and exercised by the operation of human will. God could directly intervene in human affairs, as in the case of the rule of Moses, but this was not to be envisaged in fourteenth-century Europe. Given this human-centred

---

[31] For Marsilius's career in imperial service, see Frank Godthardt, 'The philosopher as political actor – Marsilius of Padua at the court of Ludwig the Bavarian: the sources revisited', in Moreno-Riaño, *World of Marsilius*, pp. 29–46.

perspective, where else would Marsilius locate the source of ultimate authority other than in the people or citizen-body?

This model fitted the whole range of existing forms of rulership: emperors, kings, city-republics and *signori*. In particular, Marsilius's thesis applied especially to the rule of *signori* like Can Grande della Scala and Matteo Visconti, because they received grants of authority from the commune and communal constitutional forms were maintained. This has been noted by Quillet and Gregorio Piaia.[32] Marsilius discussed John XXII's persecution of Lewis's vicars and faithful subjects in Lombardy, saying of Matteo Visconti: 'He has so far singularly persecuted the generous, noble and illustrious Catholic man, unique for honesty and moral seriousness among other Italians, Matteo Visconti of good memory, by imperial authority vicar of Milan.'[33]

In a north Italian context, Marsilius's model fitted both cities that retained a genuinely republican form of government in which actual, practical sovereignty was retained by the commune, and also those cities where a signorial regime was legitimized by grants of authority from the commune. In practice, *signori* were careful to have communes confirm such grants even when these lords had obtained imperial or papal vicariates. Padua was a case in point.

Marsilius's political model was a general one of general application; it would, for instance, encompass non-Italian entities like the kingdom of France. But he was ultimately addressing the Emperor as the person who, by virtue of his office, had the right and the duty to intervene in Italy to secure the peace violated by the exercise of

---

[32] See Quillet, *La philosophie politique*, pp. 91 and 108, and Gregorio Piaia, 'The Shadow of Antenor: on the relationship between the *Defensor pacis* and the institutions of the city of Padua', in Martin Kaufhold (ed.), *Politische Reflexion in der Welt des späten Mittelalters/Political Thought in the Age of Scholasticism: Essays in Honour of Jürgen Miethke*, Studies in Medieval and Renaissance Traditions, 103 (Leiden: E.J. Brill, 2004), pp. 193–207.

[33] 'Singularius persecutus est hactenus generosum, nobilem et illustrem virum catholicum, morum honestate ac gravitate inter ceteros Ytalicos singularem, bone recordacionis Matheum Vicecomitem, imperiali auctoritate Mediolanensem vicarium' (*DP* 2.26.17, p. 512).

papal claims to plenitude of power. There was a practical point to Marsilius's writings: they were not just works of theory.

WHERE DOES LEGITIMATE AUTHORITY LIE?

The foundation of Marsilius's political theory lay in another discipline: medicine. To liken the political community to a body was of course a traditional view. But Marsilius, by a deep perception of the relevance of a biological understanding, took the analogy further. He started from this position:

> Let us assume with Aristotle in Book 1, chapter 2, and Book V, chapter 3 of his *Politics*, that a city is like an animate or animal nature. For just as an animal, well-disposed according to its nature, is composed of certain proportioned parts ordered to one another and acting in mutual communication for the good of the whole, so a city is constituted from certain such parts, when it is well disposed and instituted according to reason. The relationship therefore between the animal (and its parts) and health, is seen to be similar to that between the city or kingdom (and its parts) and tranquillity.[34]

Marsilius was concerned with the correct ordering of parts within the body politic – this resulted in its health; the ill effects of papal plenitude of power brought disease. But the significance of this analogy with an animal went deeper. He went further than the suggestions in Aristotle. Biology, he realized, was a fact with which one could not argue. By starting from the proposition that the city was like an animal, he laid the foundation of his argument, which located ultimate authority in the citizen-body itself, which like an

---

[34] 'Suscipiamus cum Aristotele primo et quinto Politice sue capitulis 2° et 3° civitatem esse velut animatam sue animalem naturam quandam. Nam sicuti animal bene dispositum secundum naturam componitur ex quibusdam proporcionatis partibus invicem ordinatis suaque opera sibi mutuo communicantibus et ad totum, sic civitas ex quibusdam talibus constituitur, cum bene disposita et instituta fuerit secundum rationem. Qualis est igitur comparacio animalis et suarum parcium ad sanitatem, talis videbitur civitatis sive regni et suarum parcium ad tranquillitatem' (*ibid.*, 1.2.3, pp. 11–12). For Marsilius's use of Aristotle, see Vasileios Syros, *Die Rezeption der aristotelischen politischen Philosophie bei Marsilius von Padua. Eine Untersuchung zur ersten Diktion des Defensor pacis* (Leiden: E.J. Brill, 2007).

animal did not require a justification outside itself. Both simply existed: the city was just there, as a fact of life. The city, like an animal, knew what was best for its own health and self-preservation.

The people or corporation of citizens possessed a range of capabilities which could best be seen as a continuum, with different aspects and functions described by different terms: for instance, consent (*consensus*: *DP* 3.3), will and election (*voluntas, eleccio*: *DP* 1.12.3) and power (*potencia coactiva*: *DP* 1.12.6). There was no real dichotomy between the people's consent and its power because they were, as it were, different points along this continuum. The question at issue is rather one of focus. If one is to attain an accurate interpretation of Marsilius's argument, how much relative weight should one attach to his notions of the origins of legitimate authority or to those of the exercise of power by such authority?

From the point of view of origins, ultimate authority lay with the people or corporation of citizens as the human legislator. This body, as its name suggests, was the source of law (*lex*). Tellingly, Marsilius understood the laws made by this body as coercive precepts:

> [Law] can be considered another way, inasmuch as there is given concerning its observance a coercive precept through penalty or reward to be distributed in this present life, or inasmuch as it is given in the form of such a precept, and considered in this way it most properly is called and is law.[35]

In stressing coercion as the element which most properly turned such a precept into law, Marsilius was clearly enunciating a concept of law as the product of power. He supported his argument with reference to a passage from Aristotle's *Nicomachean Ethics*, which he interpreted as defining law as 'an ordinance concerning the just and advantageous and their opposite through political prudence, and having coercive power, that is, concerning whose observance there is given a precept, which one is forced to observe, or made by

---

[35] 'Alio modo [lex] considerari potest, secundum quod de ipsius observacione datur preceptum coactivum per penam aut premium in presenti seculo distribuenda, sive secundum quod per modum talis precepti traditur, et hoc modo considerata propriissime lex vocatur et est' (*DP* 1.10.4, p. 50).

way of such a precept'.[36] Marsilius envisaged that usually laws would have a normative content of justice. Indeed, in his immediately preceding first definition of law he said that it could be considered 'in one way in itself, as through it is shown only what is just and unjust, advantageous and harmful, and insofar as it is of this kind, it is called the science or doctrine of right'.[37] But it was of the essence of the laws which the human legislator made that they had coercive effect – they imposed justice: that is what distinguished them from merely normative statements. Coercion made true understandings of the just and advantageous, perfect laws.[38]

But Marsilius then addressed the ensuing question of whether the element of will involved in coercion was so fundamental that an unjust law would nevertheless be valid:

Indeed, sometimes false cognitions of the just and the advantageous become laws, when a precept is given concerning their observance, or they are made by way of a precept, such as appears in the regions of certain barbarians who make it observed as just that a homicide is absolved from guilt and civil penalty by paying some fine in real property for such a crime, since this is simply unjust and in consequence their laws are not perfect simply speaking. For although they have the due form, namely a precept coercing observance, they however lack a due condition, namely the due and true ordinance of what is just.[39]

[36] 'Ordinacio de iustis et conferentibus et ipsorum oppositis per prudenciam politicam, habens coactivam potenciam, id est, de cuius observacione datur preceptum, quod quis cogitur observare, seu lata per modum talis precepti' (*DP* 1.10.4, p. 50). See Aristotle, *Ethica Nicomachea*, ed. H. Rackham, Loeb series (repr. London: Heinemann, 1968), 1180a21–2, p. 632 and the discussion in Marsilius of Padua, *The Defender of the Peace*, p. 54n11.

[37] 'Vno modo secundum se, ut per ipsam solum ostenditur quid iustum aut iniustum, conferens aut nocivum, et in quantum huiusmodi iuris scientia vel doctrina dicitur' (*DP* 1.10.4, pp. 49–50).

[38] 'Vnde iustorum et conferencium civilium non omnes vere cogniciones sunt leges, nisi de ipsarum observacione datum fuerit preceptum coactivum, seu late fuerint per modum precepti, licet talis vera cognicio ipsorum necessario requiratur ad legem perfectam' (*DP* 1.10.5, p. 50).

[39] Quinimo quandoque false cogniciones iustorum et conferencium leges fiunt, cum de ipsis datur observacionis preceptum, seu feruntur per modum precepti; sicut apparet in regionibus barbarorum quorundam, qui tanquam iustum observari faciunt homicidam absolvi a culpa et pena civili reale aliquod precium exhibentem pro tali delicto, cum tamen hoc simpliciter sit iniustum, et per consequens

This is a crux in interpretation of Marsilius's thought. It has been seen as an expression of a positivist view of law; as such, it would have been totally unusual in a medieval writer. Some modern scholars have been unwilling to accept this interpretation on the grounds that Marsilius's notion of law enshrined true cognitions of the just and the unjust. Garnett holds that Marsilius was not envisaging the possibility of a valid but unjust law within the Roman Empire.[40] It seems to me that Marsilius's meaning is clear. He preferred that laws should have the requisite moral content of justice and would expect that this would normally be the case, since the political community, like an animal, knew what was best for its own wellbeing. But he was willing to consider the kind of extreme case which he referred to here. It was not absolutely necessary for a law to be just for it to be valid: the element of coercion by legitimate authority transcended normative requirements. Legitimacy was for him more important than justice. He did express a positivist view of human law. That he should do so proceeded from the logic of his position. His location of the ultimate authority to make law in the human legislator entailed a positivist view if taken to its logical conclusion – that is, in this world, the arena of the human legislator. Such imperfect laws did exist and were binding as an observable and regrettable fact. If Marsilius had not taken this view, he would have opened the way for the interference of another power, claiming to judge the human legislator – the papacy with its pretensions to plenitude of power. He accepted that there was a higher tribunal, that of the divine law of God, but that law was only enforceable in the

ipsorum leges non perfecte simpliciter. Esto enim quod formam habeant debitam, preceptum scilicet observacionis coactivum, debita tamen carent condicione, videlicet debita et vera ordinacione iustorum' (*DP* 1.10.5, pp. 50–1).

[40] For the view that Marsilius was a positivist see, especially Gewirth, *Marsilius of Padua*, vol. i, pp. 132–75. For the contrary opinion, see Quillet, *La philosophie politique*, p. 115, and Nederman, *Community and Consent*, pp. 79–83. Marsilius clearly had the example of *wergild* in mind, hence Garnett's comment: *Marsilius of Padua*, p. 66. See also Ewart Lewis, 'The "positivism" of Marsilius of Padua', *Speculum*, 38 (1963), 541–82.

afterlife – priests could preach about it in this life but could not
enforce it. He was not saying that the will of the legislator
determined whether a law was just or not, but rather whether it
was valid. In that sense he was adopting a positivist approach
different from a later notion of positive law which would derive
the formal justice of law solely from the fact of legislation by the
correct authority in the correct manner. For Marsilius, law could
be valid but unjust rather than just, because it was valid.

The human legislator was also the source of rulership or government, that part of the body politic which put the laws into effect
by exercising coercion: the principate (*principatus*) or princely part
(*pars principans*),[41] which in turn instituted the other parts. Again,
Marsilius resorted to his basic analogy with an animal:

> From the soul of the corporation of citizens or its weightier part is first
> formed or should be formed in it [i.e. the city] one part analogous to the
> heart, in which it has indeed set up a certain virtue or form with the
> active power or authority to institute the remaining parts of the city. This
> part, however, is the principate whose virtue universal in causality is the
> law, and whose active power is the authority to judge, command and
> execute sentences concerning civil justice and benefit. On this account,
> Aristotle in *Politics*, 7.6, said that this part is the most necessary of all in
> the city.[42]

The reference to soul and heart in the context of organic imagery
applied to rulership of the community was a traditional trope of
medieval political thought, but Marsilius's precise reference was to

---

[41] The term *pars principans* is introduced in *DP* 1.9, pp. 39–47, where its institution
is discussed.

[42] 'Nam ab anima universitatis civium aut eius valencioris partis formatur aut formari
debet in ea pars una primum proporcionata cordi, in qua siquidem virtutem
quandam seu formam statuit cum activa potencia seu auctoritate instituendi
partes reliquas civitatis. Hec autem pars est principatus, cuius quidem virtus
causalitate universalis lex est, et cuius activa potencia est auctoritas iudicandi,
precipiendi et exequendi sentencias conferencium et iustorum civilium, propter
quod dixit Aristoteles 7° Politice, cap. 6°, partem hanc esse omnium aliarum
necessariissimam in civitate' (*DP* 1.15.6, pp. 88–9). See Aristotle, *Pol.*, 1328b,
13–15, p. 225.

Aristotle's theory of the relationship between body and soul.[43] The active role of the *pars principans* was analogous to the heat of the heart in the body:

Thus also the authority of ruling given to any man is analogous to the heat of the heart as its subject. Thus his armed and coercive instrumental power, analogous to heat, which we call spirit, should be regulated by the law in judging, commanding and execution concerning civil justice and advantage. For otherwise, the princely part would not act towards its due end, namely the conservation of the city.[44]

Precisely because the principate had this function of putting the laws made by the legislator into effect, it must be, as Aristotle said, the most important part of the city. Otherwise the laws would become dead letters – pious wishes: they would be mere norms.

Overall, Marsilius, in his analysis, accorded the greatest salience to the role of principate, initially in terms of the basic model in which this was set up by the human legislator and then progressively in terms of the identification of the *principatus* or *principans* with the legislator – ultimately in the person of the Roman emperor. The active role of the principate was an expression of the exercise of power.

In his summing up of the message of the *Defensor pacis* at Discourse Three, chapter 3, Marsilius made the prominence of the principate clear. Peace (the aim of the whole tract) was secured by the right laws, human and divine (reflecting God's role as *causa remota*), and the right *principatus*:

For through it [the tract *Defensor pacis*], is known the authority, cause and harmonizing of divine and human laws and every coercive principate, which

---

[43] See Alexander Aichele, 'Heart and soul of the state: some remarks concerning Aristotelian ontology and medieval theory of medicine in Marsilius of Padua's *Defensor pacis*', in Moreno-Riaño, *World of Marsilius*, pp. 163–86.

[44] 'Sic quoque auctoritas principandi alicui hominum data, caliditati cordis tamquam subiecti proporcionata. Sic etiam ipsius armata seu coactiva potestas instrumentalis, calori, quem spiritum diximus, proporcionalis, debet regulari per legem in iudicando, precipiendo et exequendo de iustis et conferentibus civilibus; aliter enim non ageret principans ad debitum finem, conservacionem scilicet civitatis' (*DP* 1.15.7, pp. 90–1). See Aristotle, *De generatione et corruptione*, II, 9, 336a13, p. 312, and *De anima*, II, 7, 418b 11–17, p. 42.

are the rules of human acts, in the unimpeded and appropriate measuring of which civil peace or tranquillity consists.[45]

Peace was therefore achieved by the correct exercise of power. At the beginning of the *Defensor pacis*, Marsilius had set himself the task of discovering what was disturbing the peace and how it could be preserved. His answer lay in revealing where legitimate authority did and did not lie.

Power can be understood in both positive and negative senses. Marsilius, in analysing the role of the principate, stressed the positive uses of power. The ruler possessing *principatus* was set up by the people, which thereby became a subject multitude:

For let the first citizen or part of the civil regime, namely the ruling one, be it one man or several, understand through those human and divine truths which have been written in this book, that only to themselves belongs the authority to command the subject multitude in whole or in part; and to constrain anyone, if it is fitting, according to laws that have been made and to do nothing beyond these (especially in difficult cases) without the consent of the subject multitude or legislator. Nor is the multitude or legislator to be provoked by injury, because the power and authority of the principate consists in its express will. But the subject multitude and any single member of it can learn from this book what kind of rulers it should institute.[46]

[45] 'Per ipsum [tractatum Defensor pacis] enim scitur auctoritas, causa et concordancia divinarum et humanarum legum et coactivi cuiuslibet principatus, que regule sunt actuum humanorum, in quorum convenienti mensura non impedita pax seu tranquillitas civilis consistit' (*DP* 3.3, pp. 611–12). For the importance of Discourse Three, see Gerson Moreno-Riaño, 'Marsilius of Padua's forgotten discourse', *History of Political Thought*, 29, 3 (2008), 441–60.

[46] 'Primus namque civis vel civilis regiminis pars, principans scilicet, sit unicus homo vel plures, comprehendet per eas que in hoc libro scripte sunt humane veritates atque divine, soli sibi convenire auctoritatem precipiendi subiecte multitudini communiter aut divisim; et unumquemque arcere, si expediat, secundum positas leges et nil preter has, arduum presertim, agere absque multitudinis subiecte seu legislatoris consensu; nec iniuria provocandam esse multitudinem seu legislatorem, quoniam in ipsius expressa voluntate consistit virtus et auctoritas principatus. Subiecta vero multitudo et ipsius singulum quodlibet ex hoc libro addiscere potest, qualem et quales instituere oporteat principantes' (*DP* 3.3, p. 612).

The power of the *pars principans* was clearly limited through being an expression of the will of the legislator and bound by its laws. Elsewhere Marsilius had made it clear that the legislator could call the principate to account.[47] But here the language of subjection revealed the gap in the exercise of power between the principate, once instituted, and the multitude which created it. This was not the same as the notion that a citizen-body could transfer its sovereignty to a ruler whose subjects it then became. Indeed, in the *Defensor minor* Marsilius went on to state that the Roman people could revoke its grant of power to the emperor. But it was a striking statement of the pre-eminence of the principate over those it ruled. The people had given the exercise of its powers away to the principate which it had in consequence to obey so long as the prescribed limits were observed.

But, above all, the role of the principate was to unify the political community. To this end, Marsilius stressed that it must be undivided. This was discussed at length in *DP* 1.17, where he said, for instance: 'I say that only this principate, the supreme one, is of necessity one in number not several, if the kingdom or city is to be rightly ordered.'[48] This reflected his conviction that there must be an undivided jurisdictional structure with the creation of law solely in the hands of the human legislator and its execution in those of the principate: church jurisdiction he saw as a divisive threat to the polity. Marsilius had a clear perception that there must be no division of sovereignty. Indeed, the principate united cities and kingdoms into one:

Furthermore, if we suppose a plurality of these principates, no kingdom or city will be one. For these are one and are called one on account of the unity of the principate, towards which and on account of which all the remaining parts of the city are ordered.[49]

---

[47] *Ibid.*, 1.18, pp. 121–5.

[48] 'Hunc autem solummodo principatum, supremum scilicet, dico unum numero ex necessitate fore, non plures, si debeat regnum aut civitas recte disponi' (*ibid.*, 1.17.2, p. 113).

[49] 'Amplius, horum sic supposita pluralitate, nullum regnum aut civitas erit una. Hec enim unum sunt et dicuntur propter unitatem principatus, ad quem et propter quem relique partes civitatis ordinantur omnes)' (*ibid.*, 1.17.7, p. 116).

More than this, the principate preserved these other parts of the political community: 'This part more amply preserves the remaining parts of the city and helps them in performing their works both proper to them and communal.'[50] Such was the importance of the principate that Marsilius expressed special concern for its preservation, including it as a second purpose of the existence of law:

> We wish to show the necessary purpose of law in its last and most proper sense. Its prime purpose is to achieve civil justice and the common benefit; but its secondary purpose is to provide some security for rulers, especially hereditary ones, and the long duration of rulership.[51]

The political community could only be secure if there were a strong and unified principate with the prospect of a secure and long-lasting tenure of power. Given Marsilius's conviction that a strong and united principate, the main part of the body politic, was necessary for the survival of the polity in peace, it is surely right to stress the power and coercion aspect of the continuum of capabilities of the corporation of citizens. The principate embodied such legitimate exercise of power for the good of the whole community. But without the exercise of such power the people could not survive.

WHERE DOES LEGITIMATE AUTHORITY NOT LIE?

The whole thrust of Marsilius's argument was to demonstrate that the church, and the papacy in particular, had no power or jurisdiction in this world – that priests and bishops only had spiritual authority. Above all, Marsilius was dedicated to destroying papal claims to plenitude of power. This he saw as the secret cause which was destroying peace and which he had to unmask. This was the

---

[50] 'Amplius conservat hec pars reliquas civitatis partes, ipsasque adiuvat in ipsarum operibus tam propriis quam communibus exercendis' (*ibid.*, 1.15.12, p. 93).

[51] 'Eius [i.e. legis] secundum ultimam et propriissimam significacionem ostendere volumus necessitatem finalem; principaliorem quidem civile iustum et conferens commune, assecutivam vero quandam principancium, maxime secundum generis successionem, securitatem et principatus diuturnitatem' (*ibid.*, 1.11.1, p. 52).

problem, which, he said, Aristotle never knew[52] and which he expressly revealed at the end of Discourse One:

This wrong apprehension of certain Roman bishops and their perhaps perverse desire for principate, which they assert is owed to them from the plenitude of power passed on to them, as they say, by Christ, is that singular cause which we have said has brought about the intranquillity or discord of city or kingdom. This is prone to creep up on all kingdoms (as I said in the proem) and has troubled the Italian kingdom for a long time by its hostile actions and continually prevents and has prevented its peace and tranquillity by prohibiting with all its might the accession or institution of its prince, that is the Roman emperor, or his action in the said empire.[53]

Marsilius's argument culminated in Discourse Two, chs. 22–30, notably in his lengthy denunciation of papal plenitude of power in *DP* 2.22.20.[54] In the context of north Italy, this view of the noxious effects of papal claims made perfect sense. Clearly, Marsilius was mainly concerned about the papacy's prevention of the exercise of imperial power in that region, but he also saw the wielding of papal plenitude of power in secular matters as a disease which was liable to spread elsewhere in Europe. This could therefore threaten the French monarchy, which had a recent memory of the conflicts between King Philip IV and Boniface VIII. Marsilius referred back to these conflicts and to *Unam sanctam*, and was supportive of the French crown.[55]

---

[52] *Ibid.*, 1.1.7, p. 8.

[53] 'Hec itaque Romanorum quorundam episcoporum extimatio non recta et perversa fortassis affeccio principatus, quem sibi deberi asserunt ex eisdem, ut dicunt, per Christum tradita plenitudine potestatis, causa est singularis illa, quam intranquillitatis seu discordie civitatis aut regni factivam diximus. Ipsa enim in omnia regna serpere prona, quemadmodum prohemialiter dicebatur, infesta sui accione dudum vexavit Ytalicum regnum, et a sui tranquillitate seu pace prohibuit prohibetque continuo principantis, scilicet imperatoris Romani, promocionem seu institucionem ipsiusque accionem in dicto imperio sui toto conamine prohibendo' (*ibid.*, 1.19.12, p. 135).

[54] *Ibid.*, 2.22.20, pp. 438–40.

[55] See, for instance, *ibid.*, 2.20.8–9, pp. 397–9; 2.21.9, pp. 411–12; 2.22.20, pp. 438–40.

Marsilius's prime target was to reveal the illegitimacy of papal pretensions to plenitude of power: that the pope had no legitimate authority in temporal matters. It is therefore crystal clear that the question of power was absolutely central to his whole argument and reason for writing. If he succeeded in destroying the intellectual and legal basis for papal claims to plenitude of power, he would have succeeded; if he did not do so, he would have totally failed – in which case, he might just as well not have taken up his pen at all.

Marsilius's thesis that law in the proper sense of a coercive precept could only be made by the human legislator or the prince by its authority entailed the consequence that the pope or any bishop or priest had no powers of jurisdiction: that canon law was not law in any proper sense. Canon law was not simply invalid – it could not exist as law at all. He referred to papal decretals as being measures 'which according to the truth are nothing other than certain oligarchic ordinances which Christ's faithful are in no way bound to obey, as such, as we demonstrated in chapter 12 of the first discourse'.[56] If Marsilius was right, the whole edifice of papal power came tumbling down: the destruction of the status of canon law was especially telling.

Marsilius's political reasoning from first principles in Discourse One ruled out church jurisdiction. In Discourse Two he relied on arguments from Scripture and history to hammer home his rejection of papal claims. He considered that, in its original and proper meaning, the term 'church' was used 'of the body of the faithful believers who invoke the name of Christ'.[57] This purely spiritual definition of its nature was his starting point, from which he sought to show that the church had taken the wrong road in developing into the ecclesiastical and hierarchical institution it

[56] 'Que secundum veritatem nihil aliud sunt, quam ordinaciones quedam oligarchice, quibus in nullo tenentur obedire Christi fideles, inquantum huiusmodi, quemadmodum ex 12° prime demonstratum est' (*ibid.*, 2.5.5, p. 189).
[57] 'De universitate fidelium credencium et invocancium nomen Christi' (*ibid.*, 2.2.3, p. 144). Marsilius referred to I Corinthians 1:2.

had become in his own day, a direction contrary to Christ's original intentions for his church:

We believe that we have shown . . . that Christ therefore abdicated principate or coercive jurisdiction over anyone in this world and forbade them by counsel or precept to his apostles and their successors, bishops or priests, and wished himself and those same apostles to be subject to the jurisdiction of secular princes.[58]

The precise moment at which the wrong route had been taken was the Donation of Constantine. This was a human measure through which the papacy had been given *principatus* or *principalitas* over the other churches. From this, papal claims to plenitude of power had developed over the centuries. Constantine had made an enormous mistake. The fourteenth-century papacy was therefore a human invention.[59]

In support of his arguments, Marsilius advocated a literal reading of Scripture, rejecting the allegorical interpretations which the papacy had relied on in support of its views. Towards the end of his denunciation of the use of papal plenitude of power in *DP* 2.22.20, he said:

Boniface VIII, amongst other Roman bishops, has expressed and asserted this claim no less rashly than prejudicially, relying on metaphorical expositions, against the literal sense of scripture, to such an extent that he decreed that it is necessary for eternal salvation for all to believe and confess that this power belongs to the Roman bishops.[60]

---

[58] 'Quod quidem igitur principatum seu coactivam iurisdiccionem cuiuscumque in hoc seculo Christus abdicaverit suisque apostolis ac ipsorum successoribus episcopis seu presbyteris interdixerit consilio vel precepto, ipsumque seipsum ac eosdem apostolos principum seculi coactive iurisdiccioni subesse voluerit . . . monstrasse nos credimus' (*ibid.*, 2.5.10, pp. 197–8). See also *ibid.*, 2.4.12, pp. 172–4.

[59] *Ibid.*, 2.22.10, pp. 429–30. It could well be that *principatus* is a loose usage by Marsilius here since he denied *principatus* to the papacy – see Marsilius of Padua, *The Defender of the Peace*, pp. 398–9.

[60] 'Hoc autem inter ceteros Romanos episcopos, non minus temerarie quam preiudicialiter et contra scripture sensum literalem, metaphoricis eius exposicionibus innisus Octavus Bonifacius intantum expressit et asseruit, ut hanc Romanis episcopis

His argument in this respect was the same as that of John of Paris and Dante.

Marsilius also advocated that priests should be poor, thus taking a position in the poverty–property debate. How much he was influenced by Franciscan ideas is debated, but his views were certainly in line with those of the Spiritual wing. Since there was a relationship between property and power and between poverty and powerlessness, Marsilius's demand that priests and bishops should be poor clearly fitted in with this denial of power and jurisdiction to them.[61] Apostolic poverty would free the church from worldly concerns so that it could pursue its spiritual mission.

By giving priority to Marsilius's interpretation of questions of power and legitimate authority we have gone to the heart of his political thought and revealed his true originality. For him, everything hung on demonstrating the right answers to the questions of who did and who did not have legitimate authority. This was the most urgent matter of all, especially in the context of the conflict between Lewis IV and the papacy, with all the harm it was doing to the peace of Italy. Marsilius believed that he had thereby revealed the true natures of the political community and of the church. The human legislator and principate exercised legitimate authority in a legal and coercive sense; the church possessed legitimate authority of a spiritual kind best fostered by poverty.

---

deberi potestatem decreverit ab omnibus credendum et confitendum esse de necessitate salutis eterne' (*DP* 2.22.20, pp. 339–40).

[61] *Ibid.*, 2.11.3–4, pp. 258–60; 2.13, pp. 275–300.

CHAPTER 4

Power and powerlessness in the poverty debates

The conflict over the question of apostolic poverty became the dominant issue in the church at the end of the thirteenth century and in the first half of the fourteenth century. In essence, the dispute was a theological one with ethical and spiritual implications – how to live the perfect Christian life. At first sight, it would not appear to be a political question at all. After all, poverty is not normally (or ever) advocated as a political prescription – rather, it is to be avoided or prevented. But, as will already be clear, this particular crisis was not a purely ecclesiastical matter: the defenders of the poverty ethos and their opponents, in addressing the whole issue of poverty and property, raised questions concerning power, powerlessness and legitimate authority which had fundamental implications for political thought.

The problem of poverty and possessions has been a perennial and central one for Christianity. The ethos of the New Testament was one of suspicion of riches. Examples abound. Christ stated that it was easier for a camel to go through the eye of a needle than for a rich man to enter heaven; he enjoined the rich young man to abandon all his possessions if he wished to be perfect and follow him; and he expressed a preferential option for the poor. The disciples sent on preaching journeys were to rely on alms and community of property was practised by the early church. Christ himself was not rich. In medieval Christianity there was a tension between the poverty ethos and the justification of possessions, including those of the church. Attitudes to property were also informed by fundamental presuppositions of medieval Catholicism: that the spiritual order was hierarchically superior to mere material things; an anti-materialism that assumed that worldly goods hindered human fulfilment; and the influence of Neoplatonic philosophy.

The injunction to a life of poverty was expressed in medieval Christianity by the institution of monasticism in which the monastery possessed property but the individual monk possessed nothing. The church's possession of property was justified, in theory, as being a charitable function for the poor. Bishops, for instance, were administrators of the property of their dioceses, not owners. Poverty movements which stressed that the imitation of the life of Christ involved an abandonment of possessions became increasingly prominent from the 1170s with the emergence of the Waldensians. Other groups, such as the Humiliati and, above all, the early Franciscans, followed. The message of St Francis (d. 1226) was twofold: the *imitatio Christi* through apostolic poverty and penitence. His ideas were simple but revolutionary: unlike monks, not only did his individual friars possess nothing but neither did the Franciscan order. With the rapid growth of the order, problems rapidly emerged over the use of property. The resulting disagreements within the Franciscan order between the majority who accepted forms of compromise over poverty and those who wished to remain true to what they imagined was the original message of their founder culminated in a conflict which became acute from the 1290s onwards.

The dispute itself was extremely complicated as it developed and the modern scholarly literature devoted to it is huge.[1] My purpose is not to give any detailed history of the dispute but to outline the

---

[1] See, in particular, Malcolm Lambert, *Franciscan Poverty: The Doctrine of the Absolute Poverty of Christ and the Apostles in the Franciscan Order, 1210–1323* (London: SPCK, 1961) and Coleman, 'Property and poverty', pp. 607–48. Amongst recent works, see Virpi Mäkinen, *Property Rights in the Late Medieval Discussion on Franciscan Poverty*, Recherches de théologie et philosophie médiévales, Biblioteca, 3 (Leuven: Peeters, 2001) and Roberto Lambertini, 'Poverty and power: Franciscans in later medieval political thought', in Jill Kraye and Risto Saarinen (eds.), *Moral Philosophy on the Threshold of Modernity* (Dordrecht: Springer, 2005), pp. 141–63 (both with extensive bibliographies).

main issues involved insofar as they are relevant to the question of legitimate authority. The papacy intervened from a very early stage, introducing a legal solution to reconcile the notion of Franciscan poverty with the actual use of property as the order grew. In 1230 Gregory IX, in his bull *Quo elongati*,[2] introduced the crucial distinction whereby Franciscans had the use (*usus*) of possessions as opposed to any property (*proprietas*) in them; he also permitted the spiritual friend (*amicus spiritualis*) to administer goods seen as necessities and introduced the office of the *nuncius* who could spend money on the friars' behalf but remained an agent of the almsgiver. Innocent IV took matters further: in his bull *Ordinem vestrum* (1245)[3] he clarified the distinction between *usus* and ownership (*dominium*) – the goods which the friars used were transferred into the ownership of the papacy. This formulation, foreshadowed by *Quo elongati*, was to be fundamental in the treatment of the poverty issue. *Ordinem vestrum* also permitted the *nuncius*, acting as an agent of the friars, to both receive and expend money on their behalf. In *Quanto studiosus* (1247)[4] Innocent permitted the friars to appoint procurators acting on behalf of the *dominus* (the pope). The next stage consolidated the work of Bonaventure who in his *Apologia pauperum* (1269) had distinguished between property (*proprietas*), possession (*possessio*), usufruct (*ususfructus*) and simple use (*simplex usus*) – that which is necessary to sustain life – with the last category alone being available to Franciscans.[5] Nicholas III in his bull *Exiit qui seminat* (1279)[6] enshrined the *usus–dominium* distinction and

[2] Gregory IX, *Quo elongati*, ed. Herbert Grundmann, *Archivum Franciscanum Historicum*, 54 (1961), 20–5.

[3] *Bullarium Franciscanum*, eds. Johannes Hyacynthus Sbaralea and Conrad Eubel, 8 vols. (Santa Maria degli Angeli: Edizioni Porziuncola, anastatic reprint, 1983 of Rome, 1759 edn), vol. I, no. 114, pp. 400–2.

[4] *Ibid.*, vol. I, no. 235, pp. 487–8.

[5] Bonaventura, *Apologia pauperum*, in *Opera omnia*, 11 vols. (Quaracchi: Ex typographia Collegii S. Bonaventurae, 1898), vol. VIII, pp. 233–330.

[6] Text in M. Jules Gay (ed.), *Les Registres de Nicholas III (1277–1280), Recueil des Bulles de ce pape*, Bibliothèque des Ecoles Françaises d'Athènes et de Rome, second series, 14, 2 (Paris: Albert Fontemoing, ed., Librairie des Ecoles Françaises d'Athènes et de Rome, December 1904), no. 564, pp. 232–41.

incorporated Bonaventure's definitions: the pope distinguished between *proprietas, possessio* and *ususfructus*, added the category of right of use (*ius utendi*) and described the Franciscan way of use without legal right as simple use of fact (*simplex usus facti*). The Franciscans held that *Exiit* was official papal approbation of their way of life of apostolic poverty.

But there still remained a split within the Franciscan order over the issue of poverty. The rigorist wing, a small minority known as the Spiritual Franciscans[7] concentrated in Italy and southern France, rejected the way in which the bulk of the friars, the Conventuals, interpreted the *usus–dominium* distinction. The Spirituals maintained that the Conventuals did not live an absolutely poor lifestyle which, they said, was enjoined by St Francis, but rather experienced a settled and secure life in community. The Spirituals stressed poor use (*usus pauper*), that is, a life of absolute destitution either as vagrant preachers with total material insecurity or as hermits. Many Spirituals also became involved with Joachite ideas, which were seen as heresy by the official church: that there were three ages of mankind – those of the Father, the Son and the Everlasting Gospel (the Spirit) – in the last of which the poor would inherit the earth, the age of which St Francis was the prophet.

The Franciscan academic, the Provençal Peter John Olivi (d. 1298), was the greatest writer used by the Spirituals. His ideas may well have been used by Nicholas III in composing *Exiit qui seminat*. Certainly, Olivi's highly sophisticated and nuanced arguments were vulgarized by Spirituals. He believed firmly that the *usus pauper* was the true Franciscan way. In his *Postilla* on the Apocalypse he referred to a conflict between the carnal church (*ecclesia carnalis*) and the spiritual church (*ecclesia spiritualis*). The Spirituals simplified Olivi's ideas by identifying the *ecclesia carnalis* with the existing church and the *ecclesia spiritualis* with themselves, who would triumph in apocalyptic circumstances. Olivi became

---

[7] See David Burr, *The Spiritual Franciscans: From Protest to Persecution in the Century after Saint Francis* (University Park, PA: Pennsylvania State University Press, 2001).

the saint of the Spirituals in Provence. A cult developed around the veneration of his tomb, where the sick were brought for cures.[8]

Relations between the Spirituals and the pope deteriorated under Boniface VIII. His immediate predecessor, the hermit Celestine V (1294), had been seen as an angelic pope by the Spirituals who were amongst those who, devastated by Celestine's resignation, did not accept the validity of Boniface's election. Boniface's enemies made common cause with the Spirituals, who were manipulated both by the Colonna and the French crown. Spirituals fuelled the propaganda which portrayed Boniface as Antichrist. On a more positive note, Boniface had included *Exiit qui seminat* in the *Liber sextus*.

Clement V (1305–14) tried to bring an end to the conflict between the Spirituals and the Conventuals. He initiated a debate within the Franciscan order on the issue of poverty: in 1309 he removed the Spirituals from the jurisdiction of their superiors and set up a three-man papal commission to examine their case. In the war of words between 1309 and 1312, the main protagonists were Ubertino da Casale on the side of the Spirituals and Raymond Fronsac and Bonagratia of Bergamo on that of the Conventuals. At the Council of Vienne in 1312, Clement accepted many of the criticisms made by the Spirituals but came down on the side of the Conventuals in not recognizing the Spirituals' interpretation of the *usus pauper* and not allowing them any right to secede on this issue. The Spirituals would not accept Clement's bull on poverty, *Exivi de paradiso*, or the bull on Olivi's theology, *Fidei catholicae fundamento*. This meant that the Spirituals were clearly disobedient to papal authority.[9]

Under John XXII (1316–34), full-scale war broke out between the papacy and the Spirituals.[10] For John, the fundamental issue was

[8] See David Burr, *Olivi and Franciscan Poverty. The Origins of the 'usus pauper' Controversy* (Philadelphia: University of Pennsylvania Press, 1989).

[9] For Clement V, see Sophia Menache, *Clement V*, Cambridge Studies in Medieval Life and Thought, fourth series, 36 (Cambridge University Press, 1998).

[10] See James Heft, *John XXII and Papal Teaching Authority*, Texts and Studies in Religion, 27 (Lewiston, NY: Edwin Mellen Press, 1986); Patrick Nold, *Pope*

obedience: he considered that the Spirituals were making far too much of poverty. In his bull *Quorundam exigit* (1317) he stated: 'Poverty is great, but integrity is greater; and obedience is the greatest good.'[11] Poverty, he held, was only concerned with material goods, whereas obedience was a matter of the mind and spirit. Superiors were given powers to regulate habits and hold granaries and vineyards. John proceeded to develop his ideas in a series of bulls which amounted to an attack on the whole Franciscan position on poverty, and not just on the Spiritual interpretation. Franciscans held the essentially Augustinian view that property was unnatural, there being no property in mankind's natural condition before the Fall, and that property was a divinely sanctioned remedy for sin, introduced after the Fall. For them, *dominium* in the form of both rulership and property were connected: rulers and governments enforced the laws concerning property. Before the Fall, mankind had the common use of material goods – the distinction between 'mine' and 'thine' was a necessary accommodation to man's sinful condition. The Franciscans, in practising poverty, were voluntarily rejecting the life of *dominium*, that of property and power. In this way, their mode of life resembled that of mankind before the Fall. In contrast, the Dominicans accepted the naturalness of property.[12] Aquinas considered that the institution of property did not infringe pre-lapsarian natural law but was an addition to it in the conditions prevailing after the Fall.[13] John XXII favoured the Dominican view and, indeed, canonized Aquinas in 1323. But Aquinas himself, in the

---

John XXII and his Franciscan Cardinal: Bertrand de la Tour and the Apostolic Poverty Controversy (Oxford: Clarendon Press, 2003); Jürgen Miethke, 'Papst Johannes XXII. und der Armutstreit', in *Angelo Clareno Francescano*, Atti del XXXIV Convegno internazionale, Assisi, 5–7 Ottobre, 2006, Atti dei Convegni della Società internazionale di studi francescani e del Centro interuniversitario di studi francescani, Nuova serie diretta di Enrico Menestò, 17 (Spoleto: Fondazione Centro Italiano di Studi sull'alto medioevo, 2007), pp. 265–313.

[11] *Bullarium Franciscanum* (Rome: Typis Vaticanis, 1898), vol. v, no. 289, p. 130: 'Magna quidem paupertas, sed maior integritas; bonum est obedientia maximum.'

[12] See, for instance, Coleman, *History of Political Thought*, pp. 122–4.

[13] *ST*, 2a 2ae, qu. 66, art, 2, ad primum: 'Proprietas possessionum non est contra ius naturale, sed iuri naturali superadditur per adinventionem rationis humanae.'

context of conflicts between the mendicants and secular clergy at Paris, had in his tract *De perfectione spiritualis vitae* produced a defence of the life of poverty which was essentially the same as that of the Franciscans.[14] Indeed, the conflict between the papacy and the Franciscans should be seen against the background not just of dissensions within that order but of the long-standing disputes between seculars and mendicants, notably at the University of Paris.[15] The intellectual debate over the issues involved in property and poverty had been honed in these disputes since the 1250s. The protagonists in the conflict between John XXII and the Franciscans were therefore using arguments which had been developed over generations.

John did not accept Nicholas III's distinction between *usus* and *dominium*, as set out in *Exiit qui seminat*, and rejected the Franciscan notion of *simplex usus facti*. John's argument was that the use of a thing involved a legal right to use it – otherwise any such use would be unjust. In other words, the Franciscans had *dominium* over everything they used – over an apple, for instance, which they consumed in use. This was pre-eminently a lawyer's view: John and the Franciscans (and certainly the Spirituals) were, so to speak, on different planets. The pope could not accept the Franciscan argument that their friars were living a life of poverty outside the legal structures of *dominium*.

In *Quia nonnunquam* (1322)[16] John removed Nicholas III's ban on discussing *usus* and *dominium*. This shocked the Franciscans, who had believed that Nicholas had given permanent papal support to their interpretation of poverty and property. A meeting of Franciscans at Perugia reiterated the Franciscan position on absolute poverty. It became clear to them, led by Michael of Cesena, that the pope was attacking not just the Spirituals but the basis of the

---

[14] See William of Ockham, *On the Power of Emperors and Popes*, ed. and trans. with an introduction by Annabel Brett (Bristol: Thoemmes Press, 1998), p. 14n21.

[15] See Virpi Mäkinen, 'The Franciscan background of early modern rights discussion: rights of property and subsistence', in Kraye and Saarinen, *Moral Philosophy*, pp. 167–8.

[16] *Extravagantes Domini Papae Johannis XXII.*, 14.2 (ed. Friedberg, col. 1224).

whole Franciscan order. In response John issued *Ad conditorem canonum* (1322),[17] which sought to destroy the Franciscan position on poverty and property. John removed papal ownership of property to be used by Franciscans. Most provocatively, in *Cum inter nonnullos* (1323)[18] he defined as heresy the doctrine of the absolute poverty of Christ and the apostles, either privately or in common. Moreover, in *Quia quorundam mentes* (1324)[19] he affirmed the sanctity of property. In *Quia vir reprobus* (1329)[20] he summed up his whole position.

John claimed that he could rescind his predecessors' use of the *usus–dominium* distinction on the grounds that it had not produced the results intended. He accused the Franciscans of not actually living the life of poverty they claimed, through giving lip service to this terminological quibble. His Franciscan opponents denied that he could overturn the bulls which thirteenth-century popes had issued in their favour, because these were infallible statements of Catholic truth. John claimed not to be infallible but sovereign. His was a lawyer's view – it gave him greater freedom of action. If the pope were infallible, the power of subsequent popes would be limited by the actions of their predecessors. If the pope were sovereign, this would not be the case. Medieval canonists did not consider that popes could make new, infallible statements. Brian Tierney first produced the argument that, paradoxically, it was the Franciscan opponents of John XXII who first enunciated the notion of papal infallibility – in opposition to the pope.[21] There has been a considerable scholarly debate about whether Tierney was right and over the minute details of what John actually claimed.[22] Certainly there is a distinction to be made between the infallibility (or indefectibility) of the Roman church and that of the pope. There was no papal claim in the fourteenth century remotely similar to the

---

[17] *Ibid.*, 14.3, cols. 1225–9.   [18] *Ibid.*, 14.4, cols. 1229–30.
[19] *Ibid.*, 14.5, cols. 1230–6.
[20] *Bullarium Franciscanum*, V, n. 820, pp. 408–49.
[21] Brian Tierney, *Origins of Papal Infallibility, 1150–1350: A Study on the Concepts of Infallibility, Sovereignty and Tradition in the Middle Ages* (Leiden: E.J. Brill, 1972).
[22] For a summary, see Heft, *John XXII*, pp. 167–201.

doctrine of papal infallibility decreed at the First Vatican Council in 1870. John himself did not consider that he could change a previous pope's decrees which included the truths of Scripture or universally accepted doctrinal definitions. He held that he had never revoked any of his predecessors' decrees which contained an article of faith.

John XXII considered that the Spiritual Franciscans had lapsed into heresy through their disobedience to papal authority: that they were willing to put their interpretation of poverty before their duty of loyalty to the papacy, instituted by Christ to lead the church to salvation. The Spirituals, in turn, believed that John was himself a heretic because of what they saw as his rejection of apostolic poverty. Inquisitorial processes took place against Spirituals between 1321 and 1325. An intransigent four were burned at Marseilles. Although the Spirituals were broken by 1325, a more moderate Franciscan opposition to John continued because of his attack on the basis of order's position, with a widening perception that the pope was a heretic. Ironically, from 1331 John (who was no more than an amateur theologian) came to express heretical views on an entirely separate theological matter – the beatific vision: he maintained that the deceased only came to behold God at the Last Judgment and not at the moment of death. This provided welcome ammunition to his opponents.

John XXII was expressing the conventional papal view that the church needed a legal and property structure for it to exist and survive in the world to fulfil its spiritual mission. From his point of view it was perfectly logical to say that obedience was more important than poverty because if ecclesiastical authority were undermined, the whole structure of the church would collapse, and with it the means to salvation. Theologically speaking, poverty could not be made a prime virtue: that lay with faith, hope and charity. He could not accept arguments that exempted Franciscans from the general condition of mankind. Most Franciscans accepted that the church rightly held property, but that such a life was not for them – by their own choice. What was crucial was the attitude to property. Both sides could agree that, for the Christian, poverty of spirit was required. The church had long condemned the desire for property. Willingness to distribute surplus to the poor was necessary. But the Franciscans maintained that poverty of spirit, that is, detachment from property actually possessed, was not enough for the full imitation of the life of Christ – poverty in real terms was required. John parted company with them on this point. In fairness to John, the Spirituals did reveal attitudes which made them suspect of heresy: they were convinced that they were right and that everyone else was wrong. The Spirituals considered themselves to be the true heirs of St Francis, but they departed from his way in that he had subordinated himself in obedience to the authority of the pope.

The main defender of the Franciscan position was the English philosopher and theologian William of Ockham (*c.*1285–1347). His voluminous works provide the best means for examining the Franciscan arguments. His was not of course the only voice and there was a range of Franciscan opinion. But his towering intellect and grasp of the range of supportive and opposing arguments made him unique. He is a pre-eminently difficult writer to understand and assess, and there is no scholarly consensus as regards the interpretation of his ideas.[23] His works can be divided into two parts. His earlier life at the University of Oxford was devoted to philosophy and theology, and he made notable contributions to the study of logic. These works were purely academic. But a radical change occurred in his writings in the second part of his life, when from the mid-1320s he devoted himself to defending the Franciscan position on poverty against John XXII – these were the so-called political

---

[23] For a recent survey of interpretations of Ockham, see Takashi Shogimen, *Ockham and Political Discourse in the Late Middle Ages* (Cambridge University Press, 2007), pp. 1–35 – see Joseph Canning's review of this in *EHR*, 124, 511 (December 2009), pp. 1478–9. See also, especially, Annabel Brett's introduction to William of Ockham, *On the Power of Emperors and Popes*, pp. 7–51; John Kilkullen, 'The political writings', in Paul Vincent Spade (ed.), *The Cambridge Companion to Ockham* (Cambridge University Press, 1999), pp. 302–25; A.S. McGrade, *The Political Thought of William of Ockham. Personal and Institutional Principles* (Cambridge University Press, 1974); Jürgen Miethke, *Ockhams Weg zur Sozialphilosophie* (Berlin: De Gruyter, 1969); and Miethke, *De potestate papae*.

(and certainly polemical) works.[24] These latter works were of two kinds: some were impersonal, in that they set forth opposing viewpoints without coming to a conclusion, instead allowing the reader to reach his or her own interpretation; others (his personal works) clearly expressed Ockham's own view. The first approach can cause frustration in the reader, although Ockham's own opinion can often be reasonably well surmised by comparison with arguments in his personal works. The method of the impersonal works had the merit of setting out opponents' arguments clearly under a veil of apparent fairness. The impersonal works included the massive *Opus nonaginta dierum* (Work of Ninety Days) (1332–4)[25] and, within the period 1334–47, the huge *Dialogus* (Dialogue)[26] and the *Octo quaestiones de potestate papae* (Eight Questions on the Power of the Pope).[27] His personal works include an *Epistola ad Fratres Minores* (Letter to the Friars Minor)[28] (1334), the *Tractatus contra Benedictum* (Against Benedict [XII]),[29] the late work *Breviloquium de principatu tyrannico* (A Short Discourse on Tyrannical Government),[30] and his

---

[24] I have used the modern critical edition, *Guilelmi de Ockham opera politica* (ed. J.G. Sikes, H.S. Offler *et al.*), 4 vols.: I–III (Manchester University Press, 1940–63), IV (Oxford University Press for the British Academy, 1997). All translations from Ockham are my own.

[25] *OP*, I, pp. 287–374; II, pp. 375–858. For a translation of part of the text of the *OND*, see William of Ockham, *A Letter to the Friars Minor and Other Writings*, eds. Arthur Stephen McGrade and John Kilcullen, trans. Kilcullen, Cambridge Texts in the History of Political Thought (Cambridge University Press, 1995), pp. 18–115.

[26] The *Dialogus* is not in *OP*: see the online critical text published by the British Academy at www.britac.ac.uk/pubs/dialogus/ockdial.html (*Auctores Britannici Medii Aevi*). For a translation of part of the text of the *Dialogus*, see William of Ockham, *Letter to the Friars Minor and Other Writings*, pp. 118–298.

[27] *OP*, I, pp. 1–221. For a translation of part of the text of the *OQPP*, see William of Ockham, *Letter to the Friars Minor and Other Writings*, pp. 300–33.

[28] *OP*, III, 6–17. For a translation of the text of the *Epistola*, see William of Ockham, *Letter to the Friars Minor and Other Writings*, pp. 3–15.

[29] *OP*, III, pp. 165–322.

[30] *Ibid.*, IV, pp. 97–260. For a translation of the *Breviloquium*, see William of Ockham, *A Short Discourse on the Tyrannical Government*, ed. Arthur Stephen McGrade and trans. John Kilcullen, Cambridge Texts in the History of Political Thought (Cambridge University Press, 1992).

final work *De imperatorum et pontificum potestate* (On the Power of Emperors and Pontiffs)[31] finished shortly before his death.

Ockham became involved in the dispute between the Franciscans and John XXII while at Avignon between 1324 and 1328. The reasons for his sojourn there and the sequence of events in his life at this point have become disputed.[32] He may or may not have been summoned there to answer accusations of heresy in his theological works. Certainly, as he said himself in the *Epistola ad Fratres Minores*, it was at Avignon that, in obedience to the command of a Franciscan superior, he examined the bulls of John XXII on the poverty issue (*Ad conditorem canonum, Cum inter nonnullos* and *Quia quorundam mentes*) and became convinced that the pope was heretical on this matter.[33] This discovery changed his life and in the spring of 1328 he fled Avignon with the Minister General of his order, Michael of Cesena, and a few other friars and sought refuge at the court of Lewis of Bavaria at Pisa and later Munich. Ockham was excommunicated for this action and treated as a heretic by John XXII and subsequent popes for opposing John's teachings on poverty.

What kind of writer are we dealing with in Ockham? He was a theologian and philosopher, and this remained the case throughout his works on the poverty dispute. The main sources he used were overwhelmingly derived from the Bible and canon law. Can he be described as a political writer? This is where there has been acrimonious dispute amongst modern scholars.[34] Certainly, his theological views had implications for what we may term political thought: he had so much to say about legitimate and illegitimate authority and power, and about property, rights and liberty – in that sense he can accurately be described as a political writer. But he expressed a scale of values which minimized the significance of politics, law and power. For him the most authentic human life was

---

[31] *OP*, IV, pp. 279–355. For a translation of *DIPP*, see William of Ockham, *On the Power of Emperors and Popes*.

[32] See Brett, introduction to William of Ockham, *On the Power of Emperors and Popes*, pp. 8–10.

[33] *OP*, III, p. 6.

[34] See Shogimen, *Ockham and Political Discourse*, pp. 6–10.

one of Christian poverty outside (and above) the world of property, law and politics – he espoused the way of powerlessness as opposed to power. In that sense he was a non-political or even an anti-political writer.[35] He was a writer who defended a life beyond and above the political but who had to address the world of law and power. He had to do this because the Franciscans were forced to fight on the papacy's ground in that they were defending themselves against a papal attack framed in terms of the law. It was not by Ockham's choice that he had to argue with an opponent of this kind who, he maintained, had fundamentally misunderstood the life of evangelical poverty by analysing it in terms of its antithesis – the law. It is also a sensible question to ask whether Ockham was a political writer, because it serves the heuristic purpose of revealing his views on the sheer limitations of the world of politics and law. For him, the way of Franciscan poverty was better than that of the world, where power and *dominium* held sway.

Ockham distinguished between two parallel orders of human life: the natural, relating to the condition of mankind in the Garden of Eden before the Fall; and the post-lapsarian one of property and rulership instituted by God as a remedy for original sin. This was a thoroughly Augustinian view which underlay the Franciscan position. The clock could not, of course, be put back and all humans suffered the effects of original sin. But Ockham and the Franciscans held that by voluntarily renouncing *dominium* in terms of property and rulership, they were living, in a sense, under the conditions of pre-lapsarian natural law: it had not been superseded if it was willingly espoused. In *Opus nonaginta dierum*, ch. 65, Ockham produced an extensive refutation of John XXII's view in *Quia vir reprobus* that any use of goods without a human legal right to do so was unjust. Ockham made a fundamental distinction between *ius poli* (the right of heaven), which was composed

---

[35] This is why I wrote in my *History of Medieval Political Thought* that 'In many ways Ockham was a non-political or even anti-political writer: he certainly did not think that politics was very important' (p. 160): the 'even' is important. Janet Coleman in her *History of Political Thought*, p. 169, considered my view to be anachronistic, but I think the distinctions I am making reflect Ockham's scale of values more accurately.

of natural and divine law, and the *ius fori* (the right of the forum), comprising positive law, human or divine, thus developing Augustine's use of these two terms:

They say that this word 'right' is sometimes taken for the right of the forum, sometimes for the right of heaven. This distinction is drawn from the words of Augustine, *De vita clericorum*, which are located in [*Decr. Grat.*, C. 17, qu. 4, c. 43]: he says, 'The bishop had it in his power not to give back, but by the right of the forum, not the right of heaven' . . . To clarify this distinction, it should be known that 'the just' which is constituted by human or explicit divine pact or ordinance is called the right of the forum. Wherefore, customary right, interpreting the word 'custom' broadly, can also be called the right of the forum . . . Natural equity however, which is consonant with right reason without any human or purely positive divine ordinance, whether it would be consonant with purely natural right reason or it would be consonant with right reason derived from those things which have been divinely revealed to us, is called the law of heaven. Accordingly, this right is sometimes called natural right, because all natural right pertains to the right of heaven. It is sometimes called divine right, because there are many things consonant with right reason derived from those things divinely revealed to us, which are not consonant with purely natural right reason.[36]

---

[36] 'Dicunt quod hoc nomen "ius" aliquando accipitur pro iure fori, aliquando pro iure poli. Ista distinctio colligitur ex verbis Augustini de vita Clericorum, quae ponuntur xvii. q. iv, c. ultimo; qui ait: "In potestate habebat episcopus non reddere, sed iure fori, non iure poli" . . . Ad istius autem distinctionis evidentiam est sciendum, quod ius fori vocatur iustum, quod ex pactione seu ordinatione humana vel divina explicita constituitur. Vnde et ius fori ius consuetudinis, large sumpto vocabulo "consuetudinis", poterit appellari . . . Ius autem poli vocatur aequitas naturalis, quae absque omni ordinatione humana et etiam divina pure positiva est consona rationi rectae, sive sit consona rationi rectae pure naturali, sive sit consona rationi rectae acceptae ex illis, quae sunt nobis divinitus revelata. Propter quod hoc ius aliquando vocatur ius naturale; quia omne ius naturale pertinet ad ius poli. Aliquando vocatur ius divinum; quia multa sunt consona rationi rectae acceptae ex illis quae sunt nobis divinitus revelata, quae non sunt consona rationi pure naturali' (*OND*, ch. 65, pp. 573–5). See Augustine's sermon *De vita clericorum*, as quoted in *Decr. Grat.* Causa 17, qu. 4, c. 43: the passage concerned the moral as opposed to the strictly legal obligation of a bishop to return goods given to the church by a man who did not expect to have heirs but then subsequently had sons. The passage from Augustine did not define *ius poli* and *ius fori* but only said: 'In potestate habebat episcopus non reddere, sed iure fori, non iure poli.' For Ockham's use of *ius poli* and *ius fori*, see the nuanced treatment of Brett in *William of Ockham, On the Power of Emperors and Popes*, pp. 35–6 and 125n2.

Natural law and non-positive divine law made up a non-legal order in a human sense and were different from the whole structure of human law. This meant that the Franciscans could licitly use goods under natural law without having any legal right to them in terms of human law, that is, any right which could be defended in court: 'It is clear that the Friars Minor, if they do not have in things a positive right common to themselves and all other believers, use whatever things they licitly use by the right of heaven and not by right of the forum.'[37] The prescriptions of the *ius poli* were perceptible by human reason, including reason applied to revelation.

Ockham was also very important in articulating the notion of subjective as opposed to objective rights. In the historical long term such a view can be seen as contributing to the development of ideas of human rights. But it would be misleading to understand Ockham in quite this way. The whole issue of his treatment of rights has been hotly disputed by historians. It is no longer possible to agree that he invented the notion of subjective rights.[38] Brian Tierney has shown that such concepts were to be found in the works of canonists from the twelfth century onwards.[39] Ockham certainly explained right (*ius*) in a subjective sense as a power (*potestas*) of

---

[37] 'Et ex hoc patet quod Fratres Minores, si non habent ius positivum in rebus commune sibi et omnibus aliis fidelibus, quibuscumque rebus licite utuntur, iure poli et non iure fori utuntur' (*OND*, ch. 65, p. 578).

[38] For the classic expression of the argument that Ockham invented the concept of subjective rights, see Michel Villey, 'La genèse du droit subjectif chez Guillaume d'Occam', *Archives de philosophie du droit*, 9 (1964), 97–127. But see now Brett, *Liberty*, p. 51, and Luca Parisoli, *Volontarismo e diritto soggetivo. La nascita medievale di una teoria dei diritti nella scolastica francescana*, Bibliotheca Seraphico-Capuccina, 58 (Rome: Istituto Storico dei Cappuccini, 1989). For the question of Marsilius of Padua's role in the development of notions of subjective right, see now Alexander Lee, 'Roman law and human liberty: Marsilius of Padua on property rights', *Journal of the History of Ideas*, 70, 1 (January 2009), 23–44.

[39] See Brian Tierney, 'Villey, Ockham and the origin of individual rights', in John Witte and Frank S. Alexander (eds.), *The Weightier Matters of the Law. Essays on Law and Religion. A Tribute to Harold J. Berman* (Atlanta, GA: Scholars Press, 1988), pp. 1–31; Brian Tierney, 'Origins of natural rights language: texts and contexts, 1150–1250', *History of Political Thought*, 10 (1989), 615–46; and Tierney, *Idea of Natural Rights*, pp. 54–69.

the individual.[40] This concept is to be distinguished from *ius* in an objective sense: that which is right. Ockham accepted both senses of *ius* – but they had different meanings. A comparison with Aquinas is instructive: on the whole, Aquinas treated *ius* in an objective and not a subjective sense.[41] Viewed in this way Aquinas can be seen to have been weak on individual rights. There was a connection in Ockham's thought between individual subjective rights and liberty.[42]

How did post-Fall *dominium*, the structure of individual property and rulership come into being? Here Ockham elaborated the Augustinian tradition. God had granted mankind the power to appropriate and to rule as a remedy for original sin. This divine grant established a condition of mankind which was then formalized by human laws:

> And thus there was a three-fold time: namely before sin, in which time they had *dominium*, such as others have never had afterwards. The second time was after sin and before the division of things; and in that time they had the power of dividing and appropriating things for themselves, and if such power may be called *dominium*, it can be conceded that they had the common *dominium* of things. The third time was after the division of things, and then began individual *dominia*, such as are now those of the inhabitants of this world.[43]

[40] See Brett, *Liberty*, p. 50, and Villey, 'Genèse du droit subjectif', pp. 117–18. See, for instance, *OND*, ch. 2: 'Ius utendi est potestas licita utendi re extrinseca qua quis sine culpa sua et absque causa rationabili privari non debet invitus' (p. 304) and 'Dominium est potestas humana principalis rem temporalem in iudicio vendicandi et omni modo, qui non est a iure naturali prohibitus, pertractandi' (p. 310).

[41] See, for instance, Tierney, 'Villey, Ockham', p. 10.

[42] For the role of Franciscan writers in this connection, see Luca Parisoli, 'La contribution de l'école franciscaine à la naissance de la notion de liberté politique: les données préalables chez Pierre de Jean Olivi', in Alain Boureau and Sylvain Piron (eds.), *Pierre de Jean Olivi (1248–1298), Pensée scolastique, dissidence spirituelle et société. Actes du colloque de Narbonne (Mars, 1999)*, Etudes de philosophie médiévale, 79 (Paris, Vrin, 1999), pp. 251–63.

[43] *OND*, ch. 14, p. 439: 'Et ita fuit triplex tempus: scilicet ante peccatum, in quo tempore habuerunt dominium, quale numquam aliqui habuerunt postea. Secundum tempus fuit post peccatum et ante rerum divisionem; et in illo tempore habuerunt potestatem dividendi et appropriandi sibi res, et si talis

In his *Breviloquium*, Ockham elaborated that God granted to human beings, whether Christian or non-Christian, the power to appropriate and to set up rulers with jurisdiction:

The aforesaid double power, that is of appropriating temporal things and instituting rulers having temporal jurisdiction, was given by God directly not only to believers, but also to unbelievers, in such a way that it falls under precept and is considered to be amongst purely moral matters, on account of which it obliges all, believers as well as unbelievers.[44]

God, ultimately, stood behind the legal structures which human beings constructed to cope with their lives as damaged, sinful creatures. Ockham was not denying the validity of legal and political systems, but, according to him, they could only cover part of human life: it was possible, voluntarily, as in the case of the Franciscans, to live outside them according to the *ius poli*. Poverty meant the renunciation of the world of power in terms of possessions and rule over others. Ockham was making a profound contribution to any discussion about what it means to be human. The whole area of human life which can be considered under categories of the legal and the political was for him only one part of our existence – and definitely not the main one. He therefore shunted off the question of legitimate legal and political authority into a limited area. This of course marked a polarized contrast with Aristotle's approach, which saw the supreme expression of human existence as being contained in the political life. Ockham's way of thinking could also be seen as being radically different from a juristic one. It has to be admitted, however, that jurists' attitudes

---

potestas vocetur dominium, potest concedi quod habuerunt dominium commune rerum. Tertium tempus fuit post divisionem rerum, et tunc inceperunt dominia propria, qualia nunc sunt mundanorum.' See also the lengthy discussion in *OND*, ch. 88. For Ockham's debt to Duns Scotus, see Brett, introduction to William of Ockham, *On the Power of Emperors and Popes*, pp. 14–15.

[44] 'Duplex potestas praedicta, scilicet appropriandi res temporales et instituendi rectores iurisdictionem habentes, data est a Deo immediate non tantum fidelibus, sed etiam infidelibus, sic quod cadit sub praecepto et inter pure moralia computatur: propter quod omnes obligat tam fideles quam etiam infideles' (*Brev.*, 3.8, pp. 180–1). See also *Brev.*, 3.7, pp. 178–80; 3.9, pp. 181–7.

varied: it was common for them to say that there was no 'mine' and 'thine' in the Garden of Eden, whereas John XXII maintained that God, before he created Eve, granted Adam individual *dominium* over all creation before the Fall.[45] Furthermore, the Franciscan case was that their understanding of poverty had been ratified in canon law. It was certainly possible for a jurist to advocate the Franciscan position, as in the case of Bonagratia of Bergamo, himself a member of the Friars Minor.[46] Ockham believed that jurists and the law had their place but that some jurists had gone beyond their competence – in particular, John XXII had pontificated on a topic which he did not understand. For Ockham, the legal and political orders had legitimacy but within their own limits, which is why he considered property and secular rulership, not least in order to reveal the illegitimacy of papal claims in these areas.

Ockham made a clear distinction between the spheres of action of temporal and spiritual power: secular rulers were left to it. The basis of his argument was clearly theological. His Augustinian approach raises fundamental questions for us concerning the models for the interpretation of late medieval political thought. The interrelated notions of a divinely granted power to appropriate (*potestas appropriandi*) and a power to rule (*potestas regendi*) presented God as the source for legitimate rulership and political and legal structures. But God had left humans to create their own arrangements for running their lives, in terms of property, laws, civil communities and government. Of course, God could intervene in human affairs at will if he so chose, but this was not the normal arrangement – it was conceivable. The divinely granted capacity of human beings to set up legal and governmental structures preceded the creation of any actual civil laws and rulership. The crucial point was that Ockham's theory justified any form of human political and legal system – pagan as well as Christian.[47] To this extent he was

---

[45] In *OND*, ch. 88, pp. 654–63, Ockham addressed John's argument in *Quia vir reprobus*.

[46] For Bonagratia of Bergamo, see Mäkinen, *Property Rights*, pp. 174–90.

[47] *Brev.*, 3.12, pp. 184–7.

reflecting the mature views of Augustine far more accurately than medieval *Augustinisme politique*. Such a theologically justified ruler-ship preceded the institution of the church, had nothing to do with it and retained its validity after the church had been set up.

When compared with the hierocratic and dualist approaches, Ockham's theory amounted to a third way of providing a theo-logical justification for legitimate power and authority. The first two were concerned solely with the relationship between temporal and spiritual power within the church understood in its wider sense as the Christian community. Rulership was Christian and under-stood to be derived from God, either through the pope (in the hierocratic interpretation) or directly (in the dualist interpretation). Of course, both approaches recognized a role for the people (what-ever that might mean) in the process of choice of a ruler. But such notions of secular Christian rulership solely within a Christian community always meant that there could be a way in for ecclesi-astical interference in the exercise of secular power. Ockham's approach avoided this pitfall, at least in his view, although the papacy would disagree. Stephen McGrade rightly described Ockham's conception of secular power as desacralized.[48]

Ockham's theory can also be looked at in another way. It provided a further argument for justifying the autonomy of secular rulership and government, and indeed of political communities.[49] As a model of interpretation it ranked beside the Aristotelian. Ockham's argument from divine grant through divine law was just as strong as any relying on Aristotelian naturalism, because it gave a theological justification for secular rulership untouched by the church's claims to power which were seen as spiritual in nature. Aristotle's works were of course used by all sides in political

---

[48] McGrade, *Political Thought of Ockham*, p. 85.
[49] In this connection, see also Matthew S. Kempshall, 'Ecclesiology and politics', in G.R. Evans (ed.), *The Medieval Theologians* (Oxford: Blackwell, 2001), pp. 331–2, for the argument that 'secularizing' tendencies in fourteenth-century scholastic writers were the result of interpretations of Augustine. See also Matthew S. Kempshall, *The Common Good in Late Medieval Political Thought* (Oxford: Clarendon Press, 1999), pp. 19–25 and 362.

discourse in our period, including hierocratic writers. But they could provide a purely this-worldly and natural explanation for the political order. How real was the difference of approach? Insofar as late medieval writers admitted that God was the ultimate origin of nature, the difference between Ockham's third way of theological explanation and a Christian Aristotelian approach might seem to begin to evaporate, because one could say that to accept that God stood behind nature was tantamount to admitting that rulership existed by divine grant through divine law. It was not necessary to have recourse to Aristotle to arrive at this position.

Ockham held that the people was the original holder of legislative power which it transferred to the ruler, whether the Roman Emperor, a king or some other – a clear reference to the *lex regia* as a model applying generally and not just to the empire:

> To clarify this, it must be first known that the power to make laws and human rights belonged first and principally to the people. Hence the people too transferred the power to make laws to the emperor; thus, also, peoples, namely the Romans as well as others, transferred the power to make laws to others, and sometimes to kings, sometimes to others of less and inferior dignity and power.[50]

Once they were instituted, secular rulers had rights which the church must respect.[51] Indeed, rights under civil law should be protected. In terms of temporal and spiritual power, the crux was the relationship between the papacy and the Roman Empire. Ockham gave extended treatment to this question, notably in the *Breviloquium* and the *De imperatorum et pontificum potestate*. He defended the legitimacy of the pre-Christian Roman Empire: the present empire was its direct continuation. Because the emperor was crowned by the pope, Ockham was at particular pains to show that the emperor was in

---

[50] 'Ad cuius evidentiam est primo sciendum quod potestas condendi leges et iura humana primo et principaliter fuit apud populum. Vnde et populus potestatem condendi leges transtulit [in] imperatorem; sic etiam populi, tam Romani videlicet quam alii, potestatem condendi leges transtulerunt in alios, et quandoque in reges, quandoque in alios minoris et inferioris dignitatis et potestatis' (*Brev.*, 3.14, p. 189).

[51] *Ibid.*, 2.16, pp. 142–5; *DIPP*, ch. 4, pp. 287–8.

no weaker a position as regards the pope than was any other ruler. According to Ockham, the power of the emperor derived ultimately from God through the choice of the Roman people which had granted power to him irrevocably: once set up, the empire depended on God alone. This remained the case throughout the pre-Christian Roman Empire, because Christ had claimed no superiority over it.[52] When the empire became Christian, it came within the church but remained the same empire as originally set up by the people under God: this was why the Christian emperor succeeded to the same rights as his non-Christian predecessors – the Christian empire did not derive from the pope.[53] The fact that the empire was within the church did not give the pope any rights over it – God was the emperor's only superior. In particular, the pope had no right to depose the emperor: indeed, the right to depose him for a secular crime lay with the princely electors (in the Senate's place) or the Roman people – the same applied in the case of heresy, where the pope only had the role of examining the case (Ockham held that this right of deposition did not mean that once instituted the empire derived from the Roman Senate or people).[54] When the emperors became Christians they did not thereby become subject to the pope for their temporal power – indeed, any emperor who accepted such subjection would be guilty of alienating the empire and would by that deed alone renounce his office – a reference to the standard Roman law objection to such alienation as being against his duty of increasing the empire.[55] The Christian emperors did not have fewer rights than their pagan predecessors, that is, the emperors had the same rights within the church as they had outside it. The limitations on the emperor were not imposed by papal power but were normative: he was constrained by natural and divine law – his powers had to be used for justice and the common good. The pope had to respect the rights and liberties of the emperor and other rulers. The Avignon

[52] See the extended discussions in *Brev.*, chs. 5–8, pp. 202–11.
[53] *Ibid.*, 4.1, p. 198; 3.16, p. 193.   [54] *Ibid.*, 6.2, pp. 250–4.
[55] *Ibid.*, 4.8, pp. 210–11.

papacy had indeed injured the empire by claiming that the emperor derived his power from the pope and by claiming more power over him than over other rulers.[56] The pope could only intervene in the emperor's sphere in case of necessity or with the assent of the Romans. Any doubts about the original legitimacy of Roman rule over others, as being based on force, were removed, because such rule had become legitimate by the time of Christ, who had accepted the legitimacy of the Roman Empire.[57]

But Ockham's main target was the papacy: his treatment of legitimate secular authority was incidental to his discussion of papal power. At a deep level, he was conservative about the papacy: in contrast to Marsilius, he recognized that the papacy was a divine institution. Ockham also accepted papal *plenitudo potestatis* but argued that it was far more restricted in extent than the Avignon papacy claimed. He acknowledged the necessity of papal authority but saw his task as defining its contents and limitations more closely. He believed in the institution of the papacy as a matter of faith but was convinced that contemporary popes had exceeded their legitimate claims to the spiritual detriment of Christendom.

Ockham set up a definition of plenitude of power to demonstrate its limitations. He denied that the pope could do anything that was not contrary to divine or natural law. This was a kind of straw man because the popes did not actually claim this capacity, but it was a starting point for showing that the term 'plenitude of power' did not mean, literally, what it appeared to signify:

But if the pope by the precept and ordinance of Christ were to have such plenitude of power that in both temporal and spiritual matters he could by right do without any exception all things which did not go against the divine law and natural law, the law of Christ would be one of the most horrible servitude, even incomparably greater than the Old Law . . . But because the statement that the evangelical law is the law of perfect liberty (from which it is clear that the pope does not have such plenitude of power) can be well and badly understood, it must be realized that the statement that the evangelical law is the law of perfect liberty should not be understood to mean that it

---

[56] *DIPP*, chs. 19 (pp. 312–13) and 17 (p. 311).   [57] *Brev.*, 4.11, pp. 215–17.

should remove all servitude and that even a Christian should not suffer this . . . But it should rather be understood negatively – that, clearly, through the evangelical law a heavy yoke is no way imposed and no one through it becomes the slave of another, nor is such a burden as regards the exteriors of the worship of God imposed on Christians as oppressed the Jews.[58]

Ockham emphasized the notion of liberty – in particular the natural liberty of the Christian, the child of the free woman and not the slave girl. This, he stressed, was the message of the Gospels: Christ brought freedom for his followers. Furthermore, he argued that the term 'whatever' in Matthew 16:19 ('Whatever you shall bind on earth . . .') could not literally signify 'whatever' without exceptions – a common anti-papal argument.[59] The popes' plenitude of power did not extend to temporal matters (except in case of necessity – the stock exception), nor did it extend to the rights, property and liberties of others in general, not just of rulers.[60] Papal authority was spiritual – an office of service to the Christian community.[61] Ockham accepted that the church needed a head that would fulfil the role of supreme judge over the faithful.[62] Although he did not use the concept, his vision of papal authority saw it as a leadership role with jurisdiction.

Ockham was given the strength to pursue his attack on John XXII's claims by his conviction that his opponent was a heretic. He

[58] 'Sed si papa per praeceptum et ordinationem Christi talem haberet plenitudinem potestatis, ut omnia tam in temporalibus quam in spiritualibus sine omni exceptione posset de iure, quae non obviant legi divinae neque legi naturali, lex Christi esset horrendissimae servitutis et incomparabiliter maioris quam fuerit lex vetus . . . Verum, quia legem evangelicam esse legem perfectae libertatis – ex quo patet papam non habere talem plenitudinem potestatis – potest bene et male intelligi, est advertendum quod legem evangelicam esse legem perfectae libertatis non debet intelligi, ut omnem servitutem tollat et nullam patiatur etiam Christianus . . . Sed debet magis intelligi negative: qua scilicet per legem evangelicam nullatenus iugum grave inducitur et nullus per ipsam fit servus alterius, nec tantum onus quoad exteriorem cultum divinum per ipsam imponitur Christianis quanto Iudaei pressi fuerunt' (*ibid.*, 2.3–4, pp. 114–16). Cp. *DIPP* ch. 1, pp. 282–4.

[59] *DIPP*, ch. 5, pp. 288–90.

[60] *Ibid.*, chs. 4, pp. 287–8; 8, pp. 298–9; 9, pp. 299–301.

[61] *Ibid.*, ch. 10, pp. 301–2.   [62] *Ibid.*, chs. 12, p. 304; 13, p. 305.

later became convinced that John and his successor, Benedict XII, were not just heretics but tyrants. Canonists had long discussed the question of what could be done about a heretical pope: Gratian held that the pope could be judged by no one 'unless he is found deviating from the faith', but the Decretists found no convincing answer to the problem of how a heretical pope could be judged and deposed.[63] Previously the issue had been theoretical; for Ockham, the nightmare had become reality. The question of papal heresy raised the most important subject in Ockham's works: how did we know what was true? At the centre of the problem was the relationship between truth and authority. Could the pope through his authority define the truths of the faith? John XXII maintained that the papal keys of knowledge and of power (binding and loosing) were combined in his hands. Ockham argued in contrast that truth was based on knowledge, not authority. His approach was a cognitive and experiential one: the reason of the individual rooted in his or her experience was the means to reach truth rather than authoritative papal interpretations, deriving their force from the ecclesiastical office of the person making them. A statement could be authoritative but not true. Ockham had confidence that the individual believer could discover the truth about the faith by honestly applying his or her reason to the Bible in the context of a respect for Catholic truth. This was an application of his epistemological theory whereby knowledge was based on signs signifying concepts derived from individual experience. In particular, Ockham, like John of Paris and Dante, was yet another thinker who followed Augustine in holding that Christian truths could only be derived from literal readings of Scripture, not from allegorical ones. The whole papal doctrine of plenitude of power rested on allegorical interpretations of Scripture based on papal authority. The proof-texts, like Matthew 16:18–19, John 21:15–17 and Jeremiah 1:10,[64] invited interpretation because they were not straightforward

---

[63] See *Decr. Grat.*, Distinctio 40, c. 6 (col. 146): 'Nisi deprehendatur a fide devius.'
[64] For Innocent III's usage of Jeremiah 1:10, see Canning, *History of Political Thought*, p. 123.

statements defining papal power. Ockham held that the individual Christian could judge the actions and statements of the pope and, if necessary, contest them. Indeed, the dutiful Catholic had a duty to speak out in the face of heresy, which was all Ockham saw himself as doing. His theological knowledge imposed this obligation on him – silence in these circumstances would itself be a sin.[65]

The most striking and indeed unique aspect of Ockham's treatment of legitimate authority concerned his views on general councils of the church which, when in session, were in canon law the only genuine alternative to papal authority. He denied the doctrinal infallibility of such councils. His philosophical nominalism led him to this position. Since he held that only individuals had reality and that any group was only the sum total of the individuals composing it, he maintained that any individual could be wrong on matters of faith and a general council, being composed of fallible individuals, could always lack the knowledge or the will to speak the truth. Truth might reside in one individual Christian, perhaps a woman or even an infant. Opponents of Ockham could accuse him of confusion, since he also held that individual Christians by the use of reason could determine the truth. Ockham was taking his argument to extremes in the case of general councils to make his point. Notoriously, he disagreed profoundly with Marsilius of Padua on the question of general councils. Marsilius, applying to the church his general model of governmental structures, located ultimate ecclesiastical authority in the faithful human legislator, which could summon a general council.[66] Such a council could make infallible doctrinal statements. Ockham, with his focus on the individual, did not share Marsilius's confidence in the right judgment of corporate bodies, be they political communities or general councils. Ockham devoted *Dialogus*, Part 3, tract 2, chs. 1 and 8, to lengthy refutations of Marsilius's view.

[65] See Brett, introduction to William of Ockham, *On the Power of Emperors and Popes*, pp. 27–9, and Coleman, *History of Political Thought*, pp. 185–9.

[66] *DP* 2.21, pp. 402–20.

Ockham's views on general councils show that he cannot rightly be seen as a forerunner of the conciliar movement in the church, although some of his ideas were used by conciliarist writers. Clearly, he was opposed in particular to juristic corporation theory and expressly rejected the juristic concept of the *persona ficta*, because he held that any group was identified with the individuals who composed it.[67] Furthermore, his third-way theological justification for an autonomous sphere for legitimate secular political authority, in the context of his views on the relationship between the worlds of *dominium* and the non-legal natural order of the *ius poli*, showed that he parted company radically with those thinkers who would derive *dominium* from grace: 'And thus what holds for lordship over temporal goods, also holds for temporal jurisdiction: that, although unbelievers and universally the wicked are unworthy of jurisdiction of this kind, they can nevertheless have true jurisdiction of this kind, whether they are unbelievers or believers who are sinners.'[68]

Overall, Ockham's elaboration of Franciscan views showed that the crisis over poverty was a dispute over fundamental values. Questions of power and legitimate authority were at issue. Ockham produced a sophisticated treatment of the nature and limits of secular and papal authority, a treatment which involved a downgrading of the importance of the political and legal order. His approach and that of the Franciscans were profoundly different from that of most jurists. But therein lay a paradox: Franciscans relied on their own interpretation of papal decretals which, they maintained, ruled in favour of their understanding of poverty and property. Indeed, the debate in which Ockham's was the pre-eminent voice was focused on the interpretation of papal decretals. Furthermore, his works were full of references to Gratian's *Decretum* and other parts of the *Corpus iuris canonici*. There was no escaping canon law.

---

[67] *Tractatus contra Benedictum*, c. 8, p. 189. For juristic corporation theory, see below, pp. 153–7.

[68] 'Et sicut est de dominio temporalium rerum, sic est de iurisdictione temporali: quod quamvis infideles et universaliter impii indigni sint iurisdictione huiusmodi, tamen veram iurisdictionem huiusmodi possunt habere tam infideles quam peccatores fideles' (*Brev.*, 3.12, p. 186).

CHAPTER 5

The treatment of power in juristic thought

The fourteenth-century writers who were pre-eminently concerned with questions of power and legitimate authority were Roman and canon law jurists. For them, jurisprudence was concerned not just with explaining the content of the law but with accommodating it to the real world. These jurists were committed to applying the law to political and social reality – with putting ideas into practice. Law was concerned not just with abstract theorizing but with action. Jurists therefore illustrated the focus on political reality characteristic of fourteenth-century political thought particularly well.

How we understand political phenomena and the categories we use to describe them tend to be expressed in terms of acknowledged or unacknowledged pre-existing systems of thought or languages. In the fourteenth century a particularly important example of the problems involved in this process was provided by Italian jurists' attempts to adapt the *ius commune* (common law) system of Roman and canon law to include emerging city-republics, kingdoms and lordships – that is, to adapt that law to changing political realities. Two kinds of problem are involved. The first was for the jurists themselves, as it were: how successfully did they manage to achieve their aim within terms of the Roman and canon law? The second is of more general interest to political theorists: how valid is the metalanguage used by modern political theorists and historians to interpret the solutions of these fourteenth-century writers? How useful are standard concepts from western political theory when applied to elucidating their ideas? Two terms in particular take centre stage in any discussion of the location of legitimate authority. Modern interpreters of these jurists' political thought have been concerned with demonstrating that they produced notions of sovereignty and state: I would include C.N.S. Woolf and Quentin Skinner, for example, and indeed my own works.[1] But might this not be to privilege concepts important from the sixteenth to the twentieth centuries but now increasingly superseded in the twenty-first century, through globalization, the European Union, the influence of the United States as a superpower, and Islamic fundamentalism? The study of the fourteenth century forces one to step back and ask whether there are consistent operating concepts of political thought at all or whether one can use terms like sovereignty and state as tools of interpretation, so long as one realizes that there are bound to be subtle differences in any application of them in specific historical circumstances. This chapter is concerned firstly with asking the general question of how useful notions of sovereignty and state are for interpreting juristic ideas of legitimate authority, and secondly with addressing the unique test case of the status of papal temporal power in the papal states.

I

The problem and its solution

The political situation which confronted these jurists was a complicated one. Italy was fragmented into three main parts. In the centre of the peninsula, the papal states stretched from coast to coast. Here the pope was temporal as well as spiritual ruler. The level of the pope's actual control was highly variable: he competed with a mass of cities and lordships (*signorie*). For most of the century, the pope was absent, being settled at Avignon from 1309 before returning to Rome in 1377. But in 1378 the Great Schism broke out, producing two papal claimants, one in Rome and the other in Avignon, and

---

[1] C.N.S. Woolf, *Bartolus of Sassoferrato. His Position in the History of Medieval Political Thought* (Cambridge University Press, 1913); Skinner, *Foundations*, vol. I, pp. 10–12; Joseph Canning, *The Political Thought of Baldus de Ubaldis*, Cambridge Studies in Medieval Life and Thought, fourth series, 6 (Cambridge University Press, 1987).

lasting until 1417. To the north of the papal lands lay a collection of city-republics and *signorie*. To the south, the kingdom of Sicily was by now divided into its mainland portion, the kingdom of Naples under the Angevins, and the island itself under the Aragonese. The Roman Emperor had real power only in parts of central Europe and nominal overlordship over Italy north of the papal states. To the west lay the kingdoms of France, England and the Iberian peninsula.

The problem which faced jurists applying the Roman law to fourteenth-century political conditions was that, having been codified in the sixth century, it had been produced for an age long past and did not cover entities which had emerged in the Middle Ages, such as city-republics and kingdoms. The *Corpus iuris civilis*, of course, discussed the Roman Republic, and also kingdoms as a genus, but that was all. Furthermore, Roman law enshrined the notion of the universal lordship of the emperor as 'lord of the world' (*dominus mundi*) – there was no place for independent cities and kingdoms within the empire. Canon law presented a different kind of problem. It certainly contained the papal claim to universal plenitude of power, but canonists disagreed over whether this included ultimate temporal power as well as spiritual power. Some papal decretals were also produced that reflected the development of the power of kings but next to nothing on city-republics.

The solution to the problem of how to reconcile the *de iure* supreme power of the emperor with the *de facto* independence of cities and kings not obeying him was worked out, within terms of the *ius commune*, by the most famous jurists of the fourteenth century: Bartolus of Sassoferrato (1313/14–57) and Baldus de Ubaldis of Perugia (1327–1400). Their argument is well known. Whereas previously jurists had accorded no legal validity to purely *de facto* power, Bartolus argued that through the exercise of their own consent, cities which did not recognize a superior achieved *de facto* the same powers within their territories as the emperor enjoyed *de iure* in the empire as a whole. Every such city, as a free people (*populus liber*), became its own emperor (*civitas sibi princeps*). Bartolus was in short according full legitimacy to *de facto* power in the case of such cities. Baldus argued somewhat differently but within the same structure and extended its application to independent kings and kingdoms. That such arguments had to be expressed in *de facto* form only made sense because they were elaborated within the overall context of the pre-existing *de iure* structure of the *ius commune*: within their own terms, they incorporated other justifications for legitimate power. There was however another approach: the Neapolitan school of jurists rejected the *de iure* claims of the emperor, seeing the Roman Empire as having been based on force. Andreas de Isernia (d. *c*.1316), for instance, held that the world had returned to its pristine condition before the conquests of Rome with a multiplicity of free kingdoms.[2]

The approach of Bartolus and Baldus raises important questions of method and interpretation. They were the pre-eminent exemplars of the school of the Commentators on the Roman and canon law, a school which applied a scholastic form of argument and treatment of authorities. The text of the law was taken as something given and no attempt was made to understand the Roman or indeed the canon law in its original historical context. This was in marked contrast to the historical school of Roman law studies which emerged under the influence of Renaissance humanist studies from the early sixteenth century. This legal humanism sought to re-establish the original meaning of the Roman law understood in the historical context in which it had been produced. The humanist jurists criticized the medieval scholastic jurists, and specifically Bartolists, for their unhistorical and therefore misleading method. But this criticism was misplaced, because the Commentators and the legal humanists were trying to do two completely different things. The Commentators did have a historical sense but used it in a different way. They sought not to elucidate the original meaning of their authoritative legal texts but to accommodate them to their late medieval contemporary society. Baldus gave the clearest example of

---

[2] Ad Feud., 2.56 (fol. 286r). See Joseph Canning, 'Law, sovereignty and corporation theory, 1300–1450', in *CHMPT*, p. 466.

a highly developed historical perspective underlying this approach. As he memorably said:

Our laws consider time and create their legal enactments in time. For time which has quite receded from human memory is for that reason thought of as if it had never been, because it has been destroyed and consumed by a different usage. What does it matter to us whether Caesar or Pompey ruled more justly? Certainly, it is nothing to us. For it was our ancestors who lived under Caesar. So let us get on with our own lives. Roots are not to be scrutinized, because man cannot find the cause of all God's works. Time which gives him life gives him law. But time which is always with us – that is what gives us custom, that is what gives us law. By time we live, are nourished and exist.[3]

For Baldus, the original context of the Roman law was irrelevant: it had been made for a different time. He considered that law was concerned with facts which emerged. He, like Bartolus, thought it necessary to interpret the Roman and canon law in a creative fashion to make it relevant to his society: to make it a living law. The letter of the law had a permanent relevance, but one which was forever changing as the conditions of life mutated. There were however two perennial foundations of the legal order of the *ius commune* – the divinely sanctioned powers of the emperor and the pope. But the relationship in which these two stood to other powers which emerged was the question at issue. The Bartolist *de iure–de facto* argument was developed precisely to answer this conundrum within terms of the Commentators' scholastic method.

Clearly, issues important for contextual interpretations of texts are raised. There is the question of how jurists in the fourteenth,

---

[3] 'Iura nostra considerant tempus, et in tempore fundant leges suas. Tempus enim quod valde recessit a memoria hominum, perinde reputatur ac si non fuisset, quoniam deletum est, et diverso usu consumptum. Quid enim attinet nobis Cesar, an Pompeius iustius regnaverit? Certe nihil ad nos. Sub Cesare enim vixerunt maiores nostri; igitur et nos vivamus. Non sunt radices perscrutande, quoniam omnium dei operum nullam potest homo invenire causam. Tempus quod dat sibi vitam, dat sibi legem. Tempus vero quod semper accedit ad nos, illud dat nobis mores, illud dat nobis legem, illo [illo *ed. Venice*, 1616; illa *ed.* [*Lyon*], *1498*] vivimus, nutrimur, et sumus' (ad D.1.3.32, fol. 18r). All references to Baldus's commentaries on the *Corpus iuris civilis* are to the Lyon, 1498 edition.

fifteenth and sixteenth centuries understood the text of the Roman law especially – whether they sought to re-establish its meaning in its original historical context or whether they treated it as a perennially valid text for creative application in the conditions of their own time. There is also the question of how we today interpret the jurists' works in the context of the moment at which they wrote. Why did the legal humanists pursue their quest at that time and with what result? The Commentators sought to interpret the law for their own time, but with what success and under what contemporary influences? Certainly, any modern approach to the history of political ideas which privileges interpretation of texts in their original historical context has a clear ancestor in the Renaissance legal humanists. Any approach which is more willing to focus on the words of the texts themselves as being primary would be sympathetic to the method of the Commentators.[4]

History tends to belong to the victors, or at least to those who were such for a while. It would be highly misleading to succumb to humanist propaganda and its withering criticisms of the Bartolists. The humanists criticized as barbarous a scholastic Latin which was in fact a honed technical language. The Commentators may not have written like Cicero but they were performing a different task. The reality was that the scholastic approach of the Commentators survived the humanist assault and side-by-side with its enemy was equally representative of Renaissance thought, remaining the pre-eminent instrument for legal practice in continental Europe into the seventeenth century.

The use by Bartolus and Baldus of the *de iure–de facto* distinction was an example of an attempt to solve a recurrent problem in political theory: how to cope with change within a given system. Obviously, it is possible to change a system by overthrowing it, as in the case of revolution. Equally, any system experiences change and development over extended periods of time. What Bartolus and Baldus were trying to do was to retain the *ius commune* system while

---

[4] For a recent discussion of these questions, see Constantin Fasolt, *The Limits of History* (Chicago University Press, 2004), pp. 155–218.

accommodating radical change within it. Given that it was a legal system, with established authority being seen as existing *de iure*, any fundamental change not sanctioned by that authority must have the label *de facto* attached to it.

Problems with the de iure–de facto *solution*

There are certain fundamental problems associated with Bartolus's and Baldus's solution which need addressing and points where misunderstandings can arise. Two groups of problems are evident, as I have said: those for the jurists themselves and those for us as their modern interpreters. To take the juristic problems first, it is an obvious objection to their argument that to accept *de facto* power would be to justify the validity of any form of government or political organization which happened to emerge.[5] Tyranny would be as valid as rule by the people. The *de facto* argument could justify anything and thus would be drained of any real meaning. In response, it is clear that neither Bartolus nor Baldus was seeking to reason in this way. The *ius commune* system was not just an intellectual structure; it was a system of justice designed to produce a moral and legal structure for the lives of human beings. To be acceptable to jurists, any emerging forms of power or legal relationships would have to adhere to the fundamental norms of that system. Bartolus distinguished between two kinds of *de facto* power and authority – legitimate and illegitimate: that of independent city-republics was legitimate, being the product of popular consent for the common good, while that of *signori* was illegitimate, being based on force, whether in the gaining of power or the exercising of it. Bartolus can be misunderstood at this point: he did not mean to justify any form of government which in fact might emerge, but only legitimate *de facto* forms which he considered to be tantamount to *de iure* ones. In reality, Bartolus developed his notion of legitimate *de facto* power only in the case

---

[5] Magnus Ryan, 'Bartolus of Sassoferrato and free cities', *Transactions of the Royal Historical Society*, sixth series, 10 (2000), 87–9; Fasolt, *Limits*, p. 194n109.

of the city-republics: it was a way of categorizing the role of popular consent which was the fundamental concept.

In broad terms, Baldus followed Bartolus's employment of the *de iure–de facto* distinction. But there were two areas of difference between their approaches. The first indeed concerned the status of the *signori*. The fourteenth century in Italy witnessed an increasing number of these lords and an accompanying decline in republics. Bartolus was unsympathetic to *signori*, joining their republican enemies in describing them as tyrants or despots. He considered that those who had obtained *de iure* power through the grant of an imperial or papal vicariate nevertheless tended to act tyrannically. Baldus, in contrast, was much more sympathetic to them, accepting that they could legitimately exercise power both on a *de iure* and a *de facto* basis. He in fact ended his career serving the greatest of them all, Giangaleazzo Visconti, lord and then, from 1395, imperial Duke of Milan.[6] But Baldus, like Bartolus, did condemn *signori* who acted in a tyrannical fashion: such rule was invalid and treason against the emperor. Nevertheless, Baldus, being pre-eminently a realist, recognized as a fact that faction-fighting, the curse of republics and the prime cause of their decline, could make a *signore* necessary:

Note that civil war is that which a people begins against itself . . . and where there is this division [i.e. in the city] . . . the sinews of the city, that is the important citizens, are torn apart. As a result, a convulsion comes upon the city and commonly leads to a tyranny being necessary, as experience teaches, because the inexperienced and ignorant mob does not stand up to pressures for long. And some wise Genoese used to say that division in the city is the entry of the worm into the cheese.[7]

---

[6] For jurists' treatment of power under the *signorie* of the Visconti and the Sforza in Milan, see now Jane Black, *Absolutism in Renaissance Milan. Plenitude of Power under the Visconti and the Sforza, 1329–1535* (Oxford University Press, 2009).

[7] 'Nota quod bellum civile est quod in se populus movet . . . et ubi est ista divisio [i.e. civitatis] . . . abscinduntur nervi civitatis, id est magni cives. Vnde civitati advenit spasmus et plerunque inducitur ad necessitatem tyrannidis sicut experientia docet quia imperitum et ignorabile vulgus non diu sustinet pressuras. Et dicebat quidam sapiens Ianuensis quod divisio in civitate est vermis ingressus in caseo' (ad C. 6.51.1, fol. 150r).

He was clearly not using tyranny in a pejorative sense but recognizing a brute fact of contemporary Italian political life. However, his argument here was one for the common good and peace. He feared that any opposition to such established lords would produce undesirable results:

Neither do I nor would I dare to turn my face to heaven to give my opinion against the might of princes, because there could follow from this opinion many bad and dangerous things to be avoided, because they would create a very great scandal.[8]

Indeed, here and in his commentary on the *Liber decretalium*,[9] Baldus was happy to call such lords 'princes' (*principes*). He simply accepted their practice of legislating by plenitude of power:

But, nevertheless, because all the Lombard *signori* through customary usage and, as it were, in theory and practice employ here the words 'by plenitude of power' and are in possession of that power, as it were, in word and deed, I think that, without substantially violating the truth, we must believe them when they use such language, because it does not appear true that they would use a deceitful mode of expression . . . Otherwise . . . the decrees of such great *signori* would become illusory.[10]

For the sake of a quiet life for all, Baldus was willing to clothe the reality of signorial power with the mantle of the most exalted language of legitimate authority, a recognition of what was by his day a fact of Italian politics.

---

[8] 'Nec audeo, nec auderem, ponere os in celum ad consulendum contra potentiam principum, quia multa ex hac opinione possent sequi valde mala et periculosa et cavenda, quia generarent valde magnum scandalum' (*Cons.*, 3.218, fol. 61v, ed. Brescia, 1491 (= *Cons.*, 1.248, ed., Venice, 1575)). A *consilium* is a juristic legal opinion and is denoted by the abbreviation '*Cons.*'. The Brescia, 1490–1 edition contains the earliest ordering of Baldus's printed *consilia*; the Venice, 1575 edition is typical of the reordering of these in later printed editions and is widely available in an anastatic reproduction (Turin, 1970).

[9] The codification of Pope Gregory IX of 1234 – also known as the *Liber extra*.

[10] 'Sed tamen quia omnes domini Lombardie de consuetudine usuali et quasi de quadam theorica et practica ponunt hic verba de plenitudine potestatis, et sunt in quasi possessione verbi et facti, puto salva substantia veritatis credendum [esse] eorum sermoni, quia non est verisimile quod falsa voce uterentur . . . Alioquin . . . illusoria fierent decreta tantorum dominorum' (*Cons.*, 3.237, fol. 70r, ed. Brescia, 1491 (= *Cons.*, 1.267, ed. Venice, 1575)).

The second point of difference raises fundamental problems and concerns property rights which were seen as being guaranteed by the law of peoples (*ius gentium*). All jurists agreed that the prince (*princeps*), specifically the emperor, could dispose of his subjects' property with a just cause. From the end of the thirteenth century and in the fourteenth there was a growing juristic view reflecting the reality that the *princeps* could and did in fact remove his subjects' property from them at will. Initially, jurists were unhappy with this development: the French jurist Jacobus de Ravannis, for instance, held that the *princeps* through his plenitude of power could remove his subjects' property without cause but sinned in so doing. Likewise, the Italian jurist Cynus de Pistoia held that the emperor could remove an individual's property 'without any cause in the world' (*sine aliqua causa de mundo*) but could not do this *de iure*, again because he was sinning in so doing.[11] Opinion began to harden among some jurists who fully accepted reality and dropped any mention of sin on the emperor's part. Jacobus Butrigarius, one of Bartolus's teachers in the 1330s, made no mention of sin when he held that the emperor could remove his subjects' property without cause and that the only limitation on such power would be a self-imposed one: if he chose not to act in this way. Bartolus disagreed expressly with this approach, maintaining that in his dealings with his subjects' property the emperor was limited by the requirements of justice, to achieve which God had instituted the imperial authority – Bartolus placed imperial power firmly within the structure of higher norms.

The extreme position was reached by Baldus and his brother Angelus, also a jurist. Baldus made use of the concept of the emperor's absolute power (*potestas absoluta*). The term 'absolute power' was a medieval invention. Canonists from Hostiensis onwards in the mid-thirteenth century had distinguished between the pope's ordained power (*potestas ordinaria* or *ordinata*) and his absolute power. The distinction, which was shared with theologians, entered into the mainstream of jurisprudence. Ordained power

---

[11] Commentary on C.1.19.7, fol. 36v (ed. Frankfurt-am-Main, 1578).

meant that exercised according to the norms of the Roman or canon law: the way in which the ruler regularly acted. Absolute power was understood to mean that of the ruler freed from the restraints of human law (*legibus solutus*) but still subject to higher norms – natural and divine law and the *ius gentium*. It did not mean power freed from any restraint whatsoever. The Italian jurist Albericus de Rosciate had already said that the emperor, by virtue of his absolute power, could remove and transfer individuals' property without cause, and that no one but God could judge whether he had just cause in any particular case. Baldus took the crucial step of maintaining that the emperor's will was all that was required to take away a subject's property; as he notoriously said, in such a case: 'Whatever reason motivates the emperor himself is cause enough.'[12] As he also said:

The goods of the individual do not belong to the *princeps* . . . The emperor can, however, dispose of these through his absolute power, as if they were his own . . . and, especially, if he has a cause.[13]

The implication was that such a cause was not essential. Baldus had extended the notion of absolute power beyond any limitation by the relevant higher norm of the *ius gentium*. Angelus took the same line in discussing property: 'The *princeps* by his absolute power can remove the rights of individuals.'[14] He also said: 'The emperor by his plenitude of power can remove our property from us even with no cause urging him to do so.'[15] What is interesting is that Angelus made it clear that he actually had the pope in mind, giving the example of the expropriation of some plebeian citizens of Perugia in favour of certain nobles. Plenitude of power, originally applied to

---

[12] 'Habetur pro causa quelibet ratio motiva ipsius principis' (ad C.1.19.7, fol. 63r).

[13] 'Bona vero singularium personarum non sunt principis . . . de his tamen imperator disponere potest ex potestate absoluta ut de propriis . . . et maxime causa subsistente' (ad C.7.37.3, fol. 201v).

[14] 'Princeps ex absoluta potestate tollere potest iura singularium personarum' (ad D.8.4.13, 1, fol. 209v (ed. Lyon, 1520)).

[15] 'Imperator de plenitudine potestatis auferre potest nobis dominium etiam nulla causa suadente' (ad D.6.1.15, 2, fol. 180r (ed. Lyon, 1520)).

the pope, was by extension applied to the emperor. Baldus too made it clear that: 'It is a privilege of the emperor alone to take away the rights of one person and give them to another through his plenitude of power.'[16]

The opinion of Baldus and Angelus marked a crucial and intriguing moment in the history of political thought and it raises fundamental questions about the concept of absolute power. In the late medieval and early modern periods, the notion of absolute power retained its limitations in terms of higher norms. Louis XIV, for instance, certainly held that his power was limited by the requirements of justice and the fundamental laws of the kingdom of France. Early modern absolutism simply did not mean the exercise of the ruler's untrammelled will. What we appear to have in Baldus's and Angelus's treatment of property rights is a deviant opinion. They clearly accepted the reality of the exercise of pure power. They accepted the validity of a *de facto* exercise of power which went against the *ius gentium*. But, of course, it was wielded by the *de iure* authority of the *princeps* and was thereby justified. We have here probably the earliest example of a notion of absolute power in the sense of the will of the ruler. Jean Bodin, whose favourite jurist was Baldus, and whose own notion of sovereignty was limited by the requirements of religion, justice and the fundamental laws of France, certainly rejected this opinion of Baldus and Angelus, seeing it as a licence for the strong to dispossess by force those weaker than themselves.[17] Why did Baldus and his brother take this view? That we cannot know, other than to see in it an acceptance of reality. Certainly, in all other respects, Baldus accepted that the ruler should act within the limitations of the civil law and higher norms, but that he could not be forced to do so.

The second juristic problem involved in the use of the *de iure–de facto* distinction is also fairly obvious: the sheer legal strength of the *de iure* position underpinning the power of emperor and pope.

[16] 'Solius enim principis privilegium est iura unius auferre et alteri dare ex plenitudine potestatis' (ad C.3.34.2, fol. 190v).
[17] *De republica*, 1.8, p. 102 (ed. Paris, 1586).

The world of both jurists was that of a Roman Empire understood in its widest sense as Catholic Christendom. Within this, the powers of pope and emperor, being divinely sanctioned, could not be changed. Bartolus, in order to produce a theory to accommodate independent city-republics, had to wrestle with a system centred on monarchy, but which did incorporate elements (such as custom) which he was able to accentuate in order to support his idea of free peoples within the empire. His solution was nothing short of audacious. It was however something of a struggle and because Bartolus's arguments were purely legal ones, it would always be possible for jurists to reject his approach. Baldus himself was glad not to be responsible for the legal situation in which cities did not recognize the emperor as their superior, seeing it as the result of imperial absence from Italy.

Baldus's approach was different from that of Bartolus in that he viewed what had been a purely legal problem from the perspective of political science and biology. He brought to jurisprudence notions concerning the meaning of politics, man's political nature and the political community. He adopted the ultimately Aristotelian notion that man was by nature a political animal and used this as philosophical underpinning for his *de facto* argument – that the ultimate justification for the independent self-government of city-*populi* (city-peoples) lay in the requirements of the political natures of the human beings composing them. Man's political nature with its capacity for self-government was simply a fact of human life. The link to the language of the *ius commune* was through Baldus's view that the *ius gentium*, itself a product of human natural reason, articulated man's political nature. The inbuilt urge towards political society existed quite apart from any divinely sanctioned authority. Other jurists in the early fourteenth century had used the term 'political', but Baldus was the first to use Aristotelian political language in a systematic way; Bartolus had made very scant use of Aristotle, claiming that the philosopher's arguments did not appeal to jurists. Baldus also used Aristotelian biological terminology producing a notion of a form of body politic. He not only stressed that man, with his political or civil nature, was a form of animal but also that the *populus* as a whole, being a congregation of political animals, became in effect a form of political animal itself. This analogy provided for city-*populi* a justification for self-government on the basis of an animal's natural capacity for self-preservation:

> A people, therefore, for the very reason that it has existence, consequently has government as part of that existence, just as every animal is ruled by its own spirit and soul . . . Moreover in as much as anything has an essential form it also has a capacity to act. But the people derives its form from itself, and therefore also the exercise of self-preservation as regards its existence and proper form. For it is natural and allowed that anything should strive after the conservation of its existence.[18]

The people preserved itself as a body politic by the exercise of the capacity for self-government which was part of its nature. The analogy with self-preservation, the strongest drive in any animal, shows how fundamental Baldus considered self-government to be for a people's existence and survival.

The biological focus on the world of facts profoundly informed Baldus's attitudes. To his mind, the body politic existed in its own right. Political communities and political life were simply fundamental aspects of human existence: they could not be erased from the make-up of the human animal. He saw the whole *de iure* structure of the *ius commune* as being superimposed on the facts of political life. But he could not allow any *de iure* objections to outweigh his basic notions about political life: he could not, for instance, be restricted by the letter of the Roman law, which would see cities such as Florence and Perugia as mere licit municipal corporations.

There were therefore similarities and differences between the theories of Bartolus and Baldus within the overall structure of the *de iure–de facto* argument. Two questions, highly relevant to political

---

[18] 'Ergo eoipso quod populus habet esse habet per consequens regimen in suo esse, sicut omne animal regitur a suo spiritu proprio et anima . . . Preterea quantum unumquodque habet de forma essentiali tantum habet de virtute activa; sed populus habet formam ex se, ergo et exercitium conservandi se in esse suo, et in forma propria; nam hoc est naturale et permissum quod unumquodque studeat conservationi sui esse' (ad D.1.1.9, fol. 9r).

theory, present themselves at this point in our interpretation of their treatment of emerging *de facto* powers. Did our two jurists operate with concepts of sovereignty? Did they produce ideas of the state? And does it matter? These are the questions for us, their modern interpreters. The arguments of Bartolus and Baldus are a case study for examining how these notions can change historically and for addressing the question of their general applicability in political theory.

Did Bartolus and Baldus operate with concepts of sovereignty?

The question at issue is whether the *de facto* entities which emerged – Italian city-republics, kings like those of France, England or the Iberian peninsula and Italian *signori* – can reasonably be described as sovereign within Bartolus's and Baldus's system. The crucial argument concerns non-recognition of a superior. As regards independent cities, both jurists accepted that these did not recognize a superior, and Baldus, in his far more extensive treatment of kingship, recognized that autonomous kings were in the same position. Since sovereignty involves having no superior, this suggests that these jurists were attributing what may reasonably be described as sovereignty in these cases. However, this is not to deny that in a sense, within the structure of the *ius commune*, the emperor remained the superior of cities, kings and *signori*, albeit an ineffective one. The element of will involved in non-recognition of a superior illustrates that, within the overall *de iure* structure of the *ius commune*, sovereignty for cities and kings could *only* be obtained *de facto*, whereas any direct grant of authority from the emperor would indeed have *de iure* validity but could not concede sovereignty, because ultimate power would remain with him. The only way in which *de iure* sovereignty for cities or kings could be established by such a grant would be if it were irrevocable. This arose, for jurists, in the case of the so-called *lex regia* (royal law) in the *Corpus iuris civilis* – the supposed original transfer of sovereignty from the Roman people to the emperor when the Empire was set up under Augustus. It was a *locus classicus* of juristic debate whether this grant was revocable or irrevocable and raises the question whether sovereignty can be alienated or not: as, for instance, in the relationship between the European Union and its Member States, to take a contemporary example. Is alienable sovereignty a contradiction in terms? Bartolus held that the *lex regia* had become irrevocable in time, Baldus that it had been irrevocable from the start but, as a source of authority, subsequently transcended by the divine source for imperial power through Christ's approbation of the empire. But there was no suggestion made by jurists that the emperor (or the pope) gave sovereignty irrevocably to any cities or kings.

In considering the relationship between these various powers I have elsewhere used the notion of a hierarchy of sovereignty to denote the connections and differences between them in a structure in which *de iure* and *de facto* powers existed in parallel. This hierarchy was best and most comprehensively expressed by Baldus. At its top is located the universal *de iure* sovereign power of the emperor in temporal matters, with all other sovereignty being essentially *de facto* (except that of the pope in the papal lands). At the next level down are sovereign kings lying outside the direct rule of the emperor but being within the empire understood in its widest sense as Christendom. Below them are cities and Italian *signori* enjoying *de facto* independence amounting to sovereignty. Parallel to these are other *signori*, exercising through *de iure* concession sovereign powers without actually being themselves sovereign but still subordinate to their superior. At the bottom are autonomous cities and lords below the level of sovereignty enjoying powers of jurisdiction *de iure*, but in a subordinate sense through imperial or papal concession. An objection to my scheme would be to say that the notion of a hierarchy of sovereignty is a contradiction in terms: that sovereignty is simply sovereignty and admits of no hierarchy of sovereign power above sovereign power. This view has a certain logic, but it does not fit the fourteenth century. Since these jurists operated with the concept of non-recognition of a superior within an overall hierarchy, it seems entirely fitting to utilize the notion of a hierarchy of sovereignty as most accurately describing their view: it is difficult to see an alternative.

Baldus also applied the language of sovereignty found in Roman and canon law to city-republics, kings and *signori*. In the case of independent cities, Bartolus, as we have seen, had already cleared the way by his formula that the city is its own emperor (*civitas sibi princeps*). Since the *princeps* was the epitome of sovereign power within Roman law, this was a means of expressing the cities' sovereignty. The model was the established notion, current from the turn of the twelfth and thirteenth centuries, that a king who recognized no superior in his kingdom was the emperor of his kingdom (*rex in regno suo est imperator regni sui*). Bartolus's formulation can appear like a stroke of genius, transposing the attributes of an individual sovereign monarch to the communitarian entity of a city, but it is a problematic flash of inspiration. It can look a bit clumsy because the city is not actually the emperor; furthermore, there could always be reservations about the formula within terms of the *ius commune* because ultimate sovereignty lay with the *princeps*, whether emperor or pope. These may be the reasons why Baldus held back from employing it. He said that the city was in the emperor's place: it acted *vice principis*. The strength of the *de facto* argument for the sovereignty of city-republics lay in its being an expression of the power of the people's consent. But the problem was that such sovereignty was in a sense provisional. It was the product of the circumstance of the emperor's prolonged absence from Italy. What would happen if the emperor happened to turn up? This occurred under Charles IV, who came down to Italy in 1355 to gain the imperial crown and returned in 1368–9. According to Baldus, when the emperor was physically present, his authority again operated in these cities, that is to say, the gaps in imperial jurisdiction which had opened up through disuse were temporarily closed. This did not affect the normal state of affairs because the sovereignty of these cities was precisely the product of imperial absence. The emperor would go away again because he had no real power in Italy anymore. Imperial overlordship over the lands of the empire (*terrae imperii*) in north and north-central Italy was simply a matter of legal theory, not political reality. Florence, for instance, in 1355 was happy to purchase from Charles IV both release from the ban of the empire under which the Emperor Henry VII had placed it during his expedition to Italy between 1310 and 1313, and the confirmation of its liberties, but was not thereby surrendering its sovereign powers. Bartolus himself led the embassy from Perugia which purchased specific liberties from the emperor, a measure aimed primarily at protecting its claims against the papacy. The emperor's power existed, but in an ultimately legitimizing sense.

There was another term denoting sovereignty which was applied by Baldus to independent city-republics: *maiestas*, the term of course which Bodin was to employ to denote sovereignty in the Latin version of his work *De republica*. In Roman law *maiestas* denoted the sovereignty of the *princeps*, the emperor, or of the Roman Republic itself (*respublica Romana*). Treason (*laesa maiestas*) could only be committed against the sovereign, whether emperor or Roman Republic – it was indeed a primary sign of sovereignty. Baldus's normal view was that *laesa maiestas* could indeed be committed against independent cities, such as Florence and Perugia, although he was not entirely consistent on this point. In applying the concept of *respublica* to such cities, he was able to reactivate the idea of the *maiestas* of the *populus* (or *respublica*) and therewith that of treason against it. Thus, *laesa maiestas* could be committed against the sovereign city both because it replaced the *princeps* and because it thereby ultimately enjoyed (within its territory) that sovereignty which the Roman people had once enjoyed but had transferred to the emperor.

In the case of kings not recognizing a superior, Baldus employed the classic formula: *rex in regno suo est imperator regni sui*. He also attributed to such kings powers which he did not allow to city-republics and which were attributes of the emperor: *suprema potestas* (supreme power) and *plenitudo potestatis* (plenitude of power). In the thirteenth century the latter had come to be applied to both emperors and kings. These terms signified sovereign power. In employing them, Baldus was placing such kings above the level of independent city-republics. He did this probably because there was no likelihood that the emperor would turn up in a kingdom like France which lay outside the empire in terms of direct imperial power, unlike the Italian *terrae imperii*, and because the emperor was the direct model for the personal sovereignty of a monarch. Baldus followed the text of the Roman law at D.1.1.5 in seeing kingdoms as being the product of the *ius gentium*. For him, the *ius gentium* in this respect did not apply just to a primitive condition before the establishment of Roman law or to peoples outside the empire (*populi extranei*); rather, it retained permanent and contemporary validity. Peoples could still elect their kings by virtue of the *ius gentium* – the Spanish were a case in point. This was another expression of the consent argument.

Signori presented a more difficult problem. In the fourteenth century such lords characteristically sought legitimation of their regimes through grants of vicariates from the emperor or the pope, depending on whether they were located in the lands of the empire or of the church. Giangaleazzo's elevation to an imperial dukedom at Milan was the first of its kind and the culmination of this development. *Signori* therefore tended to be brought within the *de iure* structure. Baldus accepted both vicariates and (as we have already seen) custom as sources for the plenitude of power of *signori*, that is, both *de iure* and *de facto* justifications for sovereign power. This would appear to present a problem for the interpretation that, for rulers and entities below the level of emperor or pope, sovereignty can only be obtained *de facto*. It was compounded by his treatment of Giangaleazzo Visconti. In Baldus's eyes, Giangaleazzo was clearly not a sovereign ruler but the emperor's subject: 'The emperor through granting a fief ennobles rulership, and it is to the advantage of the *respublica* to have just subjects rather than bad ones; and thus it is advantageous to have a subject duke rather than a tyrant.'[19]

---

[19] 'Princeps dando feudum nobilitat regnum expeditque reipublice potiori habere iustos subditos quam perversos, et sic expedit habere potius subditum ducem quam tirannum' (*Cons.*, 'Ad intelligentiam sequendorum premittendum quoddam indubitatum', ed. Kenneth Pennington, in his 'Allegationes, solutiones and dubitationes: Baldus de Ubaldis' revisions of his *consilia*', in Manlio Bellomo (ed.), *Die Kunst der Disputation. Probleme der Rechtsauslegung und Rechtsanwendung im 13. und 14. Jahrhundert*, Schriften des Historischen Kollegs, Kolloquien 38 (Munich: Oldenbourg, 1997), Appendix I, p. 58, ll. 158–62 (= *Cons.*, 3.283, fol. 88r, ed. Brescia, 1491 and *Cons.*, 1.333, ed. Venice, 1575)).

Baldus considered that the grant of the dukedom constituted a resurrection of the empire from the dead. Imperial power was thereby re-established in the territories granted to Giangaleazzo, who possessed the powers of the emperor by physically taking his place: 'Our magnificent prince should be formally and totally obeyed in those things in which obedience would be due to the emperor himself, if he were to be present in Italy in his imperial person.'[20] But Giangaleazzo was sovereign as far as his own subjects were concerned, because he exercised sovereign powers. He possessed plenitude of power, was a living law (*lex animata*) in his lands, enjoyed imperial fiscal powers, could have treason committed against him and could legitimize. He was a monarch in all but name: according to Baldus, it was the reality of power which mattered, not whether Giangaleazzo was entitled king or duke. Baldus consistently referred to him as *princeps*, applying to him passages from Roman law relevant to imperial powers. This means that Baldus attributed internal sovereignty to Giangaleazzo but not external sovereignty (at least as regards the emperor). Is this to suggest that Baldus considered that *signori* with *de facto* sovereign powers were somehow superior to Giangaleazzo? There is no suggestion that he thought this: his whole emphasis was to place his master at the pinnacle of lordship in Italy. It may be that he did not fully address this problem; it may also be a sign that the argument that sovereignty may only be obtained *de facto* within the existing *de iure* structure, while it is indeed logical, may not be strictly applied in the case of *signori*. Both forms of justification were accepted by Baldus: lords possessing sovereign power by imperial grant existed in parallel with those with *de facto* sovereign power.

The question remains whether Baldus, through accepting the claims of *signori* to exercise plenitude of power, thereby placed them above independent city-republics, which were denied this.

---

[20] 'Magnifico principi nostro debet formaliter et totaliter obediri in his in quibus esset obediendum ipsi imperatori, si eius persona principaliter et personaliter interesset in Italia' (*Cons.*, 3.276, fol. 83r, ed. Brescia, 1491 (= *Cons.*, 1.326, ed. Venice, 1575)).

This conclusion might, again, exhibit a certain logic, but there is no evidence that Baldus thought this way. It is entirely possible that, at the end of his life, he would have ranked his master, Giangaleazzo Visconti, above a city like Florence; but we cannot know this.

Overall, in Baldus's case it seems reasonable to operate with a concept of sovereignty in the elucidation of his political thought so long as one realizes that modifications are required to cope with the details and subtleties of the late medieval conditions he was seeking to accommodate. Certainly, for him, sovereignty in its fullest sense remained with the emperor or the pope; they alone possessed absolute power, including the ability to expropriate property at will. Looking at an historical case, like the thought of Bartolus or Baldus, illustrates that the concept of sovereignty may be a useful tool of interpretation, but that its meaning at any particular time is subject to variations.

Did Bartolus and Baldus operate with concepts of state?

It remains to see whether Bartolus and Baldus used concepts of state in their treatment of *de facto* political entities. The concept of state is, of course, one of the most difficult to define in political theory and one particularly prone to loose usages. Bartolus and Baldus, as we shall see, operated with state concepts which were specifically juristic and late medieval in form. Analysis of these ideas is both an historical enquiry and also serves to deepen our understanding of the range of possibilities in state theory.

Both writers used juristic corporation theory in formulating their notions of state: Bartolus for city-republics and Baldus for kingdoms as well. Whereas the earlier school of the Glossators had almost universally identified a corporation with the physical members who composed it, the Commentators considered it to be at one and the same time a body composed of a plurality of human beings and an abstract unitary entity perceptible only by the intellect. Such a corporation was a legal person distinct from the individuals composing it. Indeed, the use of the term 'person' (*persona*) to denote a legal person was an invention of thirteenth-century canonists (notably Innocent IV) and was also adopted by Roman law jurists: by the constructive use of fiction, jurists operated with the concept of a fictive person (*persona ficta*), with a purely legal existence and capabilities.

In his treatment of the city-*populus*, Baldus further developed the ideas of his master, Bartolus, to produce the most profound analysis. Baldus explained how the *populus* cannot simply be equated with the individual human beings who compose it, but is rather a collection of men into a unity:

And it does not matter that the Gloss on [D.3.4.7] says that the people is nothing other than men, because that should be understood as meaning men taken collectively. Therefore separate individuals do not make up the people, and thus properly speaking the people is not men, but a collection of men into a body which is mystical and taken as abstract, and the significance of which has been discovered by the intellect.[21]

This definition combined both the abstraction and the men who formed the material basis for this abstraction: they were no longer separated individuals but corporate men. The creative use of the phrase 'mystical body', originally employed by St Paul and applied juristically by canonists, served to distinguish clearly the *populus*, in its abstract aspect as a corporational entity understandable only by the intellect, from the bodies of its members which were real in the sense of being apprehensible by the senses.

In its abstract aspect, the city-*populus* was distinct from its members and rulers or government. Being abstract, an 'image which is perceived more by the intellect than the senses',[22] such a corporate body had an attribute denied its members: it was immortal – a 'perpetual person' (*persona perpetua*). This applied to

[21] 'Nec obstat quod Glossa dicit in [D.3.4.7] quod populus non est aliud quam homines, quia debet intelligi de hominibus collective assumptis, unde homines separati non faciunt populum, unde populus proprie non est homines, sed hominum collectio in unum corpus misticum et abstractive sumptum, cuius significatio est inventa per intellectum' (ad C.7.53.5, fol. 236r). The reference is to the Gloss of Accursius.
[22] 'Imago quedam, que magis intellectu quam sensu percipitur' (ad X.1.31.3, fol. 116r (ed. Lyon, 1551)).

any corporate body: the University of Bologna, for example. What is significant from the perspective of political theory is Bartolus's and above all Baldus's acute perception of the abstract and perpetual aspects of the *populus* of a city-republic.

Given that our jurists understood such city-republics as having sovereignty in the sense described, as ruling territories and as exhibiting independent legal systems, it seems reasonable to consider that they were operating with concepts of state. Their usage of corporation theory made their contribution distinctive: through emphasizing the abstract and perpetual aspects, they introduced a new kind of state theory. The Aristotelian tradition had tended to identify the state with its members, a view reflected in Aquinas's approach, which understood the state as a unity of order of its members. The juristic corporational approach was thus somewhat different from a straightforward organic view of the state: perhaps it could be described as abstract organic. Nominalist theologians and philosophers, such as William of Ockham, could not accept the juristic view on the grounds that any group could only be identified with the real individuals who composed it.[23]

But how did this juristic application of corporation concepts compare with what has been identified by Quentin Skinner and others as the determining characteristic of early modern state theory: that the state is an abstract locus of power distinct from its members and government?[24] The element of abstraction is common to both views, as is the distinction between the state and its members and government. The difference remains that the juristic view sees the corporation of the city-*populus* as an abstraction from the members composing it, whereas the early modern state concept entirely separates the state from its members and government: the state is operated by those who rule. Both views are entirely workable notions of state: there is no need to privilege

---

[23] See above, p. 131.

[24] See, for instance, Quentin Skinner, 'The state', in Terence Ball, James Farr and Russell J. Hanson (eds.), *Political Innovation and Conceptual Change* (Cambridge University Press, 1989), p. 112.

the early modern one. The possible objection – that to identify the city-*populus* with a corporation is to put it on the same level as any other corporate body and thus to deny by implication that it can be a state – does not affect matters, because, for Bartolus and Baldus, the state was a special kind of corporation.

The highest level of abstraction and complication that Baldus reached was in his application of corporation theory to kingdoms. He considered that the kingdom, quite apart from being a territorial entity, was identified with its members but was also distinct from them in its abstract and perpetual aspect as the corporation (*universitas*) or 'republic' of the kingdom (*respublica regni*). Baldus then applied another level of abstraction. He held that the immortal corporation of the kingdom created a similarly undying legal person, the royal office or dignity (*dignitas*), which it conferred on its mortal king to operate:

The person who concedes is not dead here, namely the *respublica* itself of the kingdom, for it is true to say that the *respublica* does nothing for itself; the ruler of the *respublica*, however, acts in virtue of the *respublica* and the office conferred on him by the same *respublica*.[25]

The king in other words was the instrument of his dignity. This was the classic formulation of what Ernst Kantorowicz called the theory of 'the king's two bodies': as Baldus said of the royal *dignitas*:

And the person of the king is the organ and instrument of that intellectual and public person; and that intellectual and public person is the principal source of action, because more attention is paid to the capacity of the principal than of the instrument.[26]

---

[25] 'Non est mortua hic persona concedens, scilicet ipsa respublica regni, nam verum est dicere quod respublica nihil per se agit, tamen qui regit rempublicam agit in virtute reipublice et dignitatis sibi collate ab ipsa republica' (*Cons.*, 1.359, fol. 109v (ed. Brescia, 1490) (=*Cons.*, 3.159, ed. Venice, 1575)).

[26] 'Et persona regis est organum et instrumentum illius persone intellectualis et publice; et illa persona intellectualis et publica est illa que principaliter fundat actus, quia magis attenditur virtus principalis quam virtus organica' (*Cons.*, 1.359, fol. 109v (ed. Brescia, 1490)). See Ernst H. Kantorowicz, *The King's Two Bodies: A Study in Medieval Political Theology* (Princeton University Press, 1957), pp. 397–401, 437–9.

If one were trying to see whether Baldus did use an early modern notion of the state as an abstract locus of power operated by the ruler or government, one would look to this nexus between the *respublica regni* and the royal *dignitas* in his theory of kingship rather than to his treatment of city-*populi*. But it does not seem quite the same view.

The usefulness of employing notions of sovereignty and state

This excursion into the political thought of fourteenth-century Italian jurists has provided a case study for the application of fundamental concepts of 'state' and 'sovereignty'. All political theories are to a degree limited by the conditions of the time in which they are produced, but in interpreting them can we apply terms which transcend historical moments? The case of Bartolus and Baldus is no different in this respect from any other. My contention is that, so long as we realize the interaction between a particular political theory and the historical circumstances in which it was produced, it is still useful to employ concepts such as state and sovereignty, so long as one sees them as the kind of tools of interpretation which they are. It is important that such tools are understood as being forms of ideal types not precisely corresponding to any particular historical reality but illuminating it from a slight distance: reality illuminates the concept, and the concept, reality. In the case of Bartolus and Baldus, this approach would avoid a purely reductionist (but safe!) interpretation solely in terms of power and government within the public community. Their political thought contained far more than that. Just as they wrestled with the language of the Roman and canon law to produce a political theory for their own time, we are faced with trying to understand them within the language of political theory. This difficult enterprise challenges us to look at our operating categories in a fresh light. We are, after all, two stages removed from the political phenomena they were describing.

II

There was however one further case relating to questions of sovereignty and state: the unique one of papal temporal rule in the papal patrimony. On this the deepest treatment was that of Baldus, who was both a civilian and canonist. He considered papal temporal jurisdiction in the papal lands to be a purely human creation: '[The church] has temporal jurisdiction from human institution and providence.'[27] He did not derive the pope's temporal power there from the vicariate of Christ, but treated it in terms of his and Bartolus's general juristic *de iure–de facto* argument concerning power.

According to Baldus, the pope operated imperial jurisdiction in the papal patrimony. The administration of imperial jurisdiction was divided between the emperor and the pope in the *terrae imperii* and the *terrae ecclesiae* respectively: '[The emperor] does not have imperial administration everywhere for he has *imperium* divided with the pope, so that the lands of the Roman church are not subject to the emperor directly or indirectly.'[28] This approach reflected Bartolus's view: 'In those lands the Roman church exercises jurisdiction which belonged to the Roman empire and it admits this. They do not therefore cease to be part of the Roman people; the administration of these provinces, however, is conceded to another.'[29] There were therefore two *principes*, with the result that Roman law texts applicable to the *princeps* (originally the emperor)

[27] '[Ecclesia habet] temporalem iurisdictionem ex institutione et providentia humana', Baldus, *additio* ad Gulielmus Durandus, *Speculum iuris*, 2.2.3, p. 248 (ed. Frankfurt, 1592).

[28] 'Non habet [imperator] ubique imperatoriam administrationem, nam divisum habet imperium cum apostolico, ita quod terre ecclesie Romane non subsunt imperatori immediate nec mediate' (Baldus, *Cons.*, 2.37, fol. 11v, ed. Brescia, 1490 (=*Cons.*, 4.40, ed. Venice, 1575)).

[29] 'Ecclesia Romana exercet illis [illas *ed. cit.* & *ed. Basel*, 1589] in terris iurisdictionem, que erat imperii [imperii *ed. Milan, 1491*; imperio *ed. cit.* & *ed. Basel, 1589*] Romani et istud fatentur; non ergo desinunt esse de populo Romano, sed administratio istarum provinciarum est alteri concessa' (Bartolus ad D.49.15.24, fol. 228r (ed. Turin, 1577)).

became applicable to the pope. Baldus's commentary on the Proem
to the *Liber extra*, for instance, provided notable evidence of this.[30]
His approach was a thoroughly *ius commune* one – in his commentary on the *Liber extra*, so much of his argument was supported by
Roman law texts.

The origins of papal temporal power

Baldus treated the origins of papal temporal power at a purely
human level. In *de iure* terms, the Donation of Constantine was
the basis of papal temporal jurisdiction in the patrimony. Through
the *lex regia*, the Roman people had irrevocably alienated its
sovereignty to the emperor, with subsequent divine approbation.
The emperor had in turn through the Donation transferred sovereignty over the papal patrimony to the pope, resulting in the
division of the administration of imperial jurisdiction. But did this
make the emperor the pope's superior in temporal matters because
he was the source of the pope's temporal jurisdiction? There was
no hint of this in Baldus's discussions – no suggestion that the
Donation was revocable. But late medieval emperors reconfirmed
the Donation at their coronations, as Baldus mentioned, although
they did so, he said, 'with the pope's authority' (*auctoritate pape*).[31]
Clearly, these repeated modern confirmations insisted on by the
popes would be seen by them as reinforcing their claims to the papal
lands. But was there more to it than that? Baldus made the intriguing following statement: 'But because the church has doubts
about the old Donation, it has had the emperor Charles make it a
new one' – a reference to Charles IV's repetition of the Donation at
his coronation in 1355.[32] One may make of this what one will: it may
well have been a straw in the wind reflecting contemporary doubts

---

[30] See Baldus ad x. Proem, 'Gregorius', n. 4, fol. 3r (ed. Lyon, 1551).

[31] Baldus ad x.2.24.33, n. 4, fol. 315r (ed. Lyon, 1551).

[32] 'Sed quia ecclesia dubitat de veteri donatione, fecit sibi de novo donari per
     imperatorem Carolum', Baldus, *additio* ad *Specul.*, 2.2.3 (p. 248). He then refers
     to this donation as 'recens', thus clearly showing he has Charles IV in mind.

about the Donation's authenticity. Other than this remark, Baldus did not show any sign that he questioned either the genuineness or validity of the original Donation, or indeed that he knew of earlier disbelief in it, as expressed by Emperor Otto III or in the early twelfth century by Gregory of Catina.[33]

There remained a further problem over the *lex regia*, despite Baldus's belief that it had been irrevocable. He described the Donation of Constantine as a new *lex regia*, passed with the consent of the senate and people of Rome:

> There is a contrary argument in favour of the Donation's validity: that it was made by Constantine together with the senate and the whole people. It is valid therefore as a result of the new *lex regia* which has been made concerning the empire, because it has not been the product of a less effective cause than the first *lex regia*, but of the same power or greater force and power . . . Thus what would not be valid on its own account is valid by the people's authority. Furthermore, because the people never dies . . . the death of Constantine does not matter . . . and thus the city of Rome belongs to the Church, not Caesar.[34]

How could this be if the original *lex regia* was irrevocable? Baldus was not being consistent here but was providing an answer to the fundamental Roman law objection to the validity of the Donation: that the empire could not be alienated. This was a very difficult (if not insoluble) problem in terms of Roman law and was Accursius's great argument against the validity of the Donation. Baldus's association of the people in the Donation made it valid where otherwise it would not have been in terms of Roman law (as he admitted) – this was a way of reading the text of the Donation in *Decr. Grat.*, D. 96, c. 14.[35] The question of sovereignty at issue was

---

[33] See Canning, *Political Thought of Baldus*, p. 52n112.

[34] 'In contrarium, quod donatio valuerit, facit quia fuit facta a Constantino cum senatu et toto populo. Valet ergo ex nova lege regia que de imperio lata est, quia non processit a minori potentia cause quam prima lex regia, sed ab eadem vi ac potestate, vel maiori . . . sic valet auctoritate populi quod per se non valeret; et quia populus nunquam moritur . . . ideo non curatur mors Constantini . . . et ideo urbs Romana est ecclesie, non Cesaris' (Baldus ad D.V. Proem, ad. v. 'Quoniam omnia', fol. 1v).

[35] See Baldus ad Feud., 2.26 (fol. 52r): 'Constantinus quando donavit urbem beato Silvestro fecit cum consensu populi ut patet in [*Decr. Grat.*, Distinctio 96, c. 14].'

whether a ruler could alienate his kingdom, empire or state. The juristic answer was that he could not, because rulership was an office, as Baldus said of the king's coronation oath.[36] Baldus considered that the powerful Roman law objections were transcended in the unique case of the Donation because it had been made for the good of the church:

> Note that a king's oath even when he is alive does not harm the rights of the kingdom. The Donation of Constantine goes against this. But in that case Constantine had not sworn not to alienate, and it was a miracle for the sake of the defence of the Catholic faith.[37]

It was essential to protect the position of the church which was fundamental to the good ordering of the world: 'Whatever is said against the universal church's wellbeing, upon which the empire and the whole world depend, is nothing but dreams.'[38]

Baldus also approached the problem of the pope's temporal jurisdiction in the papal lands from another angle: he treated it as a political fact. For him, the papal monarch in the patrimony was a king like any other. Referring to *l. Ex hoc iure* (D.1.1.5), he saw the pope's rulership there as a product of his subjects' acceptance of his monarchy on the basis of natural reason expressed through the *ius gentium*. According to Baldus, this *de facto* argument provided a fully valid legitimation of the pope's monarchical sovereignty, side-by-side with *de iure* justifications. This approach sidestepped the alienation problem. Even if the Donation was not valid (which

---

[36] See his commentary on the *locus classicus* for canonical discussion of the king's duty of non-alienation imposed by his coronation oath – Honorius III's decretal, *Intellecto* (x. 2.24.33), fols. 314v–315r (ed. Lyon, 1551).

[37] 'Nota quod iuramentum regis etiam eo vivo non officit iuribus regni. In contrarium facit donatio Constantini. Sed ibi Constantinus non iuraverat non alienare, et illud fuit miraculum propter defensionem fidei catholice' (Baldus ad x.2.24.33, fol. 315r (ed. Lyon, 1551)). See also Baldus ad Feud., Proem, ad v. 'Expedita' (fol. 2v).

[38] 'Somnia sunt quicquid dicitur contra statum universalis ecclesie, a quo dependet imperium et totus universalis orbis' (Baldus ad x.2.24.33, fol. 315r (ed. Lyon, 1551)).

Baldus said it was), the pope had prescribed his rulership because
it was accepted by his subjects:

For it is agreed that the provinces elect themselves a king according to
natural reason and the law of peoples, as in [D.1.1.5]. And thus what has been
approved from the beginning is judged to be according to the law of peoples.
But that oath of fealty to the pope himself was always approved and given by
the provinces and cities; therefore such provinces and cities are subject to the
lord pope by the law of peoples according to natural reason. And I take this
side and affirm it, because, if for argument's sake the Donation had not been
valid, the church would have nevertheless prescribed [its jurisdiction] despite
[C.4.21.20], because a subject is not prescribing as in that case, but the church
is equal to the empire.[39]

There were therefore two stages: firstly, the people was the source
of papal kingship; secondly, on this basis the pope could prescribe
imperial temporal power. Normally, prescription did not run against
the emperor's jurisdiction but the people had set up *de facto* the
pope as a monarch with supreme power:

Papal prescription weakens the right of the emperor forever . . . And
although an inferior could not prescribe regalian rights against his superior,
as in [C.7.39.6], the pope can however prescribe regalian rights against
the emperor and his subjects because he is capable of bearing supreme
power, just as one king can prescribe a king's regalian rights against
another.[40]

---

[39] 'Constat enim quod secundum naturalem rationem et secundum ius gentium
provincie eligunt sibi regem, ut [D.1.1.5]. Et ideo quod est a principio
approbatum istud censetur de iure gentium. Sed per provincias et per civitates
istud fuit semper approbatum et prestitum iuramentum fidelitatis ipsi pape; ergo
tales provincie et civitates subsunt domino pape de iure gentium secundum
naturalem rationem. Et istam partem teneo et confirmo, quia posito quod
donatio non tenuisset ecclesia tamen prescripsisset non obstante [C.4.21.20],
quia subditus non prescribit ut ibi, sed ecclesia est par imperio' (Baldus ad
C. Const., 'De novo Codice componendo', fol. 1v).
[40] 'Prescriptio pape enim enervat perpetuo ius imperatoris . . . Et licet inferior non
possit prescribere regalia contra superiorem . . . tamen papa potest prescribere
regalia contra imperatorem et subditos quia est capax supreme potestatis, sicut
unus rex potest prescribere contra alium regalia regis' (Baldus ad D.V. Proem, ad
v. 'Quoniam', fol. 1v).

The pope was therefore like any other sovereign king and could prescribe against the emperor as his equal.

Complications as regards papal sovereignty

At the level of human law and authority, Baldus treated the pope and the emperor in parallel as equal sovereigns. But Baldus also considered that, because of his spiritual authority, the pope was the emperor's superior and as the vicar of Christ could depose him. So who is the ultimate sovereign? Was there a hierarchy of sovereignty here?

Too much should not be made of this apparent problem. Baldus maintained the human nature and origin of imperial power. The church was the conserver rather than the originator of the empire: it was its conserving mother (*mater conservans*). Papal depositions of the emperor, such as that of Frederick II by Innocent IV, would be measures taken only in extreme crisis. The emperorship was of human origin and nature, but was approved by God and in this sense from God. This was not however a hierocratic argument in the pope's favour. Furthermore, full powers of imperial administration were possessed by the *Rex Romanorum* on election by the princes. But there was a sense in which the pope was the emperor's superior and the Donation was therefore a grant to a superior. Essentially, temporal jurisdiction operated at a human level with human norms and rules governing it. Thus, the papal monarchy was a human institution by its creation and it continued as such.

In the fourteenth century the papacy considered that the papal coronation of the emperor created him a feudal vassal of the pope, a claim rejected by the emperors. Baldus adhered to this pro-papal feudal view. It implied reciprocity between the two parties, with the effect that it limited papal sovereignty by giving the emperor the right of resistance to protect his rights:

And there is another reason: the church has a reciprocal obligation to its vassal, and cannot harm him [i.e. the emperor] as regards his empire. Indeed the pope shows himself unsuited to his power if he does not render such justice to the emperor who swore fealty to him . . . And the emperor can defend himself with his army.[41]

In this respect, Baldus was treating the pope as any feudal monarch.

Overall, as regards its operation, Baldus discussed papal monarchy in the patrimony at a fundamentally human level – it was a state like any other. The legitimate authority of the pope was that of a monarch like the emperor or indeed any other king in his kingdom. His freedom of action as such a monarch was limited because he had to conserve the crown and his subjects had a right of resistance against the pope if he acted tyrannically or abused his office.[42]

The ingenuity of Baldus's solutions to questions concerning the pope's temporal power in the papal states illustrated the sheer difficulty involved in trying to determine the sense in which the pope exercised legitimate temporal authority there. It was such a problem, of course, because of the nature of papal claims to temporal and spiritual power. Baldus had to address this particular issue not least because of the central position of the papal states in the political life of Italy. His treatment had enduring interest because the standing of the papal states continued as a political and legal question into the modern period. Indeed, the status of the remnant of those territories, the Vatican City, remains a problem in international law to this day. There is contemporary debate about whether the Vatican City is truly a sovereign state (like any other) and whether the pope is truly a sovereign ruler.

[41] 'Et est alia ratio quia ecclesia debet vasallo vicem, et de suo imperio non potest eum [i.e. imperatorem] ledere. Immo papa se facit alienum a potestate si talem iusticiam non reddit imperatori qui iuravit fidelitatem . . . Et imperator potest se defendere cum exercitu suo' (Baldus, *Commentarium super Pace Constantie*, ad v. 'In nomine Christi membrum', fol. 94v, ed. Pavia, 1495).
[42] See Joseph Canning, 'A state like any other? The fourteenth-century papal patrimony through the eyes of Roman Law jurists', in Diana Wood (ed.), *The Church and Sovereignty, c.590–1918. Essays in Honour of Michael Wilks*, Studies in Church History, Subsidia 6 (Oxford: Blackwell, 1991), pp. 258–9.

CHAPTER 6

The power crisis during the Great Schism (1378–1417)

The most profound crisis of authority that arose in the late Middle Ages affected the papacy: the Great Schism which lasted from 1378 to 1417 was by far the worst problem which the medieval church had to face. This Schism served as a focus for the development of two sets of ideas concerning power and legitimate authority – both sets had their origins before it. These ideas were different in kind and both were potentially deadly threats to papal claims to plenitude of power: the theory of grace-founded *dominium* and the theories of the conciliar movement. The origins of both lay before the Schism, but their time in the sun came during it.

The Great Schism posed a worse threat to the papacy than any experienced during those other watershed crises, the Investiture Contest or the conflicts between Philip IV and Boniface VIII. What was at stake was nothing less than an institutional breakdown in the governing structure of the church. Gregory XI had brought the papacy back from Avignon to Rome in January 1377, but died in March 1378. On 8 April 1378 the Archbishop of Bari, Bartolomeo Prignano, was elected pope in Rome and took the name of Urban VI. He was initially accepted as pope by the cardinals, but they became increasingly convinced of his unsuitability, largely because of his behaviour towards them. The result was that the self-same college of cardinals which had elected Urban declared that he had been uncanonically elected and that therefore the papal throne was vacant. On 20 September 1378 at Fondi, the cardinals elected one of their number, Robert of Geneva, as pope, who took the name of Clement VII. Mutual excommunications between Urban and Clement followed. Clement returned to Avignon where the bulk of the papal curia had remained all along. There were thus now two claimants to the papacy, a Roman and an Avignonese one. There had been many schisms before in the medieval church, but what was new about this one was that the same college of cardinals had elected two popes within the space of a few months.

The Schism became institutionalized because Urban VI on his death in 1389 was succeeded by Boniface IX, whereas Clement VII, in 1394, was succeeded by Benedict XIII. The latter outlived the Schism, dying in 1423, but the Roman popes had further successors: Innocent VII (1404–6) and Gregory XII (1406–15). The unprecedented length of the Schism within the western church, compounded by the political involvement of secular rulers, produced increasing distress and desperation, with the result that the cardinals of both obediences sought at the Council of Pisa in 1409 to bring an end to this ecclesiastical scandal by deposing both the Roman and the Avignon popes as schismatics and heretics, and by electing a new one, Alexander V. This initiative only made matters worse since there were then three papal claimants: the Roman, the Avignonese and the Pisan. Alexander V was succeeded in 1410 by John XXIII, who, it has to be said, was at the time accepted as the true pope by the vast bulk of western Christendom. The Schism was finally resolved by the Council of Constance which was convoked in 1414 by John XXIII, with the support of the Roman emperor-elect Sigismund. John, however, fled the council and was deposed by it in May 1415; the Roman pope, Gregory XII, resigned in July 1415 and continued to attend the council as a cardinal; the Avignon pope, Benedict XIII, was deposed in July 1417, but never accepted the council's decision. In November 1417 the council elected Cardinal Oddo Colonna, who took the name of Martin V (d. 1431).

The weak point of papal monarchy had been revealed: dispute over the election of a pope. This background of catastrophic institutional weakness laid the papal monarchy open to fundamental questioning. The turn given to the thesis of grace-founded *dominium* was in part an intensified reaction against the supposed corruption of an institution which had permitted this schism to occur. It was primarily a theological response to the way in which the fourteenth-century papacy had developed; it addressed ecclesiological questions of the nature of the church and the papal office. Conciliar theory on the other hand sought to apply permanent institutional controls and limitations on the papacy.

GRACE-FOUNDED `DOMINIUM´

The thesis of grace-founded *dominium* had a tortuous history in the late Middle Ages: as we have seen, it was first put forward by Giles of Rome as supporting an extreme pro-papal argument and involved the inclusion of both jurisdiction and ownership of property under the term *dominium* – a theological position different from the juristic view, which applied the term only to property.[1] His assumption was that the church mediated grace. The notion was further developed by Richard Fitzralph (*c*.1300–60), who used it in his attacks on the Franciscans by arguing that their claims to poverty relied upon the validity of papal ownership of property which the order used.[2] But this was a dangerous argument: if it were true, a denial that the papacy was in a state of grace would fatally undermine papal claims to *dominium*. This was the turn in the argument which emerged in the Great Schism, notably in the writings of the Englishman John Wyclif (d. 1384) and the Czech John Hus (*c*.1372–1415). Wyclif drew heavily on the ideas of Fitzralph for the development of his theory of *dominium*; Hus, in turn, made considerable use of Wyclif's arguments.

The idea of grace-founded *dominium* was different in kind from other arguments which derived power and authority from God. It all depended on what was meant by grace. The grace involved in the notion of the *rex dei gratia* signified the divine source of royal power by the exercise of God's goodwill or benevolence. Such grace was not sanctifying grace, which was necessary for salvation; it was a form of *gratia gratis data* (grace freely given). A theocratic monarch

---

[1] See above, pp. 31–6.
[2] For Fitzralph, see Katharine Walsh, *A Fourteenth-Century Scholar and Primate. Richard Fitzralph in Oxford, Avignon and Armagh* (Oxford: Clarendon Press, 1981). But see also James Doyne Dawson, 'Richard Fitzralph and the fourteenth-century poverty controversies', *Journal of Ecclesiastical History*, 34, 3 (1983), 315–44.

could therefore be in a state of mortal sin yet continue to rule legitimately – his actions as king would still retain divine sanction and justification. Similarly, the third-way Augustinian view, which recognized the divine source of all rulership, whether pagan or Christian, did not consider that the ruler's right to govern was in any way affected by the state of his soul. However, the grace-founded *dominium* argument maintained that the grace necessary for legitimate jurisdiction and ownership of property was indeed sanctifying grace – *gratia gratum faciens* (grace making someone justified, that is, united to God – in a state of grace, in short). Any sign of mortal sin vitiated a ruler's claims to legitimate *dominium*.

John Wyclif was an Oxford theologian who became increasingly involved in English politics in the 1370s. He made common cause with those critical of the church's claims to jurisdiction and property, and came under the protection of John of Gaunt, Duke of Lancaster. In 1374 Wyclif participated in a diplomatic embassy to Bruges to negotiate over papal taxation, provisions to benefices and appeals to the apostolic see. His opinions brought him into increasing opposition to leaders of the English church. But John of Gaunt's protection prevented effective ecclesiastical censure of Wyclif at an episcopal court held at St Paul's in February 1377. In May 1377 Pope Gregory XI issued a condemnation of nineteen propositions drawn from Wyclif's written work. Another trial at Lambeth Palace in March 1378 was also ineffective because of his royal patronage. The outbreak of the Great Schism and royal protection prevented further action against him. In the face of accusations of heresy he finally felt obliged to leave Oxford in 1382, withdrawing to his rectory at Lutterworth, where he died on 31 December 1384.

Wyclif used the notion of grace-founded *dominium* primarily to attack the jurisdictional and property claims of the church and the papacy in particular.[3] He was developing his argument before the

---

[3] For Wyclif's theory of *dominium*, see the seminal work of Stephen E. Lahey, *Philosophy and Politics in the Thought of John Wyclif*, Cambridge Studies in Medieval Life and Thought, fourth series (Cambridge University Press, 2003) and, for a general assessment of his thought, Stephen E. Lahey, *John Wyclif* (Oxford University Press, 2009).

Great Schism, as for instance in his *De dominio divino* (Concerning Divine Lordship), written in 1373–4, and in his *De civili dominio* (Concerning Civil Lordship) of 1375–6. But the early years of the Schism stimulated a rush of writings elaborating his thesis, including *De ecclesia* (On the Church) of 1378–9; *De officio regis* (On the Office of the King) of 1379; *De potestate papae* (On the Power of the Pope) of 1379; *De symonia* (On Symony) of 1380; *De blasphemia* (On Blasphemy) of 1381; *De dissensione paparum* (On the Dissension of the Popes) of 1382; and *De cruciata* (On the Crusade) of 1382.[4] Indeed, Wyclif as a loyal Englishman supported Urban VI against Clement VII[5] and blamed the outbreak of the Schism on those who followed their own pecuniary advantage (rather than just worked, like Wyclif, as theologians – the most reliable advisers of the church and secular rulers):

And this is the cause of the whole Schism of the church; that men too much attend to their own interests on account of lucre, and belittle or persecute those who labour in the faculty of theology. For this is the reason why there are men who out of self love desert the common good and the things of heaven.[6]

More specifically, Wyclif expressly identified the papacy's desire for temporal power and worldly goods as the root cause of the Schism.[7]

Wyclif held that the king in exercising his temporal authority was the vicar of God, whereas the priest was the vicar of Christ in his humanity:

---

[4] For the dating of Wyclif's works, see Takashi Shogimen, 'Wyclif's ecclesiology and political thought', in Ian Christopher Levy (ed.), *A Companion to John Wyclif, Late Medieval Theologian* (Leiden: E.J. Brill, 2006), pp. 199–201.

[5] See John Wyclif, *Tractatus de potestate papae*, ed. J. Loserth (London: WS, 1907), 10, p. 233.

[6] 'Et hec est causa tocius scismatis ecclesie quod homines nimis intendunt tradicionibus propriis propter lucrum, et diminuunt vel persecuntur eos qui laborant in theologica facultate. Hec enim racio quare sunt homines se ipsos amantes, bona communia et celestia deserentes' (DOR, 11, p. 257). For the role of the theological faculty in stabilizing the kingdom see DOR, 7, p. 176. For Wyclif's exalted notion of the role of theologians as the best guides to orthodoxy, see Ian Christopher Levy, 'Holy Scripture and the quest for authority among three late medieval masters', *Journal of Ecclesiastical History*, 61, 1 (January 2010), 44.

[7] See John Wyclif, *De dissensione paparum*, in *John Wiclif's Polemical Works in Latin*, ed. Rudolf Buddensieg (London: WS, 1883), vol. 11, p. 572.

God should therefore have two vicars in the church, that is to say the king in temporal matters and the priest in spiritual ones. The king however should severely coerce the rebel, just as the deity did in the Old Testament. But the priest should serve [God's] command in a mild way for the humble in the time of the law of grace, just as Christ, who was at the same time king and priest, did in his humanity. And on this matter, Augustine says that the king has the image of God but the bishop the image of Christ, undoubtedly on account of ministry. Nor is ministry to be conceived in these different words except so as to indicate that the king bears the image of the deity of Christ, just as the bishop does the image of his humanity.[8]

He made his debt to Augustine even clearer by direct quotation.[9] Wyclif accorded the king supreme authority in temporal matters precisely because of his vicariate of God and of Christ in his divinity, whereas the priesthood had greater authority in spiritual matters.[10] Sacerdotal dignity, being spiritual, was greater than that of the king, but this did not translate into any temporal superiority for the priesthood. Indeed, the king was greater than a bishop because he could command him to administer the sacraments and had general control over the church – indeed, a royal bishop acted by the king's authority[11] and the king, as '*sacerdos et pontifex regni sui*' (priest and pontiff of his kingdom), had the duty to correct his clergy and bishops.[12] Wyclif's notions only appear striking in relation to contemporary papal claims. The Augustinian notion of the king as God's vicar was common in the Carolingian period. The

---

[8] 'Oportet ergo deum habere in ecclesia duos vicarios, scilicet regem in temporalibus et sacerdotem in spiritualibus. Rex autem debet severe cohercere rebellem, sicut fecit deitas in veteri testamento. Sacerdos vero debet ministrare preceptum miti modo humilibus tempore legis gracie sicut fecit humanitas Cristi, qui simul fuit rex et sacerdos. Et huic dicit Augustinus quod rex habet ymaginem dei sed episcopus ymaginem Cristi, propter ministerium indubie. Nec est fingendum ministerium huius differencie verborum nisi quod rex gerit ymaginem deitatis Christi, sicut episcopus ymaginem sue humanitatis' (DOR, 1, p. 13).

[9] See *ibid.*, 1, p. 10: 'Dei enim ymaginem habet rex, sicut et episcopus Christi. Quamdiu igitur in eadem tradicione est, honorandus est, si non propter se, tamen propter ordinem' (referring to Augustine, *Quaestiones ex veteri testamento*, xxv); see also *ibid.*, 1, p. 12: 'Vnde Augustinus in de questionibus veteris et nove legis xx. capitulo, "Rex", inquit, "adoratur in terris quasi vicarius dei."'

[10] *Ibid.*, 6, pp. 142–3.   [11] *Ibid.*, 6, pp. 118–19; 6, p. 138.   [12] *Ibid.*, 7, p. 152.

Norman Anonymous written during the Investiture Contest, perhaps at Rouen in *c*.1100, described the king as vicar of Christ in both his royal and sacerdotal powers, with the priesthood being subject to him.

Wyclif distinguished between three kinds of *dominium*: natural, evangelical and civil. Natural *dominium* was shared by all humanity living in charity in the state of innocence before the Fall; evangelical *dominium* was established by Christ's incarnation and was in effect equated with natural *dominium*. Civil *dominium*, instituted after the Fall, covered property and rulership. The secular ruler possessed civil *dominium* but the pope and the priesthood did not.[13] The latter as vicars of Christ in his humanity should follow the example of his life on earth. Christ had been poor and had claimed no jurisdiction in this world: his kingdom was that of heaven. This argument shows the influence which the ideas of poverty movements had exerted on Wyclif. His ideas are an example of the combination of poverty ideas with the myth of the early church as being poor. This was a potent mix which posed a deadly threat to the papacy. Any claims of the papacy and the church to power and property could be presented as a betrayal of Christ and the primitive church.[14] According to Wyclif, the papacy and the contemporary church, by claiming and exercising a *dominium* which was not rightfully theirs, had fallen into mortal sin, which in itself showed that their *dominium* was not grace-founded. This was why he emphasized so much the royal duty of dispossessing the church for its own good – the constantly recurring theme in his works. He considered that poverty was fundamental to the life of a priest. Indeed, he held that 'evangelical

[13] For the forms of *dominium*, see, for instance, DCD, 1.6; 1.9; 1.18; 3.11–13. But see also John Wyclif, *De dominio divino*, ed. R.L. Poole (London: WS, 1890), 1.3, p. 15, where he distinguished between *dominium divinum*, *dominium angelicum* and *dominium humanum*, but expanded these categories in terms of *dominium naturale*, *dominium evangelicum* and *dominium coactivum*, which he termed *dominium politicum*, subdivided into *monasticum* (of a family), *civile* (of a city) and *regale* (of a kingdom or empire).

[14] See Gordon Leff, 'The making of the myth of a true church in the later Middle Ages', *Journal of Medieval and Renaissance Studies*, 1, 1 (1971), 1–15.

poverty makes a cleric far more than the character of [holy] orders'.[15] A cleric was in a higher state than a king or emperor because through poverty he more closely followed Christ.[16] Indeed, clergy were superior to laity so long as they observed evangelical poverty.[17] Such poverty was connected to the virtue of obedience and the evangelical precept to suffer injury rather than return it and not to exercise power following the example of Christ in his humanity. This explained why royal authority was greater than that of priests:

> Thus it seems to me probable that royal authority excels sacerdotal authority for a multiplicity of reasons: first, because it has a vicarious similitude to deity, and thus to claiming power, whereas sacerdotal authority has a vicarious similitude to the humanity of Christ, and thus has a reason for suffering injury.[18]

Wyclif adopted Augustine's paradoxical view of obedience. Christian humility, which priests above all should show, enjoined that the greater should obey the lesser, just as superiors owed more to their inferiors (they could certainly give them more).[19] After all, Christ, who was full of grace, was full of obedience and submitted himself to earthly authority.[20]

Wyclif was confronting the church at a fundamental level. The key question was whether the church had jurisdiction and, if so, of what kind? The papal position made jurisdiction the core of the pope's role: the church was a body which required to be governed by means of a divinely instituted hierarchy culminating in the pope. Marsilius of Padua had attacked the papacy on this point by denying jurisdiction to the church and by defining the church in terms of the belief of its members – it was comprised of all those who believed in and invoked the name of Christ.[21] Wyclif's approach was

---

[15] DCD, 3.12, p. 194.   [16] *Ibid.*, 3.12, pp. 200–1.   [17] *Ibid.*, 3.18, p. 375.
[18] 'Ideo videtur mihi probabile quod regalis auctoritas precellit auctoritatem sacerdotalem secundum rationem multiplicem. Primo quia illa habet similitudinem vicariam deitatis, et sic vindicandi potestatem; auctoritas autem sacerdotalis habet similitudinem vicariam humanitatis Cristi, et sic racionem paciendi iniuriam' (DOR, 6, p. 137).
[19] *Ibid.*, 10, p. 242.   [20] *Ibid.*, 10, p. 239.   [21] See above, p. 104.

different. He identified the church with those predestined to salvation.[22] But the identity of the predestined was unknowable in this life. This view was therefore destructive of all authority in the church. Behind Wyclif's arguments lay an ecclesiology which was fundamentally different from that of the papacy and, indeed, of the church hierarchy as a whole. Wyclif's prime concern was with the level of grace, sin, salvation and damnation, rather than with that of the mundane dimension of power and jurisdiction. For him, the fundamental question was man's relationship to God and God's to man. Mortal sin broke the link with God and precluded just human *dominium*: 'All just *dominium* towards men presupposes just *dominium* as regards God; but anyone existing in a state of mortal sin, lacks, as such, just *dominium* as regards God, and thus, in short, just *dominium*.'[23] Wyclif held that God's *dominium* was the source of all just human *dominium*, which was derived from grace and exercised in charity.[24]

Wyclif applied his notion of grace-founded *dominium* to the king as well as to the church, but in a somewhat different way. His prime target was the ecclesiastical hierarchy and he expected higher standards from the clergy, in that they should not be concerned with civil *dominium* at all. The king, however, if he were just, held such *dominium* as God's vicar. But, as Wyclif, building on a kernel of Augustinian ideas, explained in *De origine regis*, royal power existed as an order within the church in its wider sense even for a king who was one of the *prescriti*, the foreknown to damnation (as Saul had been) – such a king would lack *dominium* while still retaining the appearance of power in ruling equivocally. Unjust

---

[22] See, for instance, DCD, 1.39, p. 288: 'Accipitur ecclesia propriissime pro universitate predestinatorum, et ista vocatur corpus Christi misticum, sponsa Christi, et regnum celorum.'

[23] 'Omne dominium iustum ad homines presupponit iustum dominium quoad Deum. Sed quilibet existens in peccato mortali caret, ut sic, iusto dominio quoad Deum; ergo, et simpliciter iusto dominio' (*ibid.*, 1.1, p. 2).

[24] See Lahey, *Philosophy and Politics in Wyclif*, pp. 68–107. See Shogimen, 'Wyclif's ecclesiology', pp. 204–5, for an assessment of Lahey's novel interpretation of Wyclif's thought in terms of his metaphysics. For the role of charity, see, for instance, DCD, 1.21, p. 150: 'Nemo est sine caritatis titulo dominus alicuius.'

kings and tyrants exercised the status of power abusively and without merit, but were, nevertheless, to be obeyed out of honour, not for themselves but for their office or order which came from God. God, in other words, was to be honoured in them.[25] This nuanced argument has led to a crux in the interpretation of Wyclif's ideas on kingship. Gordon Leff held that he was showing signs of inconsistency: that Wyclif applied his notions of grace-founded *dominium* to kings as well as to the church in *De civili dominio* but that when he came to write *De officio regis*, he did not apply the rigours of grace-founded *dominium* to secular rulers.[26] Rather, he understood the king as being endowed with a scripturally sanctioned authority. But, as Stephen Lahey has persuasively argued, Wyclif, in *De origine regis*, remained true to his thesis of secular grace-founded *dominium* as argued in *De civili dominio*.[27] It seems to me that, according to Wyclif, wicked rulers did not possess *dominium* and that the essence of his earlier position was thus effectively saved. In any case, it is not clear that this difference of interpretation is that important, because Wyclif's fundamental message was that of grace-founded *dominium*. What one can say is that Wyclif's willingness to judge the ecclesiastical hierarchy on the grounds of mortal sin had been a rejection of the ancient distinction between the office and the man – a fundamental defence employed by the papacy throughout the Middle Ages, whereas in his treatment of kings, Wyclif was willing to persist with such a distinction in support of the secular ruler. He admitted, of course, that the exercise

---

[25] See the lengthy discussion of *reges discoli* and tyranny at DOR, 1, pp. 5, 10–11 and, especially, 17–20. On tyranny, see also Lahey, *Philosophy and Politics in Wyclif*, pp. 191–2, where he discusses Wyclif's argument at DCD, 1.28, that there remained the option of non-co-operation with a tyrant.

[26] See Gordon Leff, *Heresy in the Later Middle Ages* (Manchester University Press, 1967), II, 542–5, and his 'Wyclif and Hus: doctrinal comparison', in Anthony Kenny (ed.), *Wyclif in his Times* (Oxford: Clarendon Press, 1986), p. 116. Anne Hudson in her *The Premature Reformation. Wycliffite Texts and Lollard History* (Oxford: Clarendon Press, 1988), p. 360, argued that Wyclif did not apply his doctrine of *dominium* to secular rulers. See also K.B. McFarlane, *Wycliffe and English Nonconformity* (Harmondsworth: Penguin, 1972), p. 79.

[27] See, for instance, Lahey, *Philosophy and Politics in Wyclif*, pp. 200–3.

of civil *dominium* involved venial sin: 'And if it were to be asked how civil *dominium* smacks inseparably of venial sin, it is said that it is through pride or lack of charity.'[28] Certainly, he did not require of kings that they should be among the ranks of the unknowable predestined.

What we have in Wyclif's case is a classic expression of a turn which late medieval political thought took. The sheer strength and prevalence of ultimately Augustinian arguments in the fourteenth and fifteenth centuries were striking. An appreciation of this affects the models which historians apply in order to understand late medieval political thought – all of which are, of course, imposed on the past by historians in an attempt to make some sense of the variety of late medieval views. To privilege the importance of ultimately Aristotelian naturalistic political ideas is to work from an assumption about politics and the state as being essentially naturalistic and this-worldly. Similarly, to stress the significance of juristic, Stoic and Ciceronian approaches is also to prioritize a this-worldly direction in political thought.[29] Certainly, all these approaches are profoundly important for comprehending late medieval political thought. At the heart of trying to understand them is the notion of nature – one of the slipperiest concepts in the history of thought. But in the fourteenth century the rival view which derived political conclusions from theological premises was as powerful and indeed was growing in strength.[30] To employ a short-hand mode of expression, this bundle of approaches enunciated ultimately Augustinian ideas. The traditional theocratic view of rulership, encapsulated in the *rex dei gratia* formula, persisted side-by-side with the 'third way' Augustinian approach justifying both Christian and non-Christian rulership. But the grace-founded

---

[28] 'Et si queratur in quo dominium civile sapit inseparabiliter peccatum veniale, dicitur quod in superbia vel remissione caritatis' (DCD, 3.10, p. 167).

[29] For the significance of Ciceronian language in medieval political thought, see Black, *Political Thought*, p. 9; and Cary J. Nederman, 'Nature, sin and the origins of society: the Ciceronian tradition in medieval political thought', *Journal of the History of Ideas*, 49 (1988), 3–26.

[30] See the seminal article of Gordon Leff, 'The apostolic ideal in later medieval ecclesiology', *Journal of Theological Studies*, n.s., 18 (1967), 58–82.

dominium argument was indeed a new turn. Its fundamental assumption was a theological proposition: that all *dominium* belonged to God. Just human *dominium* participated in that of God – understanding dominative relationships in terms of both property and rulership. But how could human beings participate in the *dominium* of God? Clearly, of course, they could only do so by divine gift: no human had a right to such *dominium*. At this point a problem arose because there was an ambiguity in the transmission of Augustine's thought. He had said that true justice only existed in a Christian society, but in his mature thought he had left justice out of the definition of the state, on the grounds that justice was unattainable in this world. As we have seen, Ockham's 'third way' Augustinianism was in tune with this later, highly nuanced approach. The notion of grace-founded *dominium* was a misunderstanding of Augustine's final position. It was a form of the traditional medieval *Augustinisme politique* which had justified rulership within a Christian society, but it took a radically new direction by demanding that the ruler (or owner of property) be in a state of grace. The question of how one participated in the *dominium* of God was answered: the process was by the freely given grant of sanctifying grace. This was not Augustine's view. In his fight against the Donatist heretics he enunciated that the validity of the sacerdotal orders of priests did not depend upon their being in a state of grace. By extrapolation, office in church or state did not depend on the condition of the holder's soul. Rulership and property were remedies for sin in a sinful world. The predestined to salvation and the foreknown to damnation were inextricably mixed in the church and society of this world and were only to be separated eschatologically after death. By in effect distinguishing between the office and the man, Augustine was able to preserve a governmental structure for the church and the state. Wyclif, of course, parted company from him by identifying the church in this world only with the predestined to salvation. But the problem was that there was no way of knowing who they were! Faced with having to preserve some kind of structure for the church and with having to have a power capable of reforming and controlling the clergy, Wyclif had to abandon the requirement that the king be in a state of grace: he felt that he had to accept that the secular monarch, whether just or unjust, ruled by virtue of his divinely sanctioned office – with *dominium* if predestined, with power if foreknown.

But how important was Wyclif's contribution to the discussion of legitimate authority? Clearly, in terms of length and of complication, his works constituted the most thoroughgoing elaboration of the thesis of grace-founded *dominium*. Their immediate context was the political upheavals of the 1370s and 1380s in England, including the English (or Peasants') Revolt of 1381 and the Great Schism. Wyclif gained the reputation of being a heresiarch, but his precise influence on Lollard ideas is obscure, because the Lollard movement was largely not an intellectual one and is difficult to define. Wyclif's ideas came to true continental importance from the 1390s, when they were increasingly studied by the Czech reform movement in Bohemia. Wyclif's writings were used as an arsenal of material for fleshing out criticisms of the church and the papacy. The extent to which Jan Hus adopted Wyclifite arguments has long been a contentious issue amongst historians. Certainly, Hus used Wyclif's arguments heuristically in his analyses of theological and ecclesiological questions, and did incorporate passages from the Englishman's writings word-for-word in his own works, although he gave no general approval to Wyclif's ideas. There were similarities between Hus's and Wyclif's views on several points: the identification of the church with the congregation of the predestined and the exclusion from it of those foreknown to damnation; the role of the secular ruler in correcting sinful priests; and the concentration on the Bible as the source of true belief. It was in the light of this European dimension that the Council of Constance, building on previous condemnations by other councils and provincial synods, came to proscribe forty-five of Wyclif's articles as heretical in 1415 and to accuse Hus, at his trial, of holding some of his opinions.[31]

---

[31] For the relationship between Wyclif's ideas and those of the Czech reform movement and those of Hus in particular, see, for instance, Leff, *Heresy*, vol. II, pp. 606–707; František Šmahel, 'Doctor evangelicus super omnes evangelistas:

CONCILIAR IDEAS

Conciliar ideas were different in nature from those of grace-founded *dominium* and expressed a different ecclesiology. Whereas Wyclif understood the church as a spiritual body of the predestined, conciliar theory operated with a traditional model of the church understood as a body which needed to be governed. Conciliarists were concerned heavily (but not entirely) with issues of jurisdiction. Their prime concern was with church government, that is, with the structure which would best deliver unity (an end to the Schism), the suppression of heresy and reform of the church in head and members. It was imperative for them to establish where ultimate authority lay in the church. This intellectual orientation meant that a wide range of legal and political ideas and arguments were relevant to the elaboration of conciliar theory. Amongst these sources, the *ius commune* (especially canon law) and Aristotelian political science were especially important. In particular, conciliarists drew on ideas of consent and juristic corporation theory. In essence, conciliar thought expressed a radical argument within the jurisdictional model of the church, a model which insofar as it was jurisdictional was not itself radical. The conciliarist approach was in opposition to that of grace-founded *dominium*, as the works of the Parisian theologians Pierre d'Ailly (1352–1420) and Jean Gerson (1363–1429), to take leading examples, made clear: for them, the God-given power of priest or king was through *gratia gratis data*, not *gratia gratum faciens*.[32]

There were straws in the wind before the Great Schism. Emperor Frederick II had aired the idea of calling a general council of the

---

Wyclif's fortune in Hussite Bohemia', *Bulletin of the Institute of Historical Research*, 43 (1970), 16–34; Thomas A. Fudge, *The Magnificent Ride. The First Reformation in Hussite Bohemia* (Aldershot: Ashgate, 1998); Norman Housley, *Religious Warfare in Europe, 1400–1536* (Oxford University Press, 2002), pp. 37–61.

[32] See Francis Oakley, *The Political Thought of Pierre d'Ailly. The Voluntarist Tradition* (New Haven, CT and London: Yale University Press, 1964), pp. 81–2, and J.H. Burns, *Lordship, Kingship and Empire. The Idea of Monarchy, 1400–1525* (Oxford: Clarendon Press, 1992), pp. 33, 37–8. For a general survey of conciliarist ideas, see Monahan, *Personal Duties*, pp. 50–127.

church to judge the pope. During the conflicts between Philip IV and Boniface VIII, the dissident Colonna cardinals had called for the summoning of a general council to annul the pope's process against them. Furthermore, the French king's minister Nogaret had insisted that such a council should be held to judge the pope for heresy and usurpation. The threat that Philip might call a council to judge Boniface for heresy hung over the early years of the pontificate of Clement V. As we have seen, John of Paris had floated the idea that a general council could depose the pope and Marsilius, of course, had located ultimate ecclesiastical authority in the faithful human legislator which could summon a general council.[33] But the most detailed conciliar proposals which anticipated some of the main legislation at the Council of Constance were set forth by William Durant the Younger in his *Tractatus maior* (Greater Tractate) submitted as advice to Clement V before the Council of Vienne of 1311–12. William proposed that councils should be summoned automatically every ten years, thus removing a linchpin of papal control over them – the requirement in canon law that a council had to be called by the pope, entirely at his discretion. In addition, William maintained that all general legislation in the church should take place in a general council; that the pope should not be able to dispense from conciliar decrees unless a council was called; and that the pope must be under budgetary control by the council.[34] He was for the time being at least a voice crying in the wilderness.

In a way, it begs the question to talk of conciliar theory or a conciliar movement because these are umbrella terms devised by modern historians and applied to a wide range of people involved in the attempt to resolve the Schism by means of a council.[35] The first attempt, the Council of Pisa, was indeed a failure, but its significance should not be downgraded on that account, because the vast

---

[33] Above ch. 1, p. 53 and ch. 4, p. 131.

[34] See Constantin Fasolt, *Council and Hierarchy. The Political Thought of William Durant the Younger*, Cambridge Studies in Medieval Life and Thought, fourth series, 16 (Cambridge University Press, 1991).

[35] See, for instance, Philip H. Stump, *The Reforms of the Council of Constance (1414–1418)* (Leiden: E.J. Brill, 1994), p. 19.

bulk of Latin Christendom accepted both its deposition of the Roman and Avignon popes, and the validity of the elections of Alexander V and then John XXIII. In any case, by acting decisively against both the Roman and Avignonese claimants, this council did pave the way for Constance to unify the church. Pisa embodied what Francis Oakley has called the 'quasi-oligarchic' phase of conciliarism in that it was composed of the cardinals of both obediences.[36] Indeed, the members of the Council of Pisa declared themselves to be a legitimately convoked general council of the church – Pierre d'Ailly and Jean Gerson applied the Aristotelian principle of *epieikeia* (equity) in arguing that the spirit rather than the letter of canon law should be followed and sought thereby to demonstrate that the requirement that the pope must call a valid council must be ignored for the good of the church. The ecclesiology that lay behind the Pisan approach was that the Roman church consisted of the pope and the cardinals, an idea with a respectable canon law ancestry as in the thought of Hostiensis.[37] The willingness of both the Councils of Pisa and Constance to depose popes had a further deep source in the canonist discussions of how an heretical pope could be dealt with – as we have seen, canon law admitted that a pope could not be deposed except for heresy, but did not say how this penalty could be imposed.[38] By the time of Pisa and Constance, persistence in prolonging the Schism was seen as a sign of heresy on the part of the papal claimants.

The question of the legitimacy of the three papal claimants at the Council of Constance is a murky one indeed. At the time, Pisa was accepted by most people as having been a valid general council. John XXIII, having summoned the Council of Constance, was accepted by it as the true pope. The council deposed him not because it considered his papacy to be invalid but on the grounds of perjury, simony and scandalous misconduct (and thus not of heresy!). Constance did not believe that the Roman pope Gregory XII was the true pope. He was indeed asked to convoke the council

[36] See Oakley, *Conciliarist Tradition*, pp. 67–71.
[37] See, for instance, *ibid.*, p. 69.   [38] See above, p. 130.

after John's deposition, but this was as a matter of courtesy. The Avignon pope Benedict XIII was also asked to convoke the council for the same reason. The later papal interpretation of events does not fit with what contemporaries thought. The papal view came to be that Gregory XII was the true pope, whereas John XXIII was an antipope, and that Gregory had prepared the way for a solution to the Schism by convoking the council and then resigning so that another pope could be elected. This interpretation lay behind Angelo Roncalli's taking of the pontifical name of John XXIII in 1958 – a choice which implicitly treated his fifteenth-century namesake as an antipope.[39]

The actions and decrees of the Council of Constance were a clear expression of developed conciliar theory. After the flight of John XXIII, Gerson steadied the fathers' nerves by his sermon *Ambulate*, in which he reasserted the council's right to assemble without papal consent. The fundamental conciliarist decree *Haec sancta* was issued in April 1415, before the council's deposition of John. In *Haec sancta* the general council declared that it represented the Catholic church on earth; that it held power directly from Christ; that everyone, including the pope, was bound to obey it in matters concerning the faith, ending the Schism, and general reform of the church in head and members; and that anyone, even the pope, who disobeyed the decrees of this or any other legally convoked council on such matters was to be punished. The Council of Constance thus asserted its authority over the papacy while there was still a pope in office – John XXIII, whom the vast majority of its members accepted as being the valid pope. This crystal-clear assertion of conciliar claims was swiftly followed by the clearest of actions – the deposition of that pope. Further, in October, 1417 the council issued the decree *Frequens*, which changed the constitution of the church by ordering that a council should be called five years after Constance; that another one should be held seven years after that; and that finally

---

[39] The best analysis of this question remains Karl Augustus Fink, 'Zur Beurteilung des Großen Abendländischen Schismas', *Zeitschrift für Kirchengeschichte*, 73 (1962), 335–43.

councils should be called thereafter every ten years in perpetuity. This removed, at a stroke, the pope's prerogative in calling councils (or avoiding them). A second decree issued at the same time provided that, in the event of a future schism, a council must be called within a year, a council to which all contending parties must submit. The Council of Constance claimed to represent the church in that it contained within itself the church's hierarchical structure – it was in essence a prelates' council. It in no sense sought to remove the authority of the pope but defined it in a ministerial and executive sense.

The range of conciliar opinion can be divided into its theological and juristic strands. The most striking approach of theologians can be seen as a contemplation on plenitude of power. They extended this originally papal concept to the council and the church as a whole. Thus, d'Ailly, in his *Tractatus de ecclesia* (Tract on the Church) (1416), argued that plenitude of power belonged to the church 'causally and finally', to the general council in a representative way and to the pope in an executive and ministerial way. The council represented the church in its totality and had an ultimately directing and regulatory role.[40] Gerson held much the same view. In his sermon *Prosperum iter faciat nobis* (May He Have a Good Journey for Us), preached in 1415 when Sigismund had left Constance for Spain to try and bring about the abdication of Benedict XIII or his abandonment by the Spanish kingdoms, Gerson stated that the council could depose the pope whose plenitude of power was executive in nature. The council had doctrinal supremacy and had to be obeyed by the pope in matters of faith, ending the Schism and reform in head and members. Gerson indeed attributed a central role to the theologians of the University of Paris in developing orthodox teaching, but considered the general council to be the authoritative and final judge of doctrine.[41] In *De ecclesiastica*

---

[40] For d'Ailly's ideas, see also now Louis B. Pascoe, *Church and Reform. Bishops, Theologians and Canon Lawyers in the Thought of Pierre d'Ailly (1351–1420)* (Leiden: E.J. Brill, 2005).

[41] See now Levy, 'Holy Scripture and the quest', 61–8.

potestate (Concerning Ecclesiastical Power) (1416/17), Gerson gave
a detailed exposition of his views. The general council was the final
seat of ecclesiastical authority, because being composed of the
various members of the church's hierarchy, it enshrined all its
legitimate power which was greater than that of any individual
member of the hierarchy, including that of the pope, who was thus
subject to the council. The church, and the council representing it,
possessed plenitude of power; the council could determine who was
to exercise plenitude of power as pope and could oversee how he
was to use it. The council could proceed without the pope and
exercise all papal powers of jurisdiction.[42]

Jurists faced massive problems in producing conciliarist arguments. The whole tendency of Decretalist thought had been to
favour papal monarchy, with little attention given to the role of
general councils. In contrast, the older canon law, enshrined in
Gratian's *Decretum*, contained much more material useful for the
elaboration of the authority of councils – as William Durant the
Younger had realized. But the sheer stress and growing hopeless-
ness produced by the Schism led some jurists to contemplate
possible solutions which they would not have originally entertained
– they were driven by necessity. Baldus himself was a case in point.
At the beginning of the Great Schism, he had produced in 1378 and
1380 two famous *consilia* supporting the legitimacy of Urban VI,
but as the Schism dragged on, he became more and more disgusted
by the recalcitrance of the papal claimants. Right at the end of his
life, in the last few years of the 1390s, he included, in his commentary on the *Liber extra*, a range of options to end the Schism. He
proposed that emperors and kings could force both popes to submit
if they refused to end the Schism through resignation, arbitration or
a general council – Baldus's favoured option. He ended up advo-
cating that it was the emperor's role to enforce papal co-operation
in the face of a general council called by the Roman cardinals, a
council at which the emperor, kings and princes would be present

---

[42] See Louis B. Pascoe, *Jean Gerson: Principles of Church Reform*, Studies in Medieval
and Reformation Thought, 7 (Leiden: E.J. Brill, 1973).

to solve the Schism. This does not mean that Baldus had come to adopt a thoroughgoing conciliarist position – his arguments contradicted his thought on the relationship between the papacy and the empire.[43]

Baldus's pupil Petrus de Ancharano showed a similar change of mind under the pressure of events but produced more developed arguments. At heart, Petrus was a supporter of papal monarchy, holding that the pope was supreme over a general council except in matters of faith and that a council could only judge and punish the pope in case of heresy. But in six *consilia* written between 1405 and 1409 Petrus abandoned his earlier position. In reaction against Benedict XIII's and Gregory XII's ignoring of their electoral capitulations to work for an end to the Schism, he came to support the cardinals' initiative in calling the Council of Pisa. In 1408 Petrus supported the conciliar way of ending the Schism – because of the failure of the head of the church, power to convoke the council had devolved to the cardinals. But he went further than this: if the cardinals would not so act, then the power to convoke a council devolved to bishops, then clergy or, finally, the Christian people. At Pisa, he gave a speech justifying the council's legitimacy. He stressed that the original reasons for the outbreak of the Schism were by then transcended and described both papal claimants as heretics for their prolongation of the Schism. Petrus understood that the council as the living law on earth was acting in a state of emergency. He was not permanently abandoning his commitment to papal monarchy and wanted to see a return to it. But in this supreme crisis for the church, Petrus accepted that the council could use plenitude of power in order to re-establish the normal state of papal monarchy.[44]

The most thoroughgoing and systematic juristic elaboration of conciliar theory was produced by Franciscus Zabarella (*c*.1335–1417).

---

[43] See Canning, *Political Thought of Baldus*, pp. 41–3. But see also now Helmut Walther, 'Baldus als Gutachter für die päpstliche Kurie im Großen Schisma', *Zeitschrift der Savigny-Stiftung für Rechtsgeschichte*, Kanonistische Abteilung, 92 (2006), 392–409.

[44] See J.J. Sawicki, 'The ecclesiological and political thought of Petrus de Ancharano (1330?–1416)', unpublished PhD dissertation, Cornell University, 1977.

He supported the cardinals at Pisa, was made bishop of Florence in 1410 and then cardinal in 1411 by John XXIII, and was papal legate to the Council of Constance. His death at the council may well have prevented him from being elected pope – he was certainly a front-runner. In addition to his commentaries on the Clementines and the *Decretales*, he wrote *repetitiones* and *consilia*.[45] But his most important work on the Schism was his tract *De schismate* (On the Schism), which was written between 1402 and 1408 and argued in favour of a general council.

Zabarella produced a conciliar theory expressed in terms of corporation theory. He followed the mainstream theory which located jurisdiction in the corporation (*universitas*), understood as head and members, as opposed to the view which placed jurisdiction solely in the head. In *De schismate* he applied corporation theory in a conciliarist way to explain the relationship of the pope's authority to that of the rest of the church. Power lay 'as if fundamentally' (*tanquam in fundamento*) in the Christian community understood as a corporate body and in the pope 'as the principal minister' (*tanquam principali ministro*) through whom this power was deployed. The pope was made by the consent of the corporate body of Christians from whom he derived his power. Zabarella maintained that power lay with the congregation of the faithful because the Schism had caused a quasi-vacancy in the headship of the church. In these circumstances the universal church was a corporate body represented by the general council, which was itself a corporation within which the government of the church would be exercised by the weightier part of those present. One of Zabarella's crucial arguments was that it did not matter how the general council came into being – it was legitimate once assembled, because it actually represented the congregation of the faithful. Its legitimacy

---

[45] The *Clementinae* were the last authentic collection of canon law included in the *Corpus iuris canonici*: they consisted of decretals of Clement V, decrees of the Council of Vienne and one decretal each by Boniface VIII and Urban IV, and were promulgated by John XXII in 1317. *Repetitiones* were repeat lectures which sought to provide a deeper treatment of a text.

came from its congregation, not its summoning. Christ had given to the church as a whole authority which it delegated to the pope. Zabarella thus bypassed the canon law requirement that, for a council to be valid, the pope had to summon it. For Zabarella, the general council was the physical expression of the universal church for governmental purposes. He had complete confidence in such a council: it had the widest powers because it represented the whole church; it could not err; and it had instead to correct the pope if he fell into error. The inerrancy of the church was in short focused on the general council, which could judge the pope for heresy (which included prolongation of the Schism) and then depose him, because the choice of individual pope was a human one, whereas his office remained divinely instituted.

Zabarella was the prime exponent of the cardinals' version of conciliarism. He held that the Roman church had a corporate headship comprised of pope and cardinals as head and members. Plenitude of power resided in the pope and the cardinals as representing the Roman church. This meant that the pope had to consult the cardinals on all major matters, including general legislation about the condition of the church. During papal vacancies, the cardinals had the full powers of the apostolic see. They elected the pope in the name of the whole church. As representatives of the whole church, the cardinals administered preparations for any council that was called. Only a general council could depose a pope. As part of the pope's body, the cardinals ultimately derived their authority from the whole church – they represented the universal church and took its place.

In producing his juristic arguments, Zabarella was driven on by a desire to apply the canon law creatively and sensitively out of a realization that all ecclesiastical power and authority existed for the good of the church in order to aid it to achieve its ultimate and spiritual objective. He believed that councils understood in a corporational sense and incorporating a leading role for the college of cardinals best served this purpose. He held that the way in which the papal monarchy had developed had not been in the best interests of the church and had culminated in a disastrous

Schism: for him, the refusal to call councils was the root cause of the evils in the church.[46]

The conciliar movement did not come to an end with the election of Martin V in 1417 – far from it. But it began to lose momentum once it had provided the solution to the Great Schism. Those who had counselled that the election of a pope should be delayed until reform of the church had been achieved were proved right. In the months after Martin's accession, the council broke up without bringing about effective reforms. The pope managed to avoid giving official authorization to the decrees of the council, thus leaving the way open for later papal rejection of Constance's legislation and of *Haec sancta* in particular. In accordance with *Frequens*, a council did take place at Pavia-Siena in 1423–4, but the church was too exhausted for it to achieve much. As required, another council was called seven years after that – it convened at Basel in 1431 and in the event turned out to be the last council of the conciliar era.

From the outset there was bad blood between the council and Pope Eugenius IV (1431–47), who tried to dissolve it within a few months of its inception. He declared it dissolved in 1437 when he transferred the council to Ferrara in order to undertake negotiations for unity with the Greek Orthodox church. This council was then transferred to Florence, where an ill-fated act of union between the two churches was promulgated in 1439 – the Greek delegation,

[46] For Zabarella, see D. Girgensohn, 'Francesco Zabarella aus Padua. Gelehrsamkeit und politisches Wirken eines Rechtsprofessors während des großen abendländischen Schismas', *Zeitschrift der Savigny-Stiftung für Rechtsgeschichte*, Kanonistische Abteilung, 79 (1993), 232–77, and also T.E. Morrissey, 'The decree "Haec sancta" and Cardinal Zabarella. His role in its formulation and interpretation', *Annuarium Historiae Conciliorum*, 10, 2 (1978), 145–76; Morrissey, 'Franciscus Zabarella (1360–1417): papacy, community and limitations upon authority', in G. Fitch Lytle, *Reform and Authority in the Medieval and Renaissance Church* (Washington, DC: Catholic University of America Press, 1981), pp. 37–54; Morrissey, 'Cardinal Franciscus Zabarella (1360–1417) as a canonist and the crisis of his age: Schism and the Council of Constance', *Zeitschrift für Kirchengeschichte*, 96 (1985), 196–208; Morrissey, 'Cardinal Zabarella and Nicholas of Cusa. From community authority to consent of the community', in Rudolf Haubst (ed.), *Mitteilungen und Forschungen der Cusanus-Gesellschaft*, 17 (Mainz: Matthias-Grünewald-Verlag, 1986), pp. 157–76.

led by Emperor John VIII Palaeologus and the Patriarch of Constantinople, was willing to negotiate in the hope of obtaining western help against the encroachments of the Ottoman Turks. Most of the moderate members of Basel (including the bulk of the higher clergy) followed the pope's call. But the radical majority remained at Basel and rejected the papal initiative. The Council of Basel suspended Eugenius in 1438 and deposed him in 1439, and elected their own pope, Felix V, thus creating a schism between the pope and the Council.

The conciliar ideas expressed at the Council of Basel were more radical than those elaborated at Constance. Basel was based on a different ecclesiology. Membership of Constance was, as we have seen, based on the holding of office within the ecclesiastical hierarchy. Membership of Basel was based on simple incorporation into the council (so long as one was a cleric). This led to a form of equality. After 1437 the views expressed at Basel became increasingly radical. The fundamental conciliarist theory of Basel was that the council was the church's sovereign body because it represented the congregation of the faithful which was the ultimate source of authority. The council as the primary recipient of Christ's authority exercised plenitude of power over all Christians, including the pope, who was no more than the council's executive minister.

Two writers stand out as representative of the conciliarism of Basel. The first of these, John of Segovia (1393–1458), served it from his arrival in 1433 until its dissolution in 1449. John, the representative of the University of Salamanca, was a prolific writer and produced the most nuanced and sophisticated defence of the conciliar thesis. He argued that conciliar supremacy was based on the Bible and that papal sovereignty was founded on human rather than divine law. He too applied corporation theory to the government of the church, using juristic thought, including its treatment of Italian city-republics. The pope's relationship to the church was analogous to that of a *rector* to an *universitas* – the pope was the chief executor of conciliar decrees, a public person so long as he served the public good. Supreme power was located ultimately in the community of the faithful and by delegation in the council: the pope's power was derived from the sovereignty of the Christian community.[47]

The second writer, Nicholas of Cusa (1401–64), a German trained in canon law at Padua, submitted his lengthy work of ecclesiology and political theory, *De concordantia catholica* (Catholic Concordance), to the Council of Basel in 1433 or 1434.[48] He served the council until he followed the pope's summons in 1437, becoming thereafter a supporter of the papal position. In his tract, he elaborated a theory of consent. He argued that consent was the basis of all law and authority on the grounds of man's natural freedom and equality. Rulers and representatives should therefore be elected. He explained how all legitimate authority was derived from both God and the people – all ecclesiastical authority was instituted by Christ through the agency of human consent. Legitimate authority had at source the free submission of naturally free people. God had implanted natural freedom in human beings; therefore, all authority, which also derived from God, was recognized as divine when it resulted from the common consent of subjects. Within the church, the union of the faithful or the universal council representing it was superior to the pope, the church's minister. But Nicholas articulated his consent argument within the structure of a harmoniously and hierarchically differentiated society in which authority derived ultimately from God.

The split with the papacy damaged the Council of Basel irrevocably in the end – a universally recognized pope had to be part of a legitimate council. In the course of the 1440s, papal diplomacy managed progressively to remove the support of secular rulers from the council or to undermine their neutrality between the

---

[47] For John of Segovia's ideas, see Antony Black, *Monarchy and Community. Political Ideas in the Later Conciliar Controversy 1430–1450*, Cambridge Studies in Medieval Life and Thought, third series, 2 (Cambridge University Press, 1970), and his *Council and Commune. The Conciliar Movement and the Fifteenth-Century Heritage* (London: Burns & Oates, 1979), pp. 118–93.

[48] For an English translation with introduction, see Nicholas of Cusa, *De concordantia catholica*, in P.E. Sigmund, *Nicholas of Cusa. The Catholic Concordance*, Cambridge Texts in the History of Political Thought (Cambridge University Press, 1991).

pope and Basel. This led to the collapse of the authority of the council. To adhere to conciliarism required dedicated commitment to an ideological position which was no longer driven by the necessity of events, as it had been during the Great Schism. Also, it has to be said, the conciliarists were faced with the sheer institutional strength of the traditional belief in the claims of papal monarchy. In 1449 Felix V abdicated; the Council of Basel elected Eugenius IV's successor, Nicholas V, as pope and then dissolved itself.

A root problem for conciliar theory lay in its notion of representation. How could it be demonstrated that the council did represent the community of the faithful? Constance's answer was a very traditional one in terms of church office in a hierarchical structure. The fathers of Basel had not been chosen by anyone but themselves because membership of the council was by incorporation. Two arguable models of representation existed: representation by reason of office (as in the case of the bishop and his diocese) and representation by the choice of those represented (by delegation). But the members of Basel were in no sense delegates and, after 1437, few held high ecclesiastical office. Basel was always vulnerable to the claims of its opponents that it did not represent anyone but itself. There was also a further problem. The justifications for the conciliar position were elaborated in terms of juristic language and political theory because these were the concepts and arguments relevant to governmental and jurisdictional structures. But an opponent could always object that conciliarists were arguing about the church in earthly, this-worldly terms. The ultimate question which could be put to conciliarists was by what authority did the council claim such power? In the end it was a question of authority. Why should ultimate authority be located in the Christian community – what did they know? This question had particular resonance in religious matters, but of course it was the crucial one in politics. Why *should* ultimate authority lie with the people? Conciliarism made a resolute attempt to wrestle with these problems but, contrary to all signs in 1415, its day was done once the powers that be in this world abandoned it.

The Great Schism was a pre-eminent example of the way in which a devastating crisis stimulated the creative formulation of ideas concerning power and legitimate authority. The highly sophisticated level of argument reflected the development of theological and juristic thought in the fourteenth century. Wyclif's elaboration of the grace-founded *dominium* argument was truly ingenious because it attacked the very foundations of ecclesiastical claims to jurisdiction. Conciliarist writers ransacked the treasury of available intellectual authorities to produce a thoroughgoing alternative to papal monarchy. However, both Wyclif and the conciliarists did not present themselves as innovators, but rather as conservers of true (and traditional) Catholic teaching. For them, it was the papacy which had produced noxious innovations which had brought the church to this prolonged Schism.

Conclusion

This book has shown that the long fourteenth century was the most creative and original in the history of medieval political thought. In confronting the realities of power, thinkers were forced to reinterpret their inherited intellectual authorities to cope with the demands of new political crises and fundamental changes in society. Their main contribution was indeed to the elaboration of notions of power and legitimate authority, a contribution of great variety and diversity, and one which was of fundamental importance in the history of political thought.

The major characteristic of these writers was that they were interpreting inherited intellectual authorities to try and answer problems which had emerged in their own times. Knowledge of historical context is crucial for understanding their works: the conflict between Pope Boniface VIII's universalist claims and the French king's pretensions to territorial sovereignty; the parlous state of Italy at the time of Dante; the claims of the papacy, in the context of papal–imperial conflict and Italian politics, during Marsilius of Padua's lifetime; the poverty dispute which came to a head in the conflict between the papacy and the Franciscans; the problem of applying Roman and canon law to the sheer variety of political forms in fourteenth-century Europe; and the crisis of the Great Schism as a stimulus to political ideas.

The question of where legitimate authority lies is a perennial one which can be validly used as a heuristic device to interpret the works of political thinkers in any period. The question remains the same but the answers differ according to the specific historical contexts of the writers concerned. This is not to suggest that there is some disembodied or entirely abstract notion of legitimacy, power or authority existing outside time and place, but rather to see the question of legitimate authority as a useful device for facilitating the recovery of historical meaning and also for illuminating the content of present-day conceptions through comparison with those of the past. Applying this method has revealed the high level of creativity exhibited by late medieval thinkers. To recognize this, it has been necessary to understand the intellectual context of the ideas available to them and to appreciate the ways in which they applied these ideas to the practical milieu of the political and ecclesiastical life and society with which they had to deal. Only then could the meaning and significance of these texts be revealed. The writers concerned, in seeking to understand their experience in the light of revered authorities, came to a changing understanding of these authorities and to a perception of reality which was not direct but mediated by their intellectual inheritance.

In the course of writing this book, I have come to change the model which I have previously employed for understanding late medieval political thought. It remains true that the recovery of Aristotelian notions of the natural political order permitted the development of this-worldly ideas of political man, citizenship and government. But the rediscovery of this ultimately Aristotelian way of thinking only opened up the theoretical possibility of this way of justifying a naturalistic and secular political dimension – the extent to which such discourse was actually followed up by late medieval writers was another matter. Ultimately Aristotelian concepts were used to support this-worldly treatments of power and authority but also to elaborate theological approaches. This book has shown the sheer strength, sophistication and versatility of ultimately Augustinian ideas in fourteenth-century political thought. The Augustinian dimension was particularly important in fourteenth-century scholastic discourse: it existed side-by-side and in interaction with ultimately Aristotelian approaches. The Augustinian inheritance was interpreted with flexibility and originality: God could be seen as the direct source of human authority or as the ultimate and rather distant guarantor of it; he could be understood as the origin of believers' or unbelievers' rulership; those in mortal sin could legitimately rule or be deprived of their capacity to do so. The most apparently paradoxical result was the emergence of an Augustinian justification for secular authority without any reference to the church. The new model for interpreting medieval political thought accepts that both Aristotelian and August-inian languages were used for justifying the autonomy of the secular order of power and authority.

This book has also demonstrated that fourteenth-century jurists took a pre-eminent role in bringing the analysis of issues of power and authority to a higher level of sophistication. Their discussions permeated those of theologians and philosophers. Indeed, theolo-gians in particular were heavily influenced by canon law, not least because they had to cope with papal decretals.

Three further conclusions for the history of political thought have emerged in the course of this book. The first concerns ideas of state. If one starts from the assumption that fundamental political concepts are contested, one is on firm ground. Ideas of state are historically fluid and difficult to pin down. There is no one idea of the state. This book has shown that fourteenth-century jurists developed highly innovative and important ideas of state in the process of accommodating the *ius commune* to their contemporary political world.

The second concerns the overall balance in assessing fourteenth- and fifteenth-century political thought. We have seen a process of development which accords full weight to the achievements of fourteenth-century thinkers. This book has focused on scholastic writers. Scholastic approaches remained fundamental in the fifteenth and sixteenth centuries. Renaissance humanists, from their beginnings in the fourteenth century, but with added momentum in the fifteenth century, did introduce new ways of approaching political thought, but their works existed side-by-side with those of scholastics. Indeed, the Renaissance was characterized as much by scholasticism as by humanism.

The third concerns political obligation. The writers we have considered in the fourteenth century devoted a large amount of attention to this problem, so much so that it was clearly a late medieval concern and not one which emerged later in European political thought. Looked at another way, the problem of legitimate authority involved the question: why obey? The arguments that can be produced to justify the possession and exercise of power cannot be universally convincing in that, from observation, it is clear that not everyone accepts them. There is no compelling, rational solution to the problem. It all depends on what one thinks it means to be human – on what one's values are. Any justification for political power derives, ultimately, from an assertion about where final authority lies. Broadly speaking, there are two main alternatives: power can be justified as legitimate authority on the grounds either that it is derived from God in some way or that it is derived from the people (however broadly or narrowly defined) by some form of consent. As a variant, power can of course be seen as coming ultimately from God as its source, but via the people. The writers we have studied addressed a wide range of questions within these possibilities. Specific questions were discussed by some authors and not by others, but what is interesting is that these problems were raised. In what sense and how directly was God the source of authority? Did rulers have to believe in him? Did they have to be in a state of grace to rule legitimately? Still deeper questions presented themselves. By some writers, the issue was raised as to whether the Bible, as a revealed and sacred religious text, was a suitable source for justifying political authority. In other words, did religion relate to politics or did it exist on a separate, transcendent plane? In the context of examining what it meant to be human, the limits of politics were explored. For some, a purely this-worldly approach could not fulfil human nature which included both body and soul: there was a whole area of life outside and above the merely political. In particular, the ramifications of the poverty debates were central to the political thought of these years – we find them intruding time and again, and, indeed, the period cannot be understood without examining the poverty question. In terms of political thought, the issue of poverty raised the whole question of power and powerlessness. Those with apparent power in this world could be weaker than the powerless in terms of true human reality, which would include a spiritual dimension. Power could only achieve so much and could compel only those who connived with it. There could be a life quite outside the realm of law and politics. That is to say, there was an alternative to life in the political and legal order, and indeed a better and higher one. As regards the other justification for power – the people as its source – arguments were taken considerably further in this period. At a purely political level, articulated justifications were produced for autonomous political entities based on consent, notably with Italian city-republics in mind. Arguments were also produced applying the consent model to the structure of the church with fundamental implications for the ecclesiastical hierarchy and the role of the whole body of the faithful.

The world moved on from the crisis of the Great Schism. The future in the fifteenth and sixteenth centuries lay with monarchy. The notion of the king as vicar of God gained in strength and became a cornerstone of Reformation thought, notably in the form of the godly monarch. But the context for this was entirely changed. The mere fact of the spread of printed Bibles did not in itself produce this development. What was crucial was the way in which the text was interpreted. A typological interpretation of the text of the Old Testament became especially influential in the sixteenth century. Thus, the kings of Israel were seen as types for kings supporting the reformed religion. This could lead, as in the case of England, to the monarch becoming the supreme head and then the supreme governor of the church. But in Catholic countries the king could achieve control over his national church without claiming headship of it in any sense and remain in communion with Rome. A case in point was France, where the king exercised a considerable level of authority over the French church from the Pragmatic Sanction of Bourges of 1438, which subjected church benefices to royal control. Indeed, it is an irony of history that once one reaches the nineteenth century, and the period after the French Revolution, one finds that all the medieval battles for liberty of the church had been lost. The vast bulk of appointments to bishoprics in Catholic countries were in the hands of state authorities. The Vatican's centralized domination of episcopal appointments in the early twenty-first century marks a clawing back of authority by the papacy and, aided by developments in technology, has reached a level of autocratic control undreamed of by late medieval popes.

The future did not lie with the conciliar movement in the church, but its ideas did not entirely die. Conciliar ideas were much in evidence in the early sixteenth century, as the abortive cardinals' council of Pisa-Milan of 1511–12 showed, and were expressed especially at the University of Paris. Papal monarchy survived the Great Schism but was weakened and changed by it. In the fifteenth century the popes largely retreated into the role of Renaissance princes concentrating above all on the government of the papal states. The crisis of the Reformation does not make full sense without a knowledge of the Great Schism. In modern times, the memory of late medieval conciliarism was resuscitated at the time of the Second Vatican Council (1962–5) and what may be called conciliarist ideas remain to this day an ecclesiological option.

This book has sought to demonstrate the usefulness of applying the question of the location of legitimate authority. It has concentrated on the particularly fertile period of late medieval political thought. An obvious direction for future research would be to move the enquiry on into the early modern period. The knowledge provided here would serve as a firm foundation for this later study. The writers we have considered were indeed locked into their own time and place, but they were not entirely forgotten and without a familiarity with their works much of early modern political theory cannot be properly understood.

Bibliography

PRIMARY SOURCES

Aegidius Romanus, *De ecclesiastica potestate*, ed. R. Scholz. Repr. Aalen: Scientia Verlag, 1961.

Andreas de Isernia, *In usus feudorum commentaria*. Lyon, 1579.

Angelus de Ubaldis, *Lectura super Digesto veteri*. Lyon, 1520.

Aquinas, Thomas, *Catena aurea in quattuor evangelia, Expositio in Lucam*, ed. P. Angelicus Guariditi (Rome: Marietti, 1953).

    Contra errores Graecorum, in *Opera omnia*, ed. Roberto Busa, 7 vols. Stuttgart-Bad Cannstatt: Friedrich Frommann Verlag, Günther Holzboog KG, 1980, vol. III.

    Summa theologiae, ed. T. Gilby *et al.* 61 volumes. London: Eyre & Spottiswoode, 1964–80.

Aristotle, *De anima*, ed. W.D. Ross. Oxford: Clarendon Press, 1956.

    De generatione et corruptione, ed. E.S. Forster. Loeb series. Repr. London: Heinemann, 1965.

    Ethica Nicomachea, ed. H. Rackham. Loeb series. Repr. London: Heinemann, 1968.

    Politica, ed. W.D. Ross. Repr. Oxford: Clarendon Press, 1964.

Augustine of Hippo, *De civitate dei*, 4.4, Corpus Christianorum, Series Latina, vol. XLVII. Turnhout: Brepols, 1955.

Baldus de Ubaldis, *Partes I–V Consiliorum*. Brescia, 1490–1.

    Super usibus feudorum interpretatio. Pavia, 1495.

    Commentarium super Pace Constantie. Pavia, 1495.

    Lectura super prima et secunda parte Digesti veteris. [Lyon], 1498.

    Commentaria super I–V Codicis. [Lyon, 1498].

    Lectura in VI–IX Codicis. [Lyon, 1498].

    Super Decretalibus. Lyon, 1551.

    Consiliorum sive responsorum volumina I–V. Venice, 1575 (anastatic reproduction, Turin, 1970).

    In primam Digesti veteris partis commentaria. Venice, 1616.

Bartolus of Sassoferrato, *In primam et secundam Digesti novi partem*. Milan, 1491.

In primam et secundam Digesti novi partem. Turin, 1577.

In primam et secundam Digesti novi partem commentaria. Basel, 1589.

Bede, *In Lucae evangelium expositio*, in *Patrologia Latina*, vol. XCII, 1850.

Bernard of Clairvaux, *De consideratione*, in *Opera omnia*, ed. J. Leclercq, H.M. Rochais and C.H. Talbot. Rome: Editiones Cistercienses, 1963, vol. III.

Bodin, Jean, *De republica*. Paris, 1586.

Bonaventura, *Apologia pauperum*, in *Opera omnia*, 11 vols. Quaracchi: Ex typographia Collegii S. Bonaventurae, 1898, vol. VIII, pp. 233–330.

Bullarium Franciscanum, eds. Johannes Hyacynthus Sbaralea and Conrad Eubel, 8 vols. Santa Maria degli Angeli: Edizioni Porziuncola, anastatic reprint, 1983 of Rome, 1759 edn.

Cicero, *De republica*, ed. K. Ziegler., Leipzig: B.G. Teubner, 1960.

Corpus iuris canonici, vol. I: *Decretum Magistri Gratiani*, vol. II: *Decretalium Collectiones*, ed. E. Friedberg, Repr. Graz: Akademische Druck und Verlagsanstalt, 1959.

Cynus de Pistoia, *In Codicem et aliquot titulos primi Pandectarum tomi commentaria*. Frankfurt-am-Main, 1578.

Dante Alighieri, *Convivio*, ed. Franca Brambilla Ageno. Le opere di Dante Alighieri, Edizione Nazionale a cura della Società Dantesca Italiana. 2 vols. Florence: Le Lettere, 1995.

The Divine Comedy, trans. and ed. Robin Kirkpatrick. 3 vols. London: Penguin, 2006–7.

Dante, Monarchia (Latin text with introduction and English translation by Prue Shaw), Cambridge Medieval Classics, 4. Cambridge University Press, 1995.

Dante's Monarchia (English translation with an introduction and commentary by Richard Kay), Studies and Texts, 131. Toronto: Pontifical Institute of Mediaeval Studies, 1998.

Durandus, Gulielmus, *Speculum iuris* (with *additiones* of Baldus de Ubaldis and Johannes Andreae). Frankfurt, 1592.

Dyson, R.W. (ed.), *Quaestio de potestate papae (Rex pacificus)/An Enquiry into the Power of the Pope. A Critical Edition and Translation*, Texts and Studies in Religion, 83. Lewiston, NY, Queenston, Lampeter: Edwin Mellen Press, 1999.

(ed.), *Three Royalist Tracts. Antequam essent clerici; Disputatio inter clericum et militem; Quaestio in utramque partem*. Bristol: Thoemmes Press, 1999.

Gay, Jules (ed.), *Les Registres de Nicholas III (1277–1280), Recueil des Bulles de ce pape*, Bibliothèque des Ecoles Françaises d'Athènes et de

Rome, 2nd series, 14, 2. Paris: Albert Fontemoing, ed., Librairie des Ecoles Françaises d'Athènes et de Rome, December 1904.

Gregory IX, Pope, *Quo elongati*, ed. Herbert Grundmann, *Archivum Franciscanum Historicum*, 54 (1961), 20–5.

Henry of Cremona, *De potestate pape*, in Richard Scholz, *Die Publizistik zur Zeit Philipps des Schönen und Bonifaz' VIII*. Repr. Amsterdam: Editions Rodopi, 1969.

Hugh of St Victor, *De sacramentis christianae fidei*, in *Patrologia latina*, vol. CLXXVI, 1854.

James of Viterbo, *De regimine christiano*, in *Le plus ancien traité de l'Eglise, Jacque de Viterbe, De regimine christiano (1301–2), Etudes des sources et édition critique*, Critical text with an introduction by H.-X. Arquillière. Paris: Gabriel Beauchesne, 1926.

John of Paris, *De regia potestate et papali*, ed. Fritz Bleienstein, in *Johannes Quidort von Paris: Über königliche und päpstliche Gewalt (De regia potestate et papali). Textkritische Edition mit deutscher Übersetzung*, Frankfurter Studien zur Wissenschaft von der Politik, 4. Stuttgart: Ernst Kless Verlag, 1969.

Marinus da Caramanico, *Super libro constitutionum*, Proem, in F. Calasso, *I Glossatori e la teoria della sovranità*. 3rd edn. Milan: Giuffré, 1957.

Marsilius of Padua. *The Defender of the Peace*, ed. and trans. Annabel Brett, Cambridge Texts in the History of Political Thought. Cambridge University Press, 2005.

Defensor pacis, ed. R. Scholz, in *M.G.H., Fontes iuris Germanici antiqui*. Hanover: Hahnsche Buchhandlung, 1932.

Marsile de Padoue. Oeuvres mineures: Defensor minor, De translatione imperii, Latin text (ed. and trans. into French by C. Jeudy and J. Quillet). Paris: Editions du Centre National de la Recherche Scientifique, 1979.

Marsilius of Padua. Writings on the Empire. Defensor minor and De translatione imperii, ed. and trans. Cary J. Nederman, Cambridge Texts in the History of Political Thought. Cambridge University Press, 1993.

Nicholas of Cusa, *De concordia catholica*, English translation with introduction, in P.E. Sigmund, *Nicholas of Cusa. The Catholic Concordance*, Cambridge Texts in the History of Political Thought. Cambridge University Press, 1991.

Rishanger, William, *Chronica*, ed. Henry Thomas Riley, Rolls Series, 28, 2. Millwood, NY: Kraus Reprints, 1983, pp. 197–8.

Thomas of Walsingham, *Ypodigma Neustriae*, ed. Henry Thomas Riley, Rolls Series, 28, 7. Wiesbaden: Lessing-Druckerei, 1965, pp. 217–18.

Vernani, Guido, *De reprobatione Monarchie composite a Dante Alighiero Florentino* (text in Thomas Kaeppeli (ed.), *Der Dantegegner Guido Vernani, OP, von Rimini*, Quellen und Forschungen aus italienischen Archiven und Bibliotheken, 28 (1937–8), pp. 107–46.

Virgil, *Aeneid*, ed. Frederick Arthur Hertzel, Oxford Classical Texts. Oxford: Clarendon Press, repr. 1959.

William of Ockham, *Dialogus.* http://www.britac.ac.uk/pubs/dialogus/ ockdial.html (*Auctores Britannici Medii Aevi*).

    A Letter to the Friars Minor and Other Writings, ed. Arthur Stephen McGrade and John Kilcullen, trans. John Kilcullen, Cambridge Texts in the History of Political Thought (includes part of *OND* and *OQPP* and *Epistola ad fratres minores*). Cambridge: Cambridge University Press, 1995.

    On the Power of Emperors and Popes, ed. and trans. with an introduction by Annabel S. Brett. Bristol: Thoemmes Press, 1998.

    Opera politica, ed. J.G. Sikes, H.S. Offler *et al.*, 4 vols.: I–III Manchester University Press, 1940–63, IV Oxford University Press for the British Academy, 1997.

    A Short Discourse on the Tyrannical Government, ed. Arthur Stephen McGrade, trans. John Kilcullen, Cambridge Texts in the History of Political Thought. Cambridge University Press, 1992.

    Tractatus contra Benedictum, in *Opera politica*, III. Manchester University Press, 1956.

Wyclif, John, *De civili dominio liber primus*, ed. R.L. Poole. London: WS, 1885.

    De civili dominio liber secundus, ed. J. Loserth. London: WS, 1900.

    De civili dominio liber tertius, ed. J. Loserth. 2 vols. London: WS, 1903–4.

    De dissensione paparum, in *John Wiclif's Polemical Works in Latin*, ed. Rudolf Buddensieg. 2 vols. London: WS, 1883.

    De dominio divino, ed. R.L. Poole. London: WS, 1890.

    De officio regis, ed. A.W. Pollard and C. Sayle. London: WS, 1887.

    Tractatus de potestate pape, ed. J. Loserth. London: WS, 1907.

SECONDARY SOURCES

Aichele, Alexander, 'Heart and soul of the state: some remarks concerning Aristotelian ontology and medieval theory of medicine in Marsilius of Padua's *Defensor pacis*', in Gerson Moreno-Riaño (ed.), *The World of Marsilius of Padua*, Disputatio, 5. Turnhout: Brepols, 2006, pp. 163–86.

Armour, Peter, 'Dante and popular sovereignty', in John Woodhouse (ed.), *Dante and Governance*. Oxford: Clarendon Press, 1997, pp. 27–45.

Dante's Griffin and the History of the World. A Study of the Earthly Paradise (Purgatorio, Cantos XXIX–XXXIII). Oxford: Clarendon Press, 1989.

Ball, Terence, Farr, James and Hanson, Russell J. (eds.), *Political Innovation and Conceptual Change*. Cambridge University Press, 1989.

Bellomo, Manlio (ed.), *Die Kunst der Disputation. Probleme der Rechtsauslegung und Rechtsanwendung im 13. und 14. Jahrhundert*, Schriften des Historischen Kollegs, Kolloquien 38. Munich: Oldenbourg, 1997.

Black, Antony, *Council and Commune. The Conciliar Movement and the Fifteenth-Century Heritage*. London: Burns & Oates, 1979.

Monarchy and Community. Political Ideas in the Later Conciliar Controversy 1430–1450, Cambridge Studies in Medieval Life and Thought, third series, 2. Cambridge University Press, 1970.

Political Thought in Europe, 1250–1450. Cambridge University Press, 1992.

The West and Islam. Religion and Political Thought in World History. Oxford University Press, 2008.

Black, Jane, *Absolutism in Renaissance Milan. Plenitude of Power under the Visconti and the Sforza, 1329–1535*. Oxford University Press, 2009.

Blythe, James M., *Ideal Government and the Mixed Constitution in the Middle Ages*. Princeton University Press, 1992.

Boucher, David and Kelly, Paul (eds.), *Political Thinkers from Socrates to the Present*. Oxford University Press, 2003.

Boureau, Alain and Piron, Sylvain (eds.), *Pierre de Jean Olivi (1248–1298), Pensée scolastique, dissidence spirituelle et société. Actes du colloque de Narbonne (Mars, 1999)*, Etudes de philosophie médiévale, 79. Paris: Vrin, 1999.

Brett, Annabel S., 'Issues in translating the *Defensor pacis*', in Gerson Moreno-Riaño (ed.), *The World of Marsilius of Padua*, Disputatio, 5. Turnhout: Brepols, 2006, pp. 91–108.

Liberty, Right and Nature. Individual Rights in Later Scholastic Thought. Cambridge University Press, 1997.

Briguglia, Gianluca, *La questione del potere. Teologi e teoria politica nella disputa tra Bonifacio VIII e Filippo il Bello*, Filosofia e Scienza nell' Età Moderna. Milan: FrancoAngeli, 2010.

Burns, J.H. (ed.), *The Cambridge History of Medieval Political Thought, c.350–c.1450*. Cambridge University Press, 1988.

Lordship, Kingship and Empire. The Idea of Monarchy, 1400–1525. Oxford: Clarendon Press, 1992.

Burr, David, *Olivi and Franciscan Poverty. The Origins of the 'usus pauper' Controversy*. Philadelphia: University of Pennsylvania Press, 1989.

The Spiritual Franciscans: From Protest to Persecution in the Century after Saint Francis. University Park, PA: Pennsylvania State University Press, 2001.

Canning, Joseph, 'Aquinas', in David Boucher and Paul Kelly (eds.), *Political Thinkers from Socrates to the Present.* Oxford University Press, 2003, pp. 108–23.

A History of Medieval Political Thought, 300–1450. London and New York: Routledge, 1996, repr. with new introduction, 2005.

'Law, sovereignty and corporation theory, 1300–1450', in J.H. Burns (ed.), *The Cambridge History of Medieval Political Thought, c.350–c.1450.* Cambridge University Press, 1988, pp. 454–76.

The Political Thought of Baldus de Ubaldis, Cambridge Studies in Medieval Life and Thought, fourth series, 6. Cambridge University Press, 1987.

'Power and powerlessness in the political thought of Marsilius of Padua', in Gerson Moreno-Riaño (ed.), *The World of Marsilius of Padua*, Disputatio, 5. Turnhout: Brepols, 2006, pp. 211–25.

Review of George Garnett, *Marsilius of Padua and 'The Truth of History'* (Oxford University Press, 2006), in *EHR*, 125, 512 (February 2010), pp. 158–61.

Review of Takashi Shogimen, *Ockham and Political Discourse in the Late Middle Ages* (Cambridge University Press, 2007), in *EHR*, 124, 511 (December 2009), pp. 1478–9.

'The role of power in the political thought of Marsilius of Padua', *History of Political Thought*, 20, 1 (Spring 1999), 21–34.

'A state like any other? The fourteenth-century papal patrimony through the eyes of Roman Law jurists', in Diana Wood (ed.), *The Church and Sovereignty, c.590–1918. Essays in Honour of Michael Wilks*, Studies in Church History, Subsidia 6. Oxford: Blackwell, 1991, pp. 258–9.

Canning, Joseph, King, Edmund and Staub, Martial (eds.), *Knowledge, Discipline and Power in the Middle Ages: Essays in Honour of David Luscombe.* Leiden: E.J. Brill, 2011.

Cassell, Anthony K., '"Luna est ecclesia": Dante and the "Two Great Lights"', *Dante Studies*, 119 (2001), 1–26.

The Monarchia Controversy. An Historical Study with Accompanying Translations of Dante Alighieri's Monarchia, Guido Vernani's Refutation of the 'Monarchia' Composed by Dante, and Pope John XXII's Bull Si fratrum. Washington, DC: Catholic University of America Press, 2004.

Coleman, Janet, *A History of Political Thought. From the Middle Ages to the Renaissance.* Oxford: Blackwell, 2000.

'The intellectual milieu of John of Paris, OP', in Jürgen Miethke (ed.), *Das Publikum politischer Theorie im 14. Jahrhundert.* Munich: Oldenbourg, 1992, pp. 173–206.

'Property and poverty', in J.H. Burns (ed.), *The Cambridge History of Medieval Political Thought, c.350–c.1450*. Cambridge University Press, 1988, pp. 607–48.

Condren, Conal, 'Marsilius of Padua's argument from authority: a survey of its significance in the *Defensor pacis*', *Political Theory*, 5 (May 1977), 205–18.

The Status and Appraisal of Classic Texts. Princeton University Press, 1985.

Davis, Charles Till, *Dante and the Idea of Rome*. Oxford: Clarendon Press, 1957.

'Dante's vision of history', in Charles Till Davis (ed.), *Dante's Italy and Other Essays*. Philadelphia: University of Pennsylvania Press, 1984, pp. 23–41.

Dawson, James Doyne, 'Richard Fitzralph and the fourteenth-century poverty controversies', *Journal of Ecclesiastical History*, 34, 3 (1983), 315–44.

Erickson, N.N. (ed.), 'A dispute between a priest and a knight', *Proceedings of the American Philosophical Society*, 111, 5 (1967), 288–309.

Fasolt, Constantin, *Council and Hierarchy. The Political Thought of William Durant the Younger*, Cambridge Studies in Medieval Life and Thought, fourth series, 16. Cambridge University Press, 1991.

The Limits of History. University of Chicago Press, 2004.

Ferrara, Sabrina, 'Dante, Cino, il sole e la luna', *L'Alighieri. Rassegna dantesca*, n.s., 25 (2002), 27–47.

Fink, Karl Augustus, 'Zur Beurteilung des Großen Abendländischen Schismas', *Zeitschrift für Kirchengeschichte*, 73 (1962), 335–43.

Fudge, Thomas A., *The Magnificent Ride. The First Reformation in Hussite Bohemia*. Aldershot: Ashgate, 1998.

Garnett, George, *Marsilius of Padua's 'The Truth of History'*. Oxford: Oxford University Press, 2006.

Gewirth, Alan, *Marsilius of Padua*, vol. I: *Marsilius of Padua and Medieval Political Philosophy*. New York: Columbia University Press, 1951.

Giannatale, Giovanni Di, 'Papa e imperatore in "Monarchia III, 12"', *L'Alighieri*, 22, 2 (1981), 46–60.

Girgensohn, Dieter, 'Francesco Zabarella aus Padua. Gelehrsamkeit und politisches Wirken eines Rechtsprofessors während des großen abendländischen Schismas', *Zeitschrift der Savigny-Stiftung für Rechtsgeschichte*, Kanonistische Abteilung, 79 (1993), 232–77.

Godthardt, Frank, 'The philosopher as political actor – Marsilius of Padua at the court of Ludwig the Bavarian: the sources revisited', in Gerson Moreno-Riaño (ed.), *The World of Marsilius of Padua*, Disputatio, 5. Turnhout: Brepols, 2006, pp. 29–46.

Hale, John, Highfield, Roger and Smalley, Beryl (eds.), *Europe in the Late Middle Ages*. London: Faber, 1965.

Heft, James, *John XXII and Papal Teaching Authority*, Texts and Studies in Religion, 27. Lewiston, NY and Queenston: Edwin Mellen Press, 1986.

Holmes, George, '*Monarchia* and Dante's attitude to the popes', in John Woodhouse (ed.), *Dante and Governance*. Oxford: Clarendon Press, 1997, pp. 46–57.

Housley, Norman, *Religious Warfare in Europe, 1400–1536*. Oxford University Press, 2002.

Hudson, Anne, *The Premature Reformation. Wycliffite Texts and Lollard History*. Oxford: Clarendon Press, 1988.

Jones, Chris, *Eclipse of Empire? Perceptions of the Western Empire and its Rulers in Late Medieval France*, Cursor mundi, 1. Turnhout: Brepols, 2007.

Kantorowicz, Ernst H., 'Dante's "Two Suns"', in Ernst H. Kantorowicz (ed.), *Selected Studies*. New York: Augustin, 1965, pp. 325–38.

  The King's Two Bodies: A Study in Medieval Political Theology. Princeton University Press, 1957.

Kaufhold, Martin (ed.), *Politische Reflexion in der Welt des späten Mittelalters/ Political Thought in the Age of Scholasticism: Essays in Honour of Jürgen Miethke*, Studies in Medieval and Renaissance Traditions, 103. Leiden: E.J. Brill, 2004.

Kempshall, Matthew S., *The Common Good in Late Medieval Political Thought*. Oxford: Clarendon Press, 1999.

  'Ecclesiology and politics', in G.R. Evans (ed.), *The Medieval Theologians*. Oxford: Blackwell, 2001, pp. 303–33.

Kenny, Anthony (ed.), *Wyclif in his Times*. Oxford: Clarendon Press, 1986.

Kilkullen, John, 'The political writings', in Paul Vincent Spade (ed.), *The Cambridge Companion to Ockham*. Cambridge University Press, 1999, pp. 302–25.

Kohl, Benjamin G., *Padua under the Carrara, 1318–1405*. Baltimore, MD: Johns Hopkins University Press, 1998.

Kraye, Jill and Saarinen, Risto (eds.), *Moral Philosophy on the Threshold of Modernity*. Dordrecht: Springer, 2005.

Kretzmann, Norman, Kenny, Anthony, Pinborg, Jan and Stump, Eleonore (eds.), *The Cambridge History of Later Medieval Philosophy, 1100–1600*. Cambridge University Press, 1982.

Lagarde, Georges de, *La naissance de l'esprit laïque au déclin du moyen âge*, vol. III: *Le Defensor pacis*. Paris and Louvain: Nauwelaerts, 1970.

Lahey, Stephen E., *John Wyclif*. Oxford University Press, 2009.

Philosophy and Politics in the Thought of John Wyclif, Cambridge Studies in Medieval Life and Thought, fourth series, 54. Cambridge University Press, 2003.

Lambert, Malcolm, *Franciscan Poverty: The Doctrine of the Absolute Poverty of Christ and the Apostles in the Franciscan Order, 1210–1323*. London: SPCK, 1961.

Lambertini, Roberto, 'Poverty and power: Franciscans in later medieval political thought', in Jill Kraye and Risto Saarinen (eds.), *Moral Philosophy on the Threshold of Modernity*. Dordrecht: Springer, 2005, pp. 141–63.

Lambertini, Roberto and Tabarroni, Andrea, 'Le *Quaestiones super metaphysicam* attribuite a Giovanni di Jandun. Osservazioni e problemi', *Medioevo*, 10 (1984), 41–64.

Lee, Alexander, 'Roman law and human liberty: Marsilius of Padua on property rights', *Journal of the History of Ideas*, 70, 1 (January 2009), 23–44.

Leff, Gordon, 'The apostolic ideal in later medieval ecclesiology', *Journal of Theological Studies*, n.s., 18 (1967), 58–82.

Heresy in the Later Middle Ages, 2 vols. Manchester University Press, 1967.

'The making of the myth of a true church in the later Middle Ages', *Journal of Medieval and Renaissance Studies*, 1, 1 (1971), 1–15.

'Wyclif and Hus: doctrinal comparison', in Anthony Kenny (ed.), *Wyclif in his Times*. Oxford: Clarendon Press, 1986, pp. 105–25.

Levy, Ian Christopher (ed.), *A Companion to John Wyclif, Late Medieval Theologian*. Leiden: E.J. Brill, 2006.

'Holy Scripture and the quest for authority among three late medieval masters', *Journal of Ecclesiastical History*, 61, 1 (January 2010), 40–68.

Lewis, Ewart, 'The "positivism" of Marsilius of Padua', *Speculum*, 38 (1963), 541–82.

Lubac, Henri de, *Corpus mysticum: l'Eucharistie et l'Eglise au Moyen Age, Etude historique*. Paris: Aubier, 1949.

Luna, Concetta, 'Un nuovo documento del conflitto fra Bonifacio VIII e Filippo il Bello: il discorso "De potestate domini papae" di Egidio Romano (con un'appendice su Borromeo di Bologna e la "Eger cui lenia")', Documenti e studi sulla tradizione filosofica medievale, *Rivista della Società Internazionale per lo Studio del Medioevo Latino*, 3, 1–2 (1992), 167–243.

Lytle, G. Fitch, *Reform and Authority in the Medieval and Renaissance Church*. Washington, DC: Catholic University of America Press, 1981.

McFarlane, K.B., *Wycliffe and English Nonconformity*. Harmondsworth: Penguin, 1972.

McGrade, A.S., *The Political Thought of William of Ockham. Personal and Institutional Principles.* Cambridge University Press, 1974.

Mäkinen, Virpi, *Property Rights in the Late Medieval Discussion on Franciscan Poverty*, Recherches de théologie et philosophie médiévales, Biblioteca, 3. Leuven: Peeters, 2001.

'The Franciscan background of early modern rights discussion: rights of property and subsistence', in Jill Kraye and Risto Saarinen (eds.), *Moral Philosophy on the Threshold of Modernity.* Dordrecht: Springer, 2005, pp. 167–8.

Markus, R.A., *Saeculum: History and Society in the Theology of St Augustine.* Cambridge University Press, 1970.

Matteini, Nevio, *Il più antico oppositore politico di Dante, Guido Vernani da Rimini: testo critico del 'De reprobatione monarchiae'*, Il pensiero medioevale; collana di storia della filosofia, series 1, 6. Padua: CEDAM, 1958.

Menache, Sophia, *Clement V*, Cambridge Studies in Medieval Life and Thought, fourth series, 36. Cambridge University Press, 1998.

Miethke, Jürgen, *Ockhams Weg zur Sozialphilosophie.* Berlin: De Gruyter, 1969.

'Papst Johannes XXII. und der Armutstreit', in *Angelo Clareno Francescano*, Atti del XXXIV Convegno internazionale, Assisi, 5–7 Ottobre, 2006, Atti dei Convegni della Società internazionale di studi francescani e del Centro interuniversitario di studi francescani, Nuova serie diretta di Enrico Menestò, 17. Spoleto: Fondazione Centro Italiano di Studi sull'alto medioevo, 2007, pp. 265–313.

De potestate papae. Die päpstliche Amtskompetenz im Widerstreit der politischen Theorie von Thomas Aquinas bis Wilhelm von Ockham, Spätmittelalter und Reformation, 16. Tübingen: Mohr Siebeck, 2000.

(ed.), *Das Publikum politischer Theorie im 14. Jahrhundert.* Munich: Oldenbourg, 1992.

Monahan, Arthur P., *Consent, Coercion and Limit. The Medieval Origins of Parliamentary Democracy.* Leiden: E.J. Brill, 1987.

From Personal Duties towards Personal Rights. Late Medieval and Early Modern Political Thought, 1300–1600. Montreal and Kingston: McGill-Queen's University Press, 1994.

Moreno-Riaño, Gerson, 'Marsilius of Padua's forgotten discourse', *History of Political Thought*, 29, 3 (2008), 441–60.

(ed.), *The World of Marsilius of Padua*, Disputatio, 5. Turnhout: Brepols, 2006.

Morrissey, T.E., 'Cardinal Franciscus Zabarella (1360–1417) as a canonist and the crisis of his age: Schism and the Council of Constance', *Zeitschrift für Kirchengeschichte*, 96 (1985), 196–208.

'Cardinal Zabarella and Nicholas of Cusa. From community authority to consent of the community', in Rudolf Haubst (ed.), *Mitteilungen und Forschungen der Cusanus-Gesellschaft*, 17. Mainz: Matthias-Grünewald-Verlag, 1986, pp. 157–76.

'The decree "Haec sancta" and Cardinal Zabarella. His role in its formulation and interpretation', *Annuarium Historiae Conciliorum*, 10, 2 (1978), 145–76.

'Franciscus Zabarella (1360–1417): papacy, community and limitations upon authority', in G. Fitch Lytle (ed.), *Reform and Authority in the Medieval and Renaissance Church*. Washington, DC: Catholic University of America Press, 1981, pp. 37–54.

Nardi, Bruno, *Dal 'Convivio' alla 'Commedia' (Sei saggi danteschi)*, Nuovi Studi Storici, 18. Rome: Istituto Storico Italiano per il Medio Evo, repr. 1992.

Nederman, Cary J., *Community and Consent: The Secular Political Theory of Marsiglio of Padua's Defensor pacis*. Lanham, MD: Rowman & Littlefield, 1995.

'Marsiglio of Padua studies today – and tomorrow', in Gerson Moreno-Riaño (ed.), *The World of Marsilius of Padua*, Disputatio, 5. Turnhout: Brepols, 2006, pp. 11–25.

'Nature, sin and the origins of society: the Ciceronian tradition in medieval political thought', *Journal of the History of Ideas*, 49 (1988), 3–26.

Nold, Patrick, *Pope John XXII and his Franciscan Cardinal: Bertrand de la Tour and the Apostolic Poverty Controversy*. Oxford: Clarendon Press, 2003.

Oakley, Francis, *The Conciliarist Tradition. Constitutionalism in the Catholic Church, 1300–1870*. Oxford University Press, 2003.

The Political Thought of Pierre d'Ailly. The Voluntarist Tradition. New Haven, CT and London: Yale University Press, 1964.

Parisoli, Luca, 'La contribution de l'école franciscaine à la naissance de la notion de liberté politique: les données préalables chez Pierre de Jean Olivi', in Alain Boureau and Sylvain Piron (eds.), *Pierre de Jean Olivi (1248–1298), Pensée scolastique, dissidence spirituelle et société. Actes du colloque de Narbonne (Mars, 1999)*, Etudes de philosophie médiévale, 79. Paris: Vrin, 1999, pp. 251–63.

Volontarismo e diritto soggetivo. La nascita medievale di una teoria dei diritti nella scolastica francescana, Bibliotheca Seraphico-Capuccina, 58. Rome: Istituto Storico dei Cappuccini, 1989.

Pascoe, Louis B., *Church and Reform. Bishops, Theologians and Canon Lawyers in the Thought of Pierre d'Ailly (1351–1420)*. Leiden: E.J. Brill, 2005.

Jean Gerson: Principles of Church Reform, Studies in Medieval and Reformation Thought, 7. Leiden: E.J. Brill, 1973.

Passerin d'Entrèves, Alessandro, *Dante as a Political Thinker.* Oxford: Clarendon Press, 1952.

Pennington, Kenneth, 'Allegationes, solutiones and dubitationes: Baldus de Ubaldis' revisions of his consilia', in Manlio Bellomo (ed.), *Die Kunst der Disputation. Probleme der Rechtsauslegung und Rechtsanwendung im 13. und 14. Jahrhundert*, Schriften des Historischen Kollegs, Kolloquien 38. Munich: Oldenbourg, 1997, pp. 29–72.

Pope and Bishops. The Papal Monarchy in the Twelfth and Thirteenth Centuries. Philadelphia: University of Pennsylvania Press, 1984.

The Prince and the Law, 1200–1600. Berkeley, Los Angeles, Oxford: University of California Press, 1993.

Piaia, Gregorio, 'The Shadow of Antenor: on the relationship between the *Defensor pacis* and the institutions of the city of Padua', in Martin Kaufhold (ed.), *Politische Reflexion in der Welt des späten Mittelalters/ Political Thought in the Age of Scholasticism: Essays in Honour of Jürgen Miethke*, Studies in Medieval and Renaissance Traditions, 103. Leiden: E.J. Brill, 2004, pp. 193–207.

Previte-Orton, C.W., 'Marsilius of Padua and the Visconti', *EHR*, 44, 173 (April 1929), 278–9.

Quillet, Jeannine, *La philosophie politique de Marsile de Padoue.* Paris: Vrin, 1970.

Rivière, Jean, 'La dogme de la rédemption. Etudes critiques et documents', in *Bibliothèque de la Revue d'Histoire Ecclésiastique*, 5. Louvain: Bureaux de la Revue, 1931, 350–1.

Le problème de l'Eglise et de l'Etat au temps de Philippe le Bel, Etudes et documents, 8. Louvain: Spicilegium sacrum Lovaniense, 1926.

Rubinstein, Nicolai, 'Marsilius and Italian political thought of his time', in John Hale, Roger Highfield and Beryl Smalley (eds.), *Europe in the Late Middle Ages.* London: Faber, 1965, pp. 44–75.

Ryan, Magnus, 'Bartolus of Sassoferrato and free cities', *Transactions of the Royal Historical Society*, sixth series, 10 (2000), 65–89.

Sasso, Gennaro, *Dante. L'imperatore e Aristotele*, Nuovi Studi Storici, 62. Rome: Istituto Storico Italiano per il Medio Evo, 2002.

Sawicki, J.J., 'The ecclesiological and political thought of Petrus de Ancharano (1330?–1416)', unpublished PhD dissertation, Cornell University, 1977.

Scott, John A., *Dante's Political Purgatory.* Philadelphia: University of Pennsylvania Press, 1996.

Shogimen, Takashi, '"Head or Heart?" revisited: physiology and political thought in the thirteenth and fourteenth centuries', *History of Political Thought*, 28, 2 (Summer 2007), 208–29.

Ockham and Political Discourse in the Late Middle Ages. Cambridge University Press, 2007.

'Wyclif's ecclesiology and political thought', in Ian Christopher Levy (ed.), *A Companion to John Wyclif, Late Medieval Theologian.* Leiden: E.J. Brill, 2006, pp. 199–240.

Skinner, Quentin, *The Foundations of Modern Political Thought,* 2 vols. Cambridge University Press, 1978.

'The state', in Terrence Ball, James Farr and Russell Hanson (eds.), *Political Innovation and Conceptual Change.* Cambridge University Press, 1989, pp. 90–131.

Šmahel, František, 'Doctor evangelicus super omnes evangelistas: Wyclif's fortune in Hussite Bohemia', *Bulletin of the Institute of Historical Research,* 43 (1970), 16–34.

Spade, Paul Vincent (ed.), *The Cambridge Companion to Ockham.* Cambridge University Press, 1999.

Stump, Philip H., *The Reforms of the Council of Constance (1414–1418).* Leiden: E.J. Brill, 1994.

Syros, Vasileios, *Die Rezeption der aristotelischen politischen Philosophie bei Marsilius von Padua. Eine Untersuchung zur ersten Diktion des Defensor pacis.* Leiden: E.J. Brill, 2007.

Tierney, Brian, *Crisis of Church and State, 1050–1300.* Englewood Cliffs, NJ: Prentice Hall, 1964.

The Idea of Natural Rights. Studies on Natural Rights, Natural Law, and Church Law 1150–1625, Emory University Studies in Law and Religion, 5. Grand Rapids, MI: William B. Eerdmans Publishing Company, repr. 2001.

'Origins of natural rights language: texts and contexts, 1150–1250', *History of Political Thought,* 10 (1989), 615–46.

Origins of Papal Infallibility, 1150–1350: A Study on the Concepts of Infallibility, Sovereignty and Tradition in the Middle Ages. Leiden: E.J. Brill, 1972.

Religion, Law, and the Growth of Constitutional Thought, 1150–1650. Cambridge University Press, 1982.

'Villey, Ockham and the origin of individual rights', in John Witte and Frank S. Alexander (eds.), *The Weightier Matters of the Law. Essays on Law and Religion. A Tribute to Harold J. Berman.* Atlanta, GA: Scholars Press, 1988, pp. 1–31.

Took, John, '"Diligite iustitiam qui iudicatis terram": justice and the just ruler in Dante', in John Woodhouse (ed.), *Dante and Governance.* Oxford: Clarendon Press, 1997, pp. 137–51.

Turley, Thomas, 'The impact of Marsilius: papalist responses to the *Defensor pacis*', in Gerson Moreno-Riaño (ed.), *The World of Marsilius of Padua*, Disputatio, 5. Turnhout: Brepols, 2006, pp. 47–64.

Ubl, Karl, 'Johannes Quidorts Weg zur Sozialphilosophie', *Francia – Forschungen zur westeuropäischen Geschichte*, 30, 1 (2003), 43–72.

Villey, Michel, 'La genèse du droit subjectif chez Guillaume d'Occam', *Archives de philosophie du droit*, 9 (1964), 97–127.

Walsh, Katharine, *A Fourteenth-Century Scholar and Primate. Richard Fitzralph in Oxford, Avignon and Armagh.* Oxford: Clarendon Press, 1981.

Walther, Helmut, 'Baldus als Gutachter für die päpstliche Kurie im Großen Schisma', *Zeitschrift der Savigny-Stiftung für Rechtsgeschichte, Kanonistische Abteilung*, 92 (2006), 392–409.

Wilks, Michael J., *The Problem of Sovereignty in the Later Middle Ages. The Papal Monarchy with Augustinus Triumphus and the Publicists*, Cambridge Studies in Medieval Life and Thought, second series, 9. Cambridge University Press, 1963.

Witte, John and Alexander, Frank S. (eds.), *The Weightier Matters of the Law. Essays on Law and Religion. A Tribute to Harold J. Berman.* Atlanta, GA: Scholars Press, 1988.

Wood, Diana (ed.), *The Church and Sovereignty, c.590–1918. Essays in Honour of Michael Wilks*, Studies in Church History, Subsidia 6. Oxford: Blackwell, 1991.

Woodhouse, John (ed.), *Dante and Governance.* Oxford: Clarendon Press, 1997.

Woolf, C.N.S., *Bartolus of Sassoferrato. His Position in the History of Medieval Political Thought.* Cambridge University Press, 1913.

Ypma, E., 'Recherches sur la carrière scolaire et la bibliothèque de Jacques de Viterbe †1308', *Augustiniana*, 24 (1974), 247–82.

Index